A CULTURAL HISTORY
OF WORK

Volume 5

A Cultural History of Work (6 vols.)

Winner of the 2020 PROSE Award for Multivolume Reference/Humanities

A Cultural History of Work
General Editors: Deborah Simonton and Anne Montenach

Volume 1
A Cultural History of Work in Antiquity
Edited by Ephraim Lytle

Volume 2
A Cultural History of Work in the Medieval Age
Edited by Valerie L. Garver

Volume 3
A Cultural History of Work in the Early Modern Age
Edited by Bert De Munck and Thomas Max Safley

Volume 4
A Cultural History of Work in the Age of Enlightenment
Edited by Deborah Simonton and Anne Montenach

Volume 5
A Cultural History of Work in the Age of Empire
Edited by Victoria E. Thompson

Volume 6
A Cultural History of Work in the Modern Age
Edited by Daniel J. Walkowitz

A CULTURAL HISTORY OF WORK

IN THE AGE OF EMPIRE

Edited by Victoria E. Thompson

BLOOMSBURY ACADEMIC
LONDON • NEW YORK • OXFORD • NEW DELHI • SYDNEY

BLOOMSBURY ACADEMIC
Bloomsbury Publishing Plc
50 Bedford Square, London, WC1B 3DP, UK
1385 Broadway, New York, NY 10018, USA
29 Earlsfort Terrace, Dublin 2, Ireland

BLOOMSBURY and the Diana logo are trademarks of Bloomsbury Publishing Plc

First published in Great Britain 2018
This edition published in Great Britain, 2021

Copyright © Bloomsbury Publishing, 2018

Victoria E. Thompson has asserted their right under the Copyright, Designs and Patents Act, 1988, to be identified as Editor of this work.

Cover image © ACTIVE MUSEUM / Alamy Stock Photo

All rights reserved. No part of this publication may be reproduced or transmitted in any form or by any means, electronic or mechanical, including photocopying, recording, or any information storage or retrieval system, without prior permission in writing from the publishers.

A catalogue record for this book is available from the British Library.

A catalog record for this book is available from the Library of Congress.

ISBN: HB: 978-1-4742-4493-0
PB: 978-1-3502-7889-9
Set: 978-1-4742-4503-6

Series: The Cultural Histories Series

Typeset by Integra Software Services Pvt. Ltd.
Printed and bound in Great Britain

To find out more about our authors and books visit www.bloomsbury.com and sign up for our newsletters.

CONTENTS

LIST OF FIGURES	vi
CONTRIBUTORS	ix
GENERAL EDITORS' PREFACE	xi

Introduction   1
Victoria E. Thompson

1 The Economy of Work   15
 Ludovic Frobert and François Jarrige
 Translated by Victoria E. Thompson

2 Picturing Work   31
 Susan Hiner

3 Work and Workplaces   51
 Casey Harison

4 Workplace Culture   67
 Victoria E. Thompson

5 Work, Skill, and Technology   85
 François Jarrige
 Translated by Victoria E. Thompson

6 Work and Mobility   99
 Ute Chamberlin

7 Work and Society   115
 Marjorie Levine-Clark

8 The Political Culture of Work   133
 Fiona A. Montgomery

9 Work and Leisure   149
 W. Scott Haine

NOTES	164
FURTHER READINGS	189
INDEX	195

LIST OF FIGURES

CHAPTER ONE

1.1	American coal miners, c. 1912. Photo: Buyenlarge / Getty Images.	18
1.2	Weaving by power looms, 1835. Photo: Print Collector / Getty Images.	19
1.3	Silk workshop in Lyon, late nineteenth century. Photo: Christophel Fine Art / UIG via Getty Images.	21
1.4	Slaves working with an early cotton gin, 1869. Photo: MPI / Getty Images.	25
1.5	The town of New Lanark, Scotland, c. 1825. Photo: SSPL / Getty Images.	26

CHAPTER TWO

2.1	Dean Mills cotton mill, Manchester, England, 1851. © Chronicle / Alamy Stock Photo.	32
2.2	P. Lacour, *Les cris de Paris*, 1831. © INTERFOTO / Alamy Stock Photo.	36
2.3	Louis-Marie Lanté, *Paris. Repasseuse,* 1824. © Florilegius / Alamy Stock Photo.	39
2.4	Charles Philipon, *L'utile marchande de corsets*, 1830. © INTERFOTO / Alamy Stock Photo.	41
2.5	Victorian women sewing, 1888. Photo: whitemay via Getty Images.	43
2.6	Honoré Daumier, *The Burden*, or *Laundress*, 1850–3. © Peter Barritt / Alamy Stock Photo.	44
2.7	Edgar Degas, *Les repasseuses* (*Women Ironing*), 1884–6. Credit: Peter Barritt / Alamy Stock Photo.	46
2.8	Group of *catherinettes*, 1908. Courtesy of Bibliothèque nationale de France.	47
2.9	Women war workers, 1918. Credit: Chronicle / Alamy Stock Photo.	49

CHAPTER THREE

3.1	Inside the Krupp Factory, 1905. Photo: Albert Harlingue / Roger Viollet / Getty Images.	53
3.2	Picking cotton, United States, 1878. Photo: Prisma / UIG / Getty Images.	54
3.3	Nannies of the Spreewald region, c. 1903. Photo: ullstein bild / ullstein bild via Getty Images.	60

LIST OF FIGURES vii

| 3.4 | Cheshire clothing factory, 1908. Photo: Past Pix / SSPL / Getty Images. | 61 |
| 3.5 | Children pushing a coal wagon, 1869. Photo: Grafissimo via Getty Images. | 63 |

CHAPTER FOUR

4.1	Clothing prices set by master tailors, New York City, 1805. Photo: MPI / Getty Images.	70
4.2	Victorian carpenters at work. Photo: whitemay via Getty Images.	72
4.3	A journeyman arrives at a fellow felt maker's workshop, 1820. Photo: Hulton Archive / Getty Images.	75
4.4	A trade union march in Manchester, 1874. Photo: Hulton Archive / Getty Images.	81

CHAPTER FIVE

5.1	Rioting mob of Luddites, 1813. Photo: Time Life Pictures / Mansell / The LIFE Picture Collection / Getty Images.	88
5.2	Labor-saving looms, Draper Corporation Catalog, 1907. Courtesy of Wikimedia.	92
5.3	Singer's sewing machines, 1892. Courtesy of Bibliothèque nationale de France.	94
5.4	"Munitionnette" in a French war factory, 1917. Courtesy of Bibliothèque nationale de France.	98

CHAPTER SIX

6.1	Medical staff and nurses in South Africa, 1901. Photo: The Print Collector / Print Collector / Getty Images.	104
6.2	Emigrants from Europe on a ship bound for New York, c. 1910. Credit: Prisma by Dukas Presseagentur GmbH / Alamy Stock Photo.	105
6.3	East Prussian farmworkers (*Sachsengaenger*) in Berlin, c. 1907. Photo: ullstein bild / ullstein bild via Getty Images.	108
6.4	Completion of the St. Gotthard Tunnel beneath the Alps, 1880. Photo: Ann Ronan Pictures / Print Collector / Getty Images.	110
6.5	German POWs digging peat in France, 1918. Credit: Photo 12 / Alamy Stock Photo.	113

CHAPTER SEVEN

| 7.1 | Gustave Doré, a poor neighborhood in nineteenth-century Paris. Credit: Chronicle / Alamy Stock Photo. | 118 |
| 7.2 | Théophile Alexandre Steinlen, *Misère,* 1896. Courtesy of Bibliothèque nationale de France. | 125 |

7.3	A slum in the East End of London. Credit: Chronicle / Alamy Stock Photo.	126
7.4	Charles Booth, map of East End poverty, 1889. Credit: Antiqua Print Gallery / Alamy Stock Photo.	128
7.5	Mobile kitchen in Berlin, c. 1900. Credit: INTERFOTO / Alamy Stock Photo.	130

CHAPTER EIGHT

8.1	Chartist meeting, 1848. Photo: Hulton Archive / Getty Images.	138
8.2	Women coal bearers, 1829. Courtesy of Wellcome Collection via Wikimedia.	140
8.3	Benjamin Waterhouse Hawkins, *Milk*, c. 1845. Photo: Oxford Science Archive / Print Collector / Getty Images.	143
8.4	Women textile workers who struck for the ten-hour day, Crimmitschau, 1904. Photo: ADN-Bildarchiv / ullstein bild via Getty Images.	145

CHAPTER NINE

9.1	Walter Gelkie, *Fair Gamblers*, early nineteenth century. Photo: The Print Collector / Print Collector / Getty Images.	150
9.2	Reading the newspaper in the tavern, 1876. Photo: Prisma / UIG / Getty Images.	152
9.3	Music Hall patrons, c. 1830. Photo: Hulton Archive / Getty Images.	153
9.4	The Hippodrome Cinema in Paris, 1914. Courtesy of Wikimedia.	156
9.5	Newcastle United v. Sunderland, c. 1904. Photo: Bob Thomas / Popperfoto / Getty Images.	159

CONTRIBUTORS

Ute Chamberlin is Associate Professor of History at Western Illinois University, USA. She is the author of "Honour or Control? Female Recipients of Prussian State Decorations in a Civic Context," in Krista Cowman, Nina Javette Koefoed, and Asa Karlsson Sjögren, eds., *Gender in Urban Europe: Sites of Political Activity and Citizenship, 1750–1900* (2014).

Ludovic Frobert is Director of Research at the Centre national de la Recherche Scientifique (CNRS), Paris, France, and Member of the Triangle Laboratory (ENS-Lyon). His publications include (with Cyrille Ferraton) *Introduction à Albert O. Hirschman* (2017), (with George Sheridan) *Le Solitaire du ravin: Pierre Charnier (1795–1857), canut lyonnais et prud'homme tisseur* (2014), *Les Canuts ou la démocratie turbulente: Lyon 1831–1834* (2009/2017), and *John Kenneth Galbraith: La maîtrise sociale de l'économie* (2003). He recently directed (with Clément Coste and Marie Lauricella) *De la République de Constantin Pecqueur (1801–1887)* (2017) and (with Jonathan Barbier) *Une imagination républicaine: François-Vincent Raspail (1794–1878)* (2017).

W. Scott Haine is on the History Faculty at the University of Maryland University College, USA. He is the author of *Culture and Customs of France* (2006), *The History of France* (2000), and *The World of the Paris Café: Sociability among the French Working Class, 1789–1914* (1996) and coeditor (with Leona Rittner and Jeffrey H. Jackson) of *The Thinking Space: The Café as Cultural Institution in Paris, Italy and Vienna* (2013).

Casey Harison is Professor of History at University of Southern Indiana and Director of the USI Center for Communal Studies, Evansville, IN, USA. He is the author of *Feedback: The Who and Their Generation* (2015) and *The Stonemasons of Creuse in Nineteenth-Century Paris* (2008). Articles and book chapters include "The Paris Commune of 1871, the Russian Revolution of 1905, and the Shifting of Revolutionary Tradition," *History & Memory* (2007) and "The Standard of Living of English and French Workers, 1750–1850," in Christine Rider and Micheál Thompson, eds., *The Industrial Revolution in Comparative Perspective* (2000).

Susan Hiner is Professor of French and Francophone Studies on the John Guy Vassar Chair at Vassar College, Poughkeepsie, NY, USA. She is the author of *Accessories to Modernity: Fashion and the Feminine in Nineteenth-Century France* (2010), winner of the 2011 Millia Davenport Publication Award of the Costume Society of America. Recent publications include "The Modiste's Palette and the Artist's Hat," in Simon Kelly and Esther Bell, eds., *Degas, Impressionism, and the Paris Millinery Trade* (2017) and "Picturing the Catherinette: Reinventing Tradition for the Postcard Age," in Masha Belenky, Kathryn Kleppinger, and Anne O'Neil-Henry, eds., *French Cultural Studies for the Twenty-First Century* (2017). She was awarded an NEH Fellowship for her current book project, "Behind the Seams: Women, Fashion, and Work in Nineteenth-Century France."

François Jarrige is Maître de conférences en histoire contemporaine at the Université de Bourgogne, Dijon, and member of the Centre Georges Chevrier, Dijon, France. He is the author of *Technocritiques: Du refus des machines à la contestation des technosciences* (2014) and (with T. Le Roux) *La contamination du monde: Une histoire des pollutions à l'âge industriel* (2017); editor of *Dompter Prométhée: Technologies et socialismes à l'âge romantique* (2016); and coeditor of *La gamelle et l'outil: Manger au travail en France et en Europe de la fin du XVIIIe siècle à nos jours* (2016) and *Quand les socialistes inventaient l'avenir: Presse, théories et expériences (1825–1860)* (2015).

Marjorie Levine-Clark is Professor of History and Associate Dean at the University of Colorado Denver, USA. She is the author of *Unemployment, Welfare, and Masculine Citizenship: "So Much Honest Poverty" in Britain, 1870–1930* (2015) and *Beyond the Reproductive Body: The Politics of Women's Health and Work in Early Victorian England* (2004). She has published widely on gender, health, and welfare, including "The Politics of Preference: Masculinity, Marital Status, and Unemployment Relief in Post-First World War Britain," *Cultural and Social History* 7, no. 3 (2010): 233–52; and "From 'Relief' to 'Justice and Protection': The Maintenance of Deserted Wives, British Masculinity and Imperial Citizenship, 1870-1920," *Gender and History* (2010). Her current project is tentatively titled "Unemployment, Health, and the Body in Britain: From the New Poor Law to Thatcher."

Fiona A. Montgomery was, until retirement, Head of the School of Historical and Cultural Studies at Bath Spa University, Bath, UK. She has published widely on popular protest, women's history, and feminist pedagogy. Among her publications are *Women's Rights: Struggles and Feminism in Britain c. 1770–1970* (2006); (with M. Flinn) *A Vision of Learning: Edge Hill University 1885–2010* (2010); (with E. Chalus) "Women and Politics," in Hannah Barker and Elaine Chalus, eds., *Women's History, Britain, 1700–1850: An Introduction* (2005). She coedited (with Christine Collette) *The European Women's History Reader* (2002) and *Into the Melting Pot: Teaching Women's Studies in the New Millennium* (1997).

Victoria E. Thompson is Associate Professor of Modern European History and Associate Director of the Institute for Humanities Research at Arizona State University, USA. She is the author of *The Virtuous Marketplace: Women and Men, Money and Politics in Paris 1830–1870* (2000) and (with Rachel G. Fuchs) *Women in Nineteenth-Century Europe* (2005). She is currently completing a manuscript titled *Inventing Public Space, Paris 1748–1790*. She has published articles and book chapters on eighteenth- and nineteenth-century Paris focusing on urban space, travel, gender, memory, and identity.

GENERAL EDITORS' PREFACE

Issues around work and the workplace seem to be having a renaissance and are no longer embedded solely in the discourses around Marxism and labor movements. Similarly, new and fresh research has been taking place around guilds, skill, control, and gender issues. *A Cultural History of Work* takes an approach that focuses on culture in order to explore the subtleties of the character and dynamics of work and the people and relationships involved in working and the workplace in a theoretically holistic way to bring together disparate historical traditions and historiographical approaches. The aim and scope of *A Cultural History of Work* is to offer a comprehensive survey of the social and cultural construction of work across six historical periods. This approach that focuses on the *cultural* history of work provides an opportunity to explore the dynamics of work and the people and relationships involved in working and the workplace, helping to rethink boundaries and the issues of work. This is not an "economic" history of work, but a cultural one. Of course, we talk about economics, but the fundamental concept is to explain the ways in which work was situated in and influenced cultural dynamics of the western world. It is a key contribution to the process of rethinking boundaries and issues of work.

A Cultural History of Work draws on "the western world." Contributors approached their chapters with a great deal of freedom, drawing on their specific expertise in national and regional histories, but throughout the thirty-six chapters that make up the series, they have tried to embrace the "West." The series does not intend to "cover" all of western culture, or even all of Europe and North America. Authors instead have aimed at *representing* the broad trends and nuances of the culture of work from antiquity to the present. Thus *A Cultural History of Work* concentrates on the central themes in western work, with some sensitivity to areas we know less about.

This is a work of scholarly reference designed to provide scholars and students with a detailed, nuanced overview. Each contribution has been written as an original chapter presenting an *overview* of a theme in a period, but each also includes a wide range of case material and has a particular thrust or point of view (or points of view) informing the organization of the piece. The series is structured into six time periods—though historians will always quibble about what these periods mean and will blur the edges. That is part of the process of understanding the past. And time does not have the same meaning across regions, much less countries or continents. Each volume covers a long period of time and a broad geography that can and will introduce a range of variables. Each volume uses the same chapter titles so that readers can read on a theme across volumes, or read through a period exploring the range of themes and nuances that each volume presents. There are also overlaps within volumes and across them that enrich the discussion.

The editorial decision to study work rather than labor is suggestive of a broader, more encompassing field of study that lends itself more readily to different periods. For example, in particular it is more appropriate to use *labor* for periods such as antiquity and the Middle Ages because labor looks in one sense as an eighteenth- or nineteenth-century concept. English is rather unusual in having two words whose meanings overlap considerably, but are not identical. For example, there is only one word in French, *travail*, like *Arbeit* in German, *arbejde* in Danish/Swedish/Norwegian, *lavoro* in Italian. Some other languages tend to have one primary word also, for example, *trabajo* in Spanish, though there are other usable words. From a definitional point of view we can argue that *labor* means the use of mental or physical capacities/faculties, so it implies suffering and difficulty, whereas *work* has to do with the simple act or fact of doing something/ the activity/the action in progress. From the point of view of the political economy, *labor* seems to refer to the Marxist discourse; *work* is more pragmatic and less laden with cultural overtones. So, work describes the parameters of this project while *labor* is one aspect of it, which is more important in the nineteenth and twentieth centuries, and to a lesser extent in the eighteenth. Thus we argue *work* seems more neutral and general and therefore more applicable across six centuries.

Moving from the world of antiquity and into the twenty-first century, the culture of work has shifted considerably as technologies, organization, and locations have changed. Workplace relations have also undergone transformations from small-scale and familial settings to large-scale and potentially less personal environments. And yet, the world of work remains complex with great variations between national cultures, political and economic approaches to managing the fields of work, and especially in the ways that people have negotiated their own spaces and places within them. Work retains many meanings from the simple need to survive to senses of deep satisfaction for the character of the job and the creativity one can achieve. It may be valued for the income or wealth it can generate; conversely, some choose to work less and on their own terms. Part-time, job-sharing, self-employment, and the IT revolution have offered different routes for some people. Workers can, however, remain tied to an employer and though nominally slavery does not exist in the West, there are those, such as sweated immigrant workshops, and live-in domestic workers, who may feel that little has changed. *The Cultural History of Work* traces and explores many of these routes and their implications for people and their cultural experience of work.

Introduction

VICTORIA E. THOMPSON

This volume covers the cultural history of work during the "Age of Empire," defined as the period between 1800 and 1920. Like most periodization schemes, the start and end dates are imperfect. The major forces that shaped work and the lives of workers during this period—including industrialization, urbanization, and imperial expansion—were underway in some countries before 1800 and continued after 1920. This long nineteenth century is typically considered a period of transformation, and some workers, such as those who moved from farm to factory or who emigrated overseas in search of work, experienced a dramatic, and often traumatic, transformation of their working lives. For others, change was gradual, making adaptation possible. And for many, such as the peasants who worked the land of eastern and southern Europe, work largely remained an unchanging routine, similar to that of their parents and grandparents.

During the age of empire, change was uneven, coming in fits and starts according to different timetables in different parts of the western world, and existing side by side with significant continuities. The tensions produced by the encounters between continuity and change shaped the lives of workers in myriad ways, as the chapters in this volume demonstrate. Even in sectors of the economy that experienced more continuity than change, workers' lives were affected by the overall perception that new methods of production were transforming western society. Cultural attitudes concerning work and cultural practices related to work were challenged, reconceptualized, and reinvented in the period 1800–1920.

During the nineteenth century, and continuing through the First World War, the working experience of many Europeans was dramatically transformed due to a process broadly known as industrialization. Industrialization is, in the most general sense, a transition from a primarily agricultural economy to an economy organized primarily around manufacturing. The process of industrialization in the West had its roots in the eighteenth-century consumer economy, and continued well into the twentieth century. Industrialization was a long-term, structural shift in the economies of Europe and North America (and indeed, in economies throughout the world) that occurred over an extended period. Such long-term processes are not typically seen as dramatic transformations, because by definition a long-term process occurs gradually over time. However, industrialization was perceived differently. Even though the overall process of shifting from an economy based on agriculture to one based on manufacturing occurred over several generations, key aspects of that transformation occurred rapidly and with significant impact on the lives of workers. Industrialization was therefore experienced as a sudden and wide-reaching transformation of western society, and it is for this reason that the term "Industrial Revolution" came to describe this change in western economic life.

Industrialization was also a complex process that depended upon and brought about changes not only in manufacturing, but also in transportation, banking, retail, and agriculture. The cause-and-effect relationships among various sectors of economic life were complicated and not often easily identifiable. Historians still argue about the relative importance of various causes of industrialization. For contemporaries, the task of deciphering the relationships among various types of transformations that they were living through was extremely difficult, if not impossible. Instead, industrialization was perceived as centered in very specific and easily identifiable objects and locations. Foremost among these were the machine and the factory. The machine was considered a source of greater efficiency, greater profits, and potentially endless abundance. It also raised the peril of unemployment, deskilling, alienation, and bodily harm. The factory was similarly alternately celebrated and demonized. It was considered to be a site where industrial workers contributed to the modern economy and a source of profound demoralization. As Europeans and Americans attempted to make sense of the impact of industrialization, their focus on the machine and the factory encouraged a redefinition of the nature and value of work that led to larger social, political, and economic shifts that affected even those who worked in traditional sectors of the economy.

The extent and significance of economic transformation in the period 1800–1920 means that a complete overview of work in the western world is impossible to depict in a volume such as this. As a result, the chapters that follow are limited in two significant ways: they focus primarily on the European case and they deal primarily with the experience of those who worked in manufacturing. Other parts of the world and other types of employment are discussed, but they are not the main focus. This is in part a practical means of limiting the scope of each chapter but also reflects the tremendous importance of the transformation of manufacturing during this period, a process that was first evident in Great Britain and then western Europe before expanding to other parts of the world. Nonetheless, it is important to keep in mind that industrialization was a process that had an impact on the entire globe. As Ludovic Frobert and François Jarrige remind us in this volume, "British industrialization and the rise of factory work was only possible because elites controlled significant peasant populations in Scotland, Ireland, India, and Africa that could furnish the factories with the raw materials they needed." While Europeans (and others) long viewed industrialization as a process by which British and European technology was spread to other parts of the world, scholars now prefer to emphasize the "protean and polycentric" nature of industrialization.

The process of industrialization facilitated European control of overseas territories. Colonial conquest and imperial expansion would not have been possible on the same scale without the steamship, the telegraph, and the machine gun. As Europeans and North Americans gained control over increasingly large parts of the globe, the economic balance of power shifted dramatically. On the eve of the First World War, "western Europe and the United States were responsible for 82 percent of the world's industrial production."[1] As Europeans came to dominate economies in other parts of the world, these economies were geared towards producing raw materials for European markets, leading to the decline of manufacturing elsewhere. An example is Indian textiles, which dominated the world market in the late seventeenth century but were replaced by cheaper British textiles following industrialization.[2] Even those not under European control were impacted by European industrialization. Argentina depended upon British finance and on British purchase of meat, hides, and grain, and the Argentinian economy was adversely impacted by conditions in Britain that slowed these flows of money and raw materials.[3] And the acquisition and celebration of empire shaped workers' perceptions of their place in the world economy. For some workers, identification with a strong imperialist nation such as Britain or France was a source of pride that could mitigate socioeconomic inferiority at home. Others, and particularly those who adopted a Marxist perspective, viewed imperialism as evidence of bourgeois domination and exploitation.

The chapters in this volume offer us several different means of understanding the profound impact of industrialization on the cultural history of work in the period 1800–1920. In the chapters that follow we see how industrialization shaped the workplace and work processes. We see how intellectuals and politicians responded to poverty and urban overcrowding caused by industrialization, and the ways in which assumptions concerning differences between men and women shaped those responses. We come to understand the constant and creative range of responses workers adopted in an effort to retain control over their own work and workplaces. And we see how industrialization shaped life outside of the workplace, in new venues of commercialized leisure, as well as in the artistic representation of work. By way of introduction, this chapter will sketch out a broad overview of the process of industrialization in the period 1800–1920 and then will address the ways in which Europeans made sense of industrialization.

Before moving on to this discussion, it seems worthwhile to say a few words about the term "culture." This is a capacious term that has become increasingly attractive to historians over the last twenty years, as we have sought to move away from subdisciplinary boundaries that seemed too constricting in favor of more interdisciplinary analyses of the past that examine not only what people did in previous generations, but also how they experienced their own lives and times. Cultural analysis is rooted in the desire to uncover and understand a different way of looking at the world. As Lucien Febvre noted in the 1930s, the material conditions in existence at each period in history shaped the metaphors and symbols used to attribute meaning to the world. Winter and summer meant something far different in the sixteenth century than they did in the age of central heating and air-conditioning, and Febvre argues that as a consequence, we can no longer experience the difference between being cold and being warm in the same dramatic way. By extension, metaphors based on the difference between cold and warmth would not have the same force today as they did in the past. The metaphors and symbols we use to make sense of our world, metaphors and symbols based in experience as well as in traditions, myths, and beliefs handed down to us, constitute what Febvre referred to as "mental equipment"; they are the building blocks we use to create seemingly coherent explanations for why the world works in the way it does.[4] If these explanations, or what Clifford Geertz termed "webs of significance," are to have resonance beyond one person or a small group of people, they must be based upon shared experiences.[5] In order to gain acceptance, a cultural explanation for a complex and long-term process such as industrialization must appear to be plausible: it must be consistent with experience and with widely held values.

The Introduction approaches culture in this way, with its attention to how industrialization was understood. Throughout the volume as a whole culture is used more broadly to refer not only to frameworks of understanding (such as political economy) but also to social practices (such as workplace rituals) and to forms of cultural production (such as paintings and movies). Broadly held belief systems concerning differences between men and women also influenced how work was organized and experienced, while ethnic difference often determined what sorts of work were available. Cultural beliefs shaped perceptions of the worker's body as marked by sex and ethnicity and increasingly, during the age of empire, as an extension of the machine.

In taking a cultural history approach to the topic of work, the chapters in this volume build upon a significant body of scholarship on work and workers in the nineteenth century. This period has garnered a great deal of attention from labor historians working in the 1960s through to the present who were strongly influenced by the methods and questions of social history. In seeking to recover the experience of men and women who had been left out of traditional histories that focused on state politics, international relations, or major intellectual developments, these historians drew our attention to the everyday experience of workers in Europe and North America. Many of these scholars were influenced by Marxist paradigms, and thus looked to the nineteenth century to understand the process by which workers in disparate trades, governed by local and craft-based traditions, came to see themselves as members of a "working class."

For Marx, working men and women acquired class consciousness when they came to think of themselves as belonging to a specific group in society defined by its lack of ownership of the tools and other resources used in manufacturing, or the "means of production." Marx argued that under capitalism, the bourgeoisie became sole owner of the means of production, while workers lost autonomy and control over the work process. As workers' ability to provide for themselves in a way that maintained their independence, creativity, and dignity declined, conflict between workers and the bourgeoisie increased. As a result, workers came to understand the structural factors that disfavored them; they became aware of themselves as belonging to a class defined in opposition to the bourgeoisie. Armed with this understanding, they organized and fought for change.

The assumption that class consciousness was a product of one's relation to the material goods necessary for manufacturing, and the belief that such consciousness would automatically lead to organized struggle with the bourgeoisie, underlay much of the excellent work of labor historians through the 1980s and beyond. By the 1990s, however, "labour history as labour movement history by and large came to an end."[6] As Jay Winter explains, the shift in the West from an industrial to a service economy combined with a growing disenchantment with Marxist models of historical change encouraged historians of work to participate in the linguistic and anthropological turns that were transforming the entire discipline in the last two decades of the twentieth century. In French labor history, the field with which I am most familiar, the influence of new approaches and new theoretical models produced innovative scholarship, such as William Sewell's *Work and Revolution in France* and Joan Scott's essays on gender and work.[7] Sewell and Scott both focused on written texts as sources that shape identity; in their work, texts are not simply sources that historians use to uncover a preexisting reality based on material conditions, but they also worked, at the time of their creation, to influence how people understood their world and themselves. The task of the historian thus became discovering not only what happened and why, but also how people at the time understood (or misunderstood) what was happening to them and how these understandings shaped their responses to the world.

The impact of historians employing cultural methods and approaches has been significant; as Dick Geary noted, we now understand that "a host of concerns ... mitigate against and cut across the adoption of class-based identities: concerns of gender, religious confession, race, region and—at the most basic level—individual psychology."[8] Furthermore, class is itself a highly variable concept, dependent on region, religion, language, state policies, and work environment as well as on gender and ethnicity. In short, we can no longer use the term "class consciousness" as if it were self-evident what that term meant and when and why it was appropriate to use it to apply to the identities of working men and women. But how could it be otherwise when industrialization itself was a highly variable process, one that occurred rapidly in some areas of the West, slowly in others, and in some places not at all. Furthermore, industrialization was experienced differently depending on one's role in the economy, and one's role was shaped by, at the very least, one's ethnicity, age, sex, religion, family background, place of habitation, experience, and skill. Finally, during the period 1800–1920, industrialization was continually experienced as something new and unsettling; workers and bosses alike rarely thought, as Marx would have them do, that they were players on the stage of an unfolding historical dialectic whose progress was inevitable. Other ways of thinking about the world persisted and shaped the experience of workers and their understanding of the processes that we call industrialization.

INDUSTRIALIZATION AND THE ORGANIZATION OF WORK

The process of industrialization began in the eighteenth century in Great Britain, when mechanization began to alter the textile manufacturing process, allowing for higher outputs using less human labor. 1769 was a key year, in which patents were issued for James Watt's design for a steam engine that could be better adapted to a variety of uses and for Richard Arkwright's spinning machine powered by water. In the 1770s, the first cotton mills—early textile factories where spinning machines were powered by water and then steam—were established in northern England and Scotland. A combination of higher wages compared to those in other European countries (with the exception of the Low Countries) and coal reserves made mechanization attractive to manufacturers seeking to maximize profit.[9] Britain's relative prosperity meant that capital was available for technological experimentation and investment, while the existence of a strong consumer market and high demand for cotton cloth meant that industrialists had an incentive to find ways to make cloth production more efficient, and the financial means to do so. Textiles were not the only sector of the economy that drove British industrialization, however: the development of a profitable technique for making iron using coke rather than charcoal led to the expansion of coal mining, iron production, and machine manufacturing.

Mechanization in one area spurred invention in another in what David Landes termed a "sequence of challenge and response."[10] Mechanization of one part of a process of production, such as spinning thread, put a strain on other parts of the process, such as weaving that thread into cloth, thus prompting a search for greater efficiency through technology. In addition, as textile factories became more numerous the men who manufactured machines strove not only to meet demand but also to improve and invent, thus leading to new advances in mechanization.[11] Steam power and new methods of iron production also revolutionized transportation with the development of the steamship, but most dramatically for contemporaries with the railroad. Although steam-powered railcars had been used at coal fields since the start of the nineteenth century, longer-distance commercial and passenger railway transport was inaugurated in 1830 with the opening of the Liverpool and Manchester Railway. As a contemporary wrote in 1831, rail transportation advanced industry by providing a means of overcoming the natural rhythms that limited transport by water: "Owing to the deficiency of water in summer, barges cannot carry their usual freights; and from the operation of frost, in winter, the canals are frequently for weeks unnavigable."[12] As with the mechanization of textiles, the development of the railroads entailed the creation of new trades and profession, and encouraged further refinements in technology. In Britain and throughout the world, railroads also allowed for the development of markets "far exceeding in volume and scope the international trade of the preindustrial era," thereby increasing demand for a wide array of goods and providing further incentives for mechanization.[13]

In addition to mechanization, industrialization depended upon new forms of organizing work and workers in a single space; this space was most famously the factory, but as Ludovic Frobert and François Jarrige remind us, sugar processing on plantations in the Caribbean was done in settings where large numbers of workers were brought together in one place and subject to factory-like supervision and discipline. This "centralization of manufacturing" also took place in convents around Lyon, where young women working in the silk trade were subjected to strict discipline and harsh punishment by supervising nuns.[14] Thus while steam-powered spinning machines in a textile mill still epitomize for many the early stages of industrialization, much broader changes in the nature of work were evident in the early decades of the nineteenth century.

Another of these changes has been characterized by Christopher Johnson as "proletarianization": the decline of working conditions and wages due to a division of labor and concomitant deskilling.[15] Johnson's study of Parisian tailors in the 1830s and 1840s showed that although the tailoring trade was not subject to mechanization at this time (the sewing machine would not have an impact on tailoring until the 1860s), the work process was increasingly divided into smaller tasks requiring less skill and for which lower piece rates were paid. Tailoring thus became less of a craft requiring extensive knowledge and artistry, and more of a series of discrete tasks requiring a limited, and typically less complex, set of skills. Master tailors still worked with clients to design their clothes, but at the lowest rung of the trade men and women with basic sewing skills worked from their homes to make cuffs or collars for a wage that barely allowed them to survive. One of the reasons for this shift was the rise of ready-to-wear clothing, which depressed prices in the tailoring industry. As Johnson notes, the manufacture of ready-to-wear clothing "was labor-intensive and relied upon cheap labor for its success." And it was a success; despite a far higher number of bespoke tailors in Paris, the manufacturers of ready-to-wear men's clothing averaged a significantly higher amount of gross sales measured in French francs.[16] Not only were workers in ready-to-wear less skilled and more poorly paid, but they had few means of combating the "flexible specialization" of the garment trade, where seasonal slowing and the dictates of fashion created a workforce that could be sped up or let go at will, which was highly desirable for employers.[17]

The employment of women and children at jobs requiring less skill and paying lower wages was an important aspect of industrialization. The cotton mills of England and Scotland, as well as those established in the United States and continental Europe, drew a large part of their workforce from women and children in the surrounding countryside. Yet as Deborah Simonton notes, "factories never employed the majority of workers, nor even the majority of women," a statement that remains true throughout the age of empire.[18] Cottage industry—the "putting-out" system whereby manufacturers contracted with workers laboring in their homes to weave and sew—existed alongside the factories. Indeed, in trades such as tailoring, ready-to-wear manufacturers depended upon the labor of women working out of their homes for their profits. By the second half of the nineteenth century, work opportunities for women were expanding. Yet as several of the chapters indicate, throughout the period, women tended to be placed in lower-skilled positions, paid lower wages, and offered few opportunities for advancement. Women's disadvantage in the workplace was justified by the belief that women were never the primary breadwinners for their families, a belief that did not accord with reality. Women also faced sexual harassment and assault in the workplace, and if an unmarried woman worker was unlucky enough to get pregnant, she would find herself out of a job and with no means to support herself other than prostitution or begging.

As industrialization spread throughout continental Europe and the United States, mechanization, the division and deskilling of labor, and the feminization of the labor force continued apace. A few examples will have to suffice here: In the Rhineland (Germany) in 1861, there were 5,200 cotton handlooms and 1,200 mechanical looms; by 1880, the number of handlooms had dropped to 1,000 while the number of mechanical looms had increased to 7,000. By 1875, women workers in cotton mills in this area outnumbered men by 32 percent.[19] The sewing machine facilitated an increase of women working in their homes for low wages in the garment industry, a trend we see in other trades as well in the second half of the nineteenth century, such as the fabrication of shoes, hosiery, and artificial flowers. In Paris at the end of the nineteenth century, over 80 percent of workers in artificial flowers were women, and by 1906 almost 38 percent of these women worked in their homes. While some women made a good living in this trade, in the early twentieth century only 27 percent made subsistence wages or higher.[20] The division of labor and deskilling were systematized with the development of Taylorism, a management technique in which the work process was broken down into simple, easily taught tasks in order to increase efficiency. The First World War magnified these trends. The shift to wartime manufacturing encouraged mechanization and brought ever larger numbers of women into the factories at jobs where they were paid less than male workers, often based on the justification that their work required less skill.

These processes were facilitated by other changes that occurred in the late eighteenth and early nineteenth centuries. Again, the garment industry provides an instructive example. In France, the abolition of the guilds during the French Revolution contributed to the transformation of tailoring, as cloth merchants could legally establish ready-to-wear workshops—or send work out to low-paid workers toiling in their homes—because regulations concerning apprenticeships and wages could no longer be enforced by the guilds. Workers' ability to set wages and working conditions were similarly curtailed in Great Britain with the passage of the Combination Acts in 1799 and 1800. This did not mean that workers did not protest change; they did, repeatedly, as several of the chapters in this volume discuss. But it did mean that manufacturers had the legal ability to reorganize the work process through mechanization, the division of labor, and the hiring of lower-paid workers. New forms of retailing including early incarnations of what would become, in the second half of the nineteenth century, the department store, where lower-priced, ready-made goods were attractively displayed for purchase, and advances in transportation with the steamboat and railroad, that made moving raw materials and finished goods less costly, also contributed to the rise of ready-made clothing manufacturing. Advances in agriculture meant that fewer workers were needed on the farm and men and women sought work in the cities, where low-paid but unskilled employment in trades such as tailoring was available.

As the example of tailoring suggests, proletarianization—encompassing deskilling, falling wages, and loss of control over the work process—was the result of a variety of interrelated processes that over the course of the nineteenth century changed the nature of work for many men and women in the West. It is for this reason that Robert

Allen writes that the "Industrial Revolution" was in fact a series of transformations in technology, demography, urbanization, agriculture, commerce, transport, and finance.[21] The complexity of industrialization still engenders disagreements about what factors were most important in Great Britain's "take off": its dramatic transformation of the manufacturing process in the late eighteenth and early nineteenth century. Jeff Horn, Leonard N. Rosenband, and Merritt Roe Smith write that although economic historians do not agree on the relative importance of various causes of British industrialization, they do agree in general that "the kingdom's highly productive and responsive agriculture; its abundant and accessible supplies of minerals, particularly coal; foreign trade, sustained by massive and cost-effective state investment in naval power; and, last but not least, technological discovery and innovation" were all significant factors.[22] Britain's economic growth spurred emulation and competition throughout the West.

MAKING SENSE OF INDUSTRIALIZATION, 1800–48

If historians today still argue over the causes of industrialization, how much more difficult was it for those who lived through the experience to make sense of it. Artisan journeymen who experienced proletarianization as an often-catastrophic decrease in wages and dashed hopes for advancement to the status of independent master, targeted both the masters of their trade who attempted to lower wages and other workers who accepted lower wages, as the responsible parties for a deterioration of their working conditions. They did not, nor could they possibly, understand the variety of interrelated factors transforming their trade. They, like other workers, did the best they could to find reasonable explanations for what was happening to them. Thus, François Jarrige draws our attention to the tendency of workers whose ability to make a living was adversely affected by mechanization to attack the machines themselves, while, Fiona A. Montgomery and Marjorie Levine-Clark remind us that workers subject to the process of proletarianization often argued that the solution to falling wages was to exclude women from the workforce. None of these responses were irrational. They were the result of workers' attempts to make sense of the dramatic transformations in their working lives, based on what they observed: masters were lowering wages to compete; other workers, and particularly women, were accepting lower wages to survive; and machines were making inroads into various trades, often with the result of deskilling, the hiring of women and children to operate machines, and falling wages.

In Great Britain, but also in the parts of France, Belgium, and some of the German territories that were beginning the process of industrialization in the early nineteenth century, workers protested these changes. Machine-breaking incidents were widespread in the first decades of the nineteenth century, most dramatically in the Luddite riots. These protests were an attempt to maintain control over a trade being transformed by mechanization, and far from an irrational outbreak of vandalism, the 1812 Declaration of Framework Knitters reveals a logic to the machine breaking. In this declaration, an Act of Parliament that made the destruction of knitting machines a felony is declared "fraudulent" and the result of "deceit," and thus null and void. The declaration reveals that knitters, like many artisans in the first decades of the nineteenth century, did not accept mechanization and its consequences as valid or inevitable. It thus proclaims that "we do hereby declare to all Hosiers lace Manufactirou's and proprieters of frames that we will break and distroy all manner of frames Whatsoever that do not pay the regular prises heretofore Agree'd to by the Masters and Worckman."[23]

Traditionally, workers had been able to maintain some control over their trade and wages through organization in guilds, although of course not all workers could organize in this way. The majority of workers in the early nineteenth century were employed in agriculture and domestic service, where they had much less control. Other workers, such as itinerant peddlers, had a greater degree of independence even if they, like those who engaged in low-paid menial labor or worked in the sex trade, worked as a means to survive. With their tradition of organization, artisans took the lead in creating friendly societies and mutual aid societies that could serve to soften the financial blows of industrialization while also providing a framework for political action. By the 1830s, artisans had begun to organize across trade boundaries. In 1833, workers in New York City founded a General Trades Union and in 1834 a meeting in London gave rise to the Grand National Consolidated Trades Union (GNCTU). Both sought to bring together workers in various trades as a means to pressure employers to limit work hours and pay higher wages. The former spread from New York City to other major cities of the northeastern United States, including Philadelphia and Boston, but fell apart in 1837. Similarly, the GNCTU was short-lived, riven by disagreement over whether confrontation or cooperation with employers was the best tactic to adopt. Despite the ultimate failure of these unions, these early efforts to organize were spurred by a belief that workers could improve their situation by means of organized protest (including strikes) and negotiation.

One of the obstacles workers faced in organizing was a deteriorating economic situation. In the United States, the Panic of 1837, a banking crisis, led to a recession that lasted well into the 1840s. In Europe, economic downturn in the 1830s gave way to subsistence crises in the mid-1840s, the most severe of which was the Irish Potato Famine that led to mass migrations out of Ireland and the death of about one million people. As Ute Chamberlin discusses, migration was an option that many workers exercised, despite the emotional and financial hardship it often entailed, as a means to improve their lives. For those who stayed in place, work slowdowns or stoppages (strikes) were a means used to pressure employers to raise wages or improve working conditions. Yet the widespread economic hardship of the 1830s and 1840s made it more difficult for workers to sustain such actions, or to organize. Nonetheless, these decades lay the foundation for later, more successful efforts. They also gave rise to movements that focused on political rights. In England, the Chartist movement demanded political rights for workers, both the right to vote and the right to hold political office. The Great Charter, a petition presented to Parliament repeatedly without success, looked to political reform as a means to better workers' lives.

One reason protest was so widespread in the first half of the nineteenth century was that many believed it was possible to stop, or even reverse, the process of industrialization. As Maxine Berg has noted of this period in Britain, "it was far from clear whether [mechanization] was a portent of inevitable economic revolution, or but one course of development among several ... Its consequences were equally hard to determine."[24] And indeed, in 1848, industrialization was far from dominant. In 1851, 64 percent of the French workforce was employed in agriculture. In industrialized regions of the Rhine province of Prussia, about 40 percent of the population worked on farms.[25] Even in Britain, overall economic growth slowed in the period 1770–1840 in comparison to growth in the middle of the eighteenth century.[26] Furthermore, industrialization was accompanied by deindustrialization; in the early nineteenth century, workers in manufacturing increased in the northern counties of England by almost 62 percent but decreased in the southern counties by about 25 percent.[27] And, as noted above, older forms of manufacturing, such as cottage industry, were sometimes expanded as a result of industrialization; in continental Europe, as David Landes has shown, "a great expansion of rural putting-out [was] paradoxically accelerated by the mechanization of some ... of the stages of manufacture."[28] Finally, greater availability of mass-produced goods enhanced the value of artisanal products that came to be associated with luxury. Economic growth in certain regions, notably Paris, was dependent upon continued demand for luxury goods, and small workshops with a highly skilled workforce continued to produce these goods well beyond 1920. Casey Harison gives us an overview of the wide variety of workplaces during this period, from the street to the construction site to the workshop, helping us understand how artisans subject to the process of industrialization moved in and out of different workplaces, and lived side by side with others whose lives remained more closely tied to tradition. If this was still true in 1920, it was even more the case in the 1840s.

Yet despite these continuities, it was evident to many that the economy was undergoing a profound transformation. The 1830s and 1840s were thus also a period of intellectual ferment, as writers from various backgrounds attempted to make sense of these changes. Both workers and other observers were troubled by what appeared to be the profound contradictions of industrialization. One of the most significant cultural changes of the nineteenth century was the growing belief that work was a source of value beyond the economic benefit it brought to society. As Frobert and Jarrige note, while labor had traditionally been associated with a servile state, "work was exalted in an unprecedented manner in the modern period." In a process that began in the eighteenth century but accelerated in the period after 1800, work was redefined as a source of creativity and dignity, particularly for men. Workers' efforts were crucial to economic growth, yet workers themselves often lived in dire poverty. Workers manufactured goods that generated profits as well as jobs in other sectors, such as retail, yet also hindered the functioning of the economy by participating in actions from slowdowns to strikes to revolutions. It is thus not surprising that while work gained in cultural importance, it also was a category of social life that some dreamed of eliminating altogether. In the 1830s, utopian socialists imagined a society in which work was a means of personal fulfilment rather than daily toil. They drew inspiration from the work of Henri de Saint-Simon, who saw industry as a means of bringing about an endless abundance shared by worker and employer alike. Socialists, from the utopian socialists of the early nineteenth century to Marx and other "scientific" socialists, argued that workers had the right to an equal share of the fruits of their labor.

Unlike the Luddites, who threatened to break weaving machines if they were unable to retain control over their trade, the utopian socialists did not wish to stop industrial progress. Rather, they wanted to find a way for industrialization to benefit workers, as well as employers and consumers. They and their supporters were influenced not only by their own experience, but also by the growing number of depictions of work that revealed the hardships faced by laboring men and women. Consider Friedrich Engels' description of the St. Giles neighborhood in London in 1844, the home of the "poorest of the poor," where "the walls are crumbling, doorposts and window-frames loose and broken, doors of old boards nailed together, or altogether wanting in this thieves' quarter, where no doors are needed, there being nothing to steal. Heaps of garbage and ashes lie in all directions, and the foul liquids emptied before the doors in stinking pools."[29] Or these words of a tailor, published in the early 1830s: "We work 14 to 18 hours per day, in the most painful posture; our body becomes deformed and broken; our limbs become numb and lose their ability to move ... our health is ruined, and we only leave the workshop for the hospital."[30]

In the writings of those who condemned industrialization, factories were compared to penal colonies and prisons, and industrial work likened to slavery. The metaphor of slavery was a powerful means of communicating the loss of control over the work process that workers in both factories and more traditional sectors of the economy were experiencing in the nineteenth century. According to Friedrich Engels,

> the proletarian has to sell himself by the day and by the hour. The slave is the property of one master and for that very reason has a guaranteed subsistence, however wretched it may be. The proletarian is, so to speak, the slave of the entire bourgeois *class*, not of one master, and therefore has no guaranteed subsistence, since nobody buys his labour if he does not need it.[31]

Some abolitionists in the United States rejected the comparison on the grounds that it minimized the evils of slavery. Yet as Jonathan Earle has argued, those active in the early labor movement supported "core values [that] were fundamentally at odds with the institution of slavery."[32] These values were often rooted in artisanal experience. But slavery was not just a metaphor during this period. Many countries, including the United States, banned the slave trade early in the nineteenth century. Slavery itself was not banned in British colonies until 1833, in French colonies until 1848, and in Dutch colonies until 1860. It was banned in the United States in 1865 and in Brazil in 1888. Nonetheless, unfree and coerced labor remained common throughout the nineteenth century; indentured and other forced workers were crucial to the functioning of colonial economies that supplied raw materials to Europe. This was true in Europe as well. Russia abolished serfdom in 1861, yet peasants were often unable to redeem themselves and remained tied to the land. Despite the continued importance of unfree labor to industrialization, employers and political economists emphasized the new contractual nature of work, and justified slavery and forced labor using racist arguments.

While socialists argued either for a reorganization of work that would allow the worker greater control and a share of the profits, or, in the second half of the nineteenth century, for the revolutionary overthrow of the bourgeoisie in order to place the means of production in workers' hands, political economists developed another important framework for making sense of industrialization. As Emma Rothschild notes, nineteenth-century economic thought was "identified as 'political' economy because it was concerned with the policies of national states."[33] While political economists differed in their assessment of the costs and benefits of industrialization, in general, their work sought to make sense of economic transformation by placing it within a framework of values and beliefs that were gaining ground in the nineteenth century, including the importance of the individual, the need to preserve the family unit, a faith in progress, and competition among nation-states. The adoption and expansion of these beliefs can be considered part of the cultural revolution of work during this period. In the work of the political economists of the nineteenth century we see, as Frobert and Jarrige observe, "an obsessive attention to industrial labor, that of artisans and of the new proletarians of big industrial concerns."[34] The size and scale of factory production prompted reflections on the ways in which the concentration of labor in a single locale, its rationalization, and the adoption of machinery could revolutionize the work experience and expand the economy. The factory soon came to embody the values cherished by nineteenth-century political economists: discipline, rationalization, and progress.

Advances in printing technology and the expansion of the art market allowed for greater dissemination of visual images of work. As Susan Hiner notes, representations of work are "never free of an ideological position," and this was all the more true in the period 1800–1920 because work was undergoing such a major transformation in sectors such as textiles and the garment trades. Work was not an entirely new topic for artists in this period, but interest in depicting both traditional forms of work (agriculture, street vendors) and new forms of work (factory work) increased beginning in the 1840s. Workers' protests against mechanization, fascination with the factory system, and widespread suffering during the economic crisis of the 1840s made work a compelling subject for artists, who often sought, as Hiner argues, to render workers less threatening and to downplay the intense physical toll of manual labor. And as Marjorie Levine-Clark discusses, women's work was particularly threatening at a time when middle-class beliefs about the sanctity of the family and motherhood were gaining cultural dominance, even as more women entered the workforce than ever before over the course of the nineteenth century. In France, visual images of women workers sought to reconcile these tensions by emphasizing the sexual attractiveness (and imagined sexual availability) of women workers, thereby "romanticizing and mythologizing" women's manual labor. British images of textile workers, on the other hand, were frequently sentimentalized as a means of emphasizing that women's natural state was to be "protected by a wage-earning man."[35] These images of women workers were echoed in workers' publications, where men argued that higher wages were necessary to support a wife and children.

INVENTING THE INDUSTRIAL REVOLUTION

The economic hardship of the 1830s and 1840s, the continued processes of industrialization, and the failure of efforts to organize workers all contributed to the revolutions that erupted across Europe in 1848. The failure of these revolutionary efforts and the establishment of strong governments that followed, alleviated some anxiety among employers and politicians that workers' efforts to combat industrialization would permanently hinder continued economic growth. In the 1850s and 1860s, optimism concerning industrialization was spreading among the middle classes of Great Britain. An important source of Britain's economic success was its export of manufactured goods, including textiles. Until the First World War, two-thirds of British cloth was exported to continental Europe, the Americas, and Asia.[36] These exports depressed prices and wages in importing countries, which then sought to industrialize in order to compete. In the German states in the 1820s, British cotton yarn was 43 percent cheaper and pig iron 25 percent less expensive.[37] In order to survive, German manufacturers needed to adopt British technology, which soon became another important export to the continent. The British also exported capital, which they invested in the development of railroads in continental Europe and the United States. British machinery and engineers helped build those railroads. Eric Hobsbawm has argued that as a result of British success, manufacturers as well as those who benefited indirectly from industrialization (for example, those living off the profits of money invested abroad in the railroads) experienced greater confidence that industrialization was overall a benefit to humanity, and that the economic transformation experienced by Britons would not be reversed.[38]

One result of this confidence was a willingness on the part of employers and politicians to invest money and effort into improving the lives of the working classes. Chapter Four discusses the policies of paternalism as a means to secure the industrial workforce. By the century's end, employers, often under pressure from workers, were providing cleaner facilities in which workers could eat and wash up, and organizing activities from dinners to brass band performances. Protective legislation, so-called because it first concerned efforts to limit working hours for children and women, became increasingly common throughout Europe over the course of the nineteenth century, discussed in Chapters Seven and Eight. In the latter decades of the nineteenth century and beginning of the twentieth, as working-class political parties were formed and unions legalized, this legislation was expanded. Compensation for injuries, shorter work weeks, and safety inspections were designed to improve working conditions and care for workers hurt while on the job. They were also meant to stem the tide of political unrest that characterized the decades preceding the First World War. Yet François Jarrige notes, as mechanization advanced, more powerful machines meant that injuries remained a common hazard in factories despite greater attention to safety.

By the end of the nineteenth century, Britons in particular were aware that their economy had been transformed. It was at this time that the term "Industrial Revolution" gained ground as a description of the changes that had occurred in the late eighteenth and early nineteenth centuries. The term "revolution" had been used earlier in the nineteenth century to refer to changes in the process of manufacturing. As early as 1819, the statesman and promoter of French industry, Jean-Antoine Chaptal had written that the mechanization of spinning in the woollens industry had "effected a great revolution."[39] Yet as Anna Bezanson noted, the use of the term "revolution" to apply to manufacturing referred at this time simply to any evident change in one part of the production of goods, without implying an overall structural transformation of the economy.[40] This latter meaning of the term "revolution" when applied to the economy became popular after it was used by Arnold Toynbee in a series of lectures at Balliol College, Oxford, published after his death in 1884.

In introducing his history of the Industrial Revolution, Toynbee begins not with facts and figures, but with ideas. Toynbee's outline of the three stages of the Industrial Revolution is centered around the work of three political economists: Adam Smith, Thomas Malthus, and David Ricardo. These thinkers were crucial for Toynbee, who argued that the historian of economic transformation must not simply document the facts but must also, "explain many phenomena like those attending the introduction of enclosures and machinery, or the effects of different systems of currency, which without [the] assistance [of political economy] would remain unintelligible."[41] What mattered was the explanation for economic transformation, for it drove policy and politics. Yet for Toynbee, what he called the "old political economy"—that of Smith, Malthus, and Ricardo—was too wedded to the belief in the benefits of laissez-faire to account for the human costs of industrialization. What was needed was a new political economy, or a new interpretive framework, shaped by fact and able to explain economic transformation in a way that would ameliorate the suffering of workers and the poor.

By the late nineteenth century, when Toynbee wrote his lectures, the time was ripe for a new interpretive framework. In the midst of a severe economic downturn that began in 1873, what we refer to as the Second Industrial Revolution was underway. Larger and more powerful machinery, the growth of the steel and chemical industries, the invention of electricity and the internal combustion engine, along with the spread of industrialization across the European continent and in the United States both encouraged a continuation of the view that technology was key to progress and changed Britain's position vis-à-vis other western economies. The emergence of mass political parties dedicated to furthering the interests of workers, the legalization of trade unions, and increased strike activity coincided with a growing concern, fuelled by social Darwinist thought, with national degeneration to make the question of employer–labor relations a pressing issue. Daniel C. S. Wilson has argued that these changes shaped British understandings of industrialization, both by making comparative analyses of industrialization possible and by encouraging thinkers such as Toynbee to use the First Industrial Revolution as a lens through which to examine both Britain's role in relation to other western nations and social problems.[42] Interest in the causes of British industrialization was spurred by a growing awareness that the country's industrial supremacy was diminishing. By the end of the nineteenth century, Germany and the United States dominated international steel markets, and Germany had become a leader in machine manufacturing.

As industrialization advanced in the last decades of the nineteenth century and into the twentieth, factory life became the norm for growing numbers of workers. Industrialization was still spotty, and as industries rose in some regions of Europe, they declined in others. Machines and factories still caused concern and even shock. Yet by the 1880s, it was clear to all that industrialization was a process that could not be stopped or reversed. This realization underlay workers' efforts at organization, and by all accounts, the end of the nineteenth century witnessed a greater sense of solidarity among workers in different trades. The struggles of the first half of the nineteenth century had often seemed local and limited, but as these struggles were reported on and documented in a growing periodical press, as workers travelled from location to location as part of their training or in search of work, and as those who advocated new models of organizing work shared their ideas with others, workers increasingly became aware of the structural factors that created similar tensions in different trades. By the late nineteenth century, an organized labor movement and political parties that represented workers furthered this sentiment that workers in different trades were more similar than they were different, what Marx called a "class consciousness."

At the same time, however, by the end of the period under consideration in this volume, work became increasingly only a part of workers' lives. As W. Scott Haine discusses in Chapter Nine, in cities in particular workers could escape the drudgery of the work day at the music hall, the cinema, and in the pages of a detective story. The expansion of voting rights to working-class men prompted increased interest and involvement in political organizations. The spread of compulsory education shortened the working life span of men and women, and gave workers the means to read and write and think about things other than work. Of course, workers' identities had always been, as was noted at the beginning of this chapter, rooted in more than their labor. Community, family, and religion, as well as leisure and the discussion of ideas, were—throughout this period as in the periods before and after—significant dimensions of workers' lives. By looking at the cultural history of work, we see only a piece of a more complex experience of what it meant to labor for a living in the age of empire.

CHAPTER ONE

The Economy of Work

LUDOVIC FROBERT AND FRANÇOIS JARRIGE

TRANSLATED BY VICTORIA E. THOMPSON

Work was reevaluated and redefined in the nineteenth century. Long an object of suspicion, seen as suffering and stigma in an Old Regime organized by estates and legal privilege, where work was associated with servitude and exclusion, work was exalted in an unprecedented manner in the modern period. Beginning in the eighteenth century, Diderot and d'Alembert's *Encyclopédie* rehabilitated manual labor, proclaiming in an article on "idleness" that work was a source of pleasure at a time when the words "artisan" and "artist" were nearly synonymous.[1] In the nineteenth century, as the realities of labor continuously evolved within a context of widening differentials of global development, an ideology of work emerged. In Europe in particular, work became seen as a creative freedom, promising a more just social order based on the contributions of each human being, a guarantee of the social contract, and a true collective effort. At the same time, work was repeatedly at the heart of social and political debates, as workers—proletarians—came together in "dangerous masses," always at the limits of barbarism, while the cry of Lyon's *canuts* in 1831, "Live working or die fighting," frightened the elites.[2] By contrast, outside of Europe and other areas of rapid industrialization, such as the United States, "work" as a conceptual category was often absent, invisible, or at least never as central as it became in industrialized countries where it was progressively theorized by political economists. As part of this process, the increasingly autonomous discipline of political economy debated the meaning of work and attempted to clarify its importance. As an abstract concept, work developed within the context of larger discussions concerning global trade, a triumphant liberalism, social inequalities, technical developments, and new ideas concerning progress and emancipation.

This extraordinarily rich context, both concrete and abstract, prompts two brief reflections: The first, very succinct and thus imperfect, is an acknowledgement of the diversity of work in this long nineteenth century, shaped as it was by chronology, geography, region (city/countryside), gender, and juridical status. The second is a reminder that at least two discourses attempted to interpret these various phenomena and to bring them together in a coherent manner for specific purposes. The first, dominant, discourse was that of the *experts*, both liberal and socialist economists. Naturally, there were endless antagonisms, and often chasms, among these various expert opinions. But, equally attached to the idea of progress, especially in technology, they all taught that work was at the heart of modernity, and while the majority of workers would become impoverished as the rational use of machines increased, they believed that the beneficial outcome of this impoverishment would be the disappearance of labor. Paradoxically, work was central, but *progressively* its qualitative aspect would be lost in the hope of diminishing its quantitative importance. But in the margins, another discourse emerged. Profane and muted because unknown or censured, it came most notably from those subject to work and to the domination of experts but also from certain utopians. The nineteenth century gave birth to the myth of work as personal fulfilment and of the possible liberation from the alienation of labor. It dreamt of a society where work became a work of art, a vital necessity. Its utopian energies were directed towards the sphere of production, seen from an original perspective indissociably linking work and material and technical *creation*, as well as the political, social, and moral creation of a common world, that of coproducers or *associés*.

A NEW UTOPIA OF WORK AS CREATION

If 1798 is known for the pessimistic predictions and moral sermons of Reverend Thomas Malthus's *An Essay on the Principle of Population*, in the following years journalists celebrated the inexorable retreat of famine thanks to work. The ancestral reality of parsimony, suffering, and work seemed little by little to dissipate. Economists developed a new science, independent of morality and politics, detailing the subtle mechanisms of production, distribution, and circulation. The driving element, however, was production and a celebration of the power of human labor in itself or accumulated in the form of capital, reinforced by promises of new sciences and technologies that heralded a world without poverty. Only the distribution of wealth, class division, or sociopolitical disorganization could hinder, slow, or perturb the accumulation of wealth and the yield of labor. Luxury, the special province of the idle and the parasite, was now stigmatized and said to belong to the barbaric past. Jean-Baptiste Say put paid to a world of aristocrats and warriors where "rags of misery" were side by side with "signs of wealth."[3] The classical economists, from David Ricardo to John Stuart Mill, also pointed to the physical limits of growth, and showed that unresolvable antagonisms existed between different capitalists, as well as between capitalists and workers, and were therefore unable to deny that workers menaced by machines would, during a time of transition, suffer.

European socialists, from Robert Owen in his *Book of the New Moral World* (1836) to Étienne Cabet's *Voyage en Icarie* (1839–42), stated most strongly that with proper organization, and with a foundation of solidarity and association among producers made possible by the shared control over property, that the power of human labor was without limits. And as engineers and agronomists produced new knowledge, as technical experiments multiplied and as the marvels of technology, from the telegraph to the railroad, were praised, many believed that abundance was within reach. In France, it was the flamboyant followers of Charles Fourier who expressed this most strikingly. Clarisse Vigoureux took on those who were stuck in a past of suffering and parsimony, asking, "have they ever known, have they ever dared to affirm THAT HAPPINESS WAS AN OBLIGATION?" This happiness could be realized within the new context of the phalanstery:

Work?
Work, is happiness or misfortune.
Work, is peace or war.
Work, is wealth or misery.

Work, is liberty or oppression.
Work, is life or death.
Work, is the great question, which calls for a great and new science.⁴

Each of these commentators were reflecting on what all could observe. Industrialization accelerated globally in the nineteenth century and profoundly transformed the ways in which work was thought about and studied; it favored an intensification of production, a mutation of technology, and the advent of a new discipline of time and space. It drove a growing segment of the world's population to consecrate their labor to the production of manufactured goods, abandoning growing crops or fishing. Work became the central reality of political economy because contemporaries were struck by the changing scale of industrial production. Agriculture, the focus of the Physiocrats, was supplanted by an obsessive attention to industrial labor, that of artisans and of the new proletarians of big industrial concerns, on the part of economists and social investigators. Some estimate a growth in global industrial production of 4 percent per year during the second half of the nineteenth century, or a sevenfold increase of global industrial output between 1860 and 1913. Before 1850, however, industrialization remained limited and experts often downplayed its impact by highlighting how—even in Great Britain—the growth of Gross Domestic Product (GDP) remained weak, not more than 1.5 percent, and the proportion of artisanal and agricultural work remained significant. Moreover, domestic rural industry could be found throughout the world; in India, China, and Europe peasants became "workers" while at home, working with their families for markets that were often far away. At the beginning of the nineteenth century, few great differences existed between this cottage industry in India, China, and Europe.⁵ In the early modern period, industrialization began with the intensification of rural work produced for export, whether it was that of weavers in Brittany, Yorkshire, or the Yangtze Delta. Breton peasants exported their linens to America; Indian artisans from a multitude of villages wove high-quality textiles at a low cost that were exported by means of the East India Company to Europe and America. Indeed, some historians have suggested that British industrialization was a response to the efficiency and the low cost of Indian textiles in the eighteenth century.⁶

Over the course of the nineteenth century, global inequality grew and profound redistributions of production took place: if at the outset of the century European industry was not fundamentally different from that of Asia, the gap rapidly widened. The early industrialization of Great Britain had a major impact on its colonies and on the international division of labor; from 1830 on, the English worker that so fascinated economists produced on his spinning jennies three hundred and fifty times more cotton thread an hour than the Indian artisan with his spinning wheel. While India imported less than a million meters of English textiles in 1814, imports rose to over 1.8 billion meters in 1890. In 1913, western Europe and the United States were responsible for 82 percent of the world's industrial production. By this date, a great differentiation had occurred within the worlds of labor, and new groups emerged and gradually became central in the analysis of work. This is the case with coal miners, celebrated in literature and increasingly emblematic of the new, virile proletarian (see Figure 1.1). From Appalachia in the United States to the Ruhr in western Germany, the miner's work became the symbol of the new dynamism of industry; while twelve thousand miners extracted 1.5 million metric tons of coal from the Ruhr valley in 1850, in 1910 four hundred thousand miners extracted 110 million metric tons, making the region the leading center of the steel industry.

FIGURE 1.1 American coal miners, c. 1912. Photo: Buyenlarge / Getty Images.

At the time, it seemed clear that industrialization and the redefinition of work that accompanied it occurred first in western Europe, then in the United States, before spreading in successive stages throughout the world, while still retaining European commercial and political supremacy. In this understanding, the nineteenth century witnessed the deepening of inequalities between what historians call the "pioneering" countries—England followed by northwestern Europe and the United States—where industrialization occurred in the beginning of the century, and the "late-comers"—including southern Europe, settlement colonies such as Canada and Australia, as well as Japan—which did not begin industrializing until after the 1860s, and finally a last group—comprising the rest of the world—where industrialization would not begin until the early twentieth century, if not later. However this view of industrialization, based on a model of diffusion, has been profoundly rethought in the last thirty years, as new understandings of the ways in which work has been organized globally have emerged.[7] Whether one calls it the "great transformation," the "great divergence," or the classic "Industrial Revolution," the question of the origins of global industrialization continues to haunt the historiography.[8] The oldest interpretations, based on the concept of "revolution," have been replaced by more gradualist approaches, and a model based on the diffusion of European industry throughout the world has been supplanted by the discovery of industrialization's protean and polycentric character. National frameworks are no longer considered the most apt for analysis, and the European experience is no longer thought of as unique and exceptional in relation to other trajectories. As with other European developments, the "Industrial Revolution" has been provincialized, that is, reinscribed within a global framework.[9]

ARTISANAL, DOMESTIC, AND CENTRALIZED WORK

In his *Philosophy of Manufactures*, Andrew Ure vaunted the Factory System as superior to older models of the artisanal workshop and dispersed domestic manufacturing. He praised "the progression of the British system of industry, according to which every process peculiarly nice, and therefore liable to injury from the ignorance and waywardness of workmen, is withdrawn from handcraft control, and placed under the guidance of self-acting machinery."[10] Disciplining labor and promising its strict control, the Factory System was a response both to the analyses of classical economists and to the moral and political complaints of Victorian society. The great mechanized looms where work was rationalized became the symbol of the System, as images from the period, such as in the work of Edward Baines, celebrated the order presiding over the organization of work in these new factories full of huge machines (see Figure 1.2).[11] As Charles Babbage stated in 1837, the importance of a manufacturing system in which workers were centralized and which was founded on the possibilities of calculation could be summed up as a "struggle against time"; in France, the economist Adolphe Blanqui applauded Babbage's work as a "hymn to the machine."[12]

In the workshop and more generally in more dispersed manufacturing systems, time remained the property of the artisan and of his expertise. Control over production still ensured the artisan control over his life. However, influenced by the perception that the dangerous masses were incapable of measuring up to the values of modern industrial society, the Factory System, mechanization, the division of labor, and more generally the process of rationalization were meant to control and tame the working population. In England, Charles Dickens painted in *Hard Times* (1854) the image of a society where the narrow, venal utilitarianism of some was opposed to the misery, alienation, and suffering of others. Among other critics of the emerging economic horror caused by industrialization, Jules Michelet contrasted the lively world of the workshop where the

FIGURE 1.2 Weaving by power looms, 1835. Photo: Print Collector / Getty Images.

artisan "could dream" while creating "an endless variety of products that bear the imprint of his human personality" with the large factories, where "the vital equilibrium, noise, cries, movement" were absent and in which "a small, miserable people of men-machines create only to die," subjected to "the invariability of this steel being," the machine.[13] It was to defend these different dimensions of a life over which they retained some control and by which they were still able to protect themselves, their wives, and their children from the cadences of modern life that artisans fought. Among these were the *sublimes* and *sublissimes*—Parisian workers who refused to submit either to their bosses or to bourgeois moral codes—stigmatized by Denis Poulot.[14] And this struggle focused notably on the fight to retain a dispersed manufacturing system, which numerous economists declared obsolete but which artisans defended as rational.

Indeed, outside of the abstract theories of economists celebrating the centralized factory and inventing "work" as an autonomous reality and a category of analysis central to their emerging science, actual work remained extremely diverse and complex, shaped by time and space. First, it is worth mentioning that protoindustrialization and rural manufacturing reached its apogee in Europe in the mid-nineteenth century and became increasingly important in Asia over the entire century.[15] European economists were primarily interested in factories and other forms of organizing work judged to be the most modern, and therefore neglected the importance of cottage industry, seen as an archaic residue destined to disappear. Factory work often came to symbolize industrialization in works of political economy, where its presumed superiority was based on the minute division of labor and the reinforcement of discipline it made possible, as well as on the massive use of complex, coordinated machines used to increase productivity. This vision was particularly strong among liberal economists. The Genovese Sismondi deplored the fact that "capitalists are on the alert to discover the means of centralizing in the same way [as in the factory] all industry, to suppress everywhere the trades in order to replace them with factories."[16] But belief in the superiority of new forms of centralized manufacturing or of the factory over the older and more complex system of dispersed production was also at the heart of certain projects of reformers. Thus, in his *Propagande communiste*, Étienne Cabet explained that, in the new society, the principal rule in the matter of production and work could be summed up in two words: "*simplify* and *centralize*."[17] In the first half of the nineteenth century, certain regions such as Manchester in Lancashire, England or Lowell in New England, United States saw the rise of huge mechanized textile factories, employing workers who were often unskilled and from the countryside, and producing a mass of standardized products. In the great cotton-producing regions of Europe and the United States, textile mills—symbols of the first modern factories—employed several hundred workers on average in the 1830s (over three hundred in Alsace, France, and in Lancashire, England, around 1840) and already in 1816 over a thousand workers were employed in two factories in Manchester, England. Nineteenth-century observers were struck by these examples.

Nonetheless, one must not exaggerate the importance of large factories, nor allow them to mask the essential fact that until the beginning of the twentieth century work in small, disseminated settings was often most important, even in England. It is not possible to see industrialization as a linear and necessary path from agricultural, artisanal, and manual labor to a technological society; a more apt image is a "branching tree," with various possible paths, in the case of both technology and the organization of work.[18] Charles Sabel and Jonathan Zeitlin have notably insisted on the persistence—alongside mass production using specialized machinery and unskilled workers to produce standardized goods—of a "flexible" production mobilizing skilled workers and adaptable artisanal technologies which enhanced expertise and allowed the artisan to apply his skills to the production of an increasingly varied range of products.[19] The most common and usual form of industrial production remained urban artisanal workshops or microestablishments integrated into rural life, which maintained the industrial dynamics inherited from the eighteenth century. The so-called "Birmingham" model, based on subcontracting and small enterprises working with artisanal methods could be found in ironmongery in Saint-Étienne and Saint-Chamond, France; in cutlery in Sheffield, England, and Solingen, Germany; in the textile industry of Philadelphia, United States; as in capital cities with important consumer markets, such as London and Paris. Similarly, in the early nineteenth century, several artisanal trades in the Ottoman Empire, such as weaving in Damascus and Aleppo, were known for the dynamism of their production. According to this model, industrialization occurred because of the valorization of artisanal knowledge, technological flexibility, and the malleability of the organization of labor, allowing for a more rapid adaptation to changing markets. Industrialization is linked to the role of markets and the evolution of consumerism, characterized by gradual shifts and a diversity of trajectories. Technical innovations in production and consumption are essential, but are often linked to important political and social changes.

Among skilled urban artisans, the regulation of workshops in order to maintain high standards of quality allowed for experimentation with new institutions. In 1827 to 1828, weavers in the *Grande Fabrique* (silk industry) of Lyons, France (see Figure 1.3), founded a mutualist association as a way to have a voice in local decisions concerning their industry, and particularly in the court of prud'hommes, where disputes between merchants and heads of workshops were decided. Here, as in other skilled urban industries, such action provided artisans with a political apprenticeship, where practice in participation,

FIGURE 1.3 Silk workshop in Lyon, late nineteenth century. Photo: Christophel Fine Art / UIG via Getty Images.

deliberation, and negotiation produced, in the absence of a true political citizenship, a democracy of the workshop.[20]

If work in centralized factories was far from dominant in the nineteenth century, neither is it certain that this type of organization emerged first in Europe, as Eurocentric accounts, often the heirs of works by nineteenth-century economists, affirm. Historians of sugar plantations have noted that the first prototypes of the factory—a closed space where workers labor in great numbers together and in an intense and coordinated manner—should be sought in the sugar manufactories of Latin American and the Antilles, where sugar was prepared for exportation to Europe. The first workers required to adapt to factory discipline were slaves rather than wage-earning Europeans. In the early nineteenth century, agro-industrial plantations combined, under one roof, agriculture and the transformation of agricultural products, with an abundant labor force and heavy discipline. Diverse elements in this system seem to anticipate the functioning of industrial capitalism: the interchangeability of tasks, the importance of time in gauging production, and the separation of production and consumption as well as of the worker and his tools. On the Île Bourbon, Réunion, one sees an early use of steam-powered machines in the first half of the nineteenth century in the sugar industry; at the outset of the 1830s more steam engines could be found on this island in the Indian Ocean than in any administrative unit (*département*) of metropolitan France. The simplicity of the work undertaken, the absence of a trade-based tradition, the strict control of the workforce, and intense international competition pushed sugar manufacturers and engineers to industrialize production precociously. From the 1820s on, they developed a unique form of industrialization, using "indigenous mechanization" adapted to local conditions, and fed by technological transfers that were not limited to transfers from home country to colony but that instead circulated among the sugar-producing territories.[21]

These plantation-factories multiplied, expanding and becoming more efficient, and with an enslaved and exploited workforce. Indeed, until the early 1830s, industrialization was based on the purchase of adult men sold illegally into slavery. These proletarian slaves of various origins—"Creole," Madagascan, Indian, or Malay—were subject to an increasing rationalization of their work. Far from being manual labor, their work became more complicated, technical, and was similar in many ways to that of European factory workers. Like them, they faced an intensification of the pace of work and an increase in surveillance—symbolized by the use of the bell—in the name of increasing productivity. Slaves in the sugar factories experienced, sometimes even before European workers, a degradation of working conditions. In the first half of the century, philanthropists, as well as working-class and socialist journalists, repeatedly compared the situation of slaves in the Americas to those of European proletarians.[22]

If the factory is the exception, if it emerged in a polycentric manner, it was also not the natural result of an inevitable process as economists had argued. The factory, mechanization, and the new forms of work that came with them were highly contested at the beginning. Historians have demonstrated the extent of workers' insubordination: the turnover of the workforce in the first factories, the repeated machine breaking, as well as the long survival of artisanal tools and practices.[23] These realities invite us to ask about the negotiated and conflictual process of industrialization, and the daily and multiple accommodations by which it occurred. Given this reality, it is significant that women were also subject to an early centralization of manufacturing. Many of the elements of the factory-plantations of the colonies were echoed in the factory-convents that brought together a young, unskilled, and thus new workforce in a single location. Women's work in textiles especially, which previously, in both cities and countryside, was characterized by a diversity of tasks and the importance of the family as a unit of production, was one of the first to shift to large factories with machines powered by steam. And despite the pessimistic warnings of observers and social philanthropists, from Villermé to Jules Simon, women's factory work spread to several new industries, such as the chemical industries, food production, and light metalwork after mid-century.

The refusal of the factory, which was frequently compared to a penal colony, occurred in diverse regions. In England, textile workers rioted repeatedly, breaking machines and burning down factories during the Luddite period (1811–12) and with the revolt of hand weavers in 1826. In France, the long persistence of rural cottage industry and the dispersion of textile production delayed the adoption of centralized and mechanized factories. However, global events had an impact on local conditions, as when in the 1860s cloth manufacturers in Elbeuf, France, postponed modernizing their machinery because the American Civil War (1861–5) raised the price of cotton while the massive export of wool from La Plata, Argentina, allowed them to keep their prices low. Similarly, in the Ottoman Empire as in China, yarn produced by local artisans was only very gradually replaced by machine-woven yarn imported from Europe. And even though imports increased greatly after 1870—tripling in China between 1870 and 1883—they never represented more than 10 percent of the yarn used in the country because of the endemic hostility of the workforce to European imports. In the Anatolian provinces of the Balkans, workers protested the opening of modern factories financed by European investment. In the 1850s, the opening of factories equipped with steam-powered machinery created unrest in Bursa while hand spinners protested similar attempts in Usak in the 1880s.

FREE AND UNFREE LABOR

From the very beginning of the nineteenth century, both classical economists and socialist theoreticians in Europe viewed free labor and industry as the source of emancipation and general enrichment. For David Ricardo in *On the Principles of Political Economy and Taxation* (1817), work taken on freely was at the basis of his concept of economic value, which served as a touchstone for the new economic science built around the categories of production, distribution, and consumption, considered separate from morality and politics. In this same period, Henri de Saint-Simon called for a new world with no war and no castes, and also without the shortages of the old world that he saw disappearing. "The golden age, which blind tradition has until now situated in the past, is before us," he claimed.[24] In his *Nouveau Christianisme*, he announced the advent of a society where a surplus of morality combined with the power of industry and science would bring about "improvement in the moral and physical existence of the poorest class."[25] Euthanizing the idle and those who lived from their investments would allow for the birth and then the rational organization of a vast social workshop, a globe connected by railroads, communication networks, and financial flows, consecrating "a peaceful army of workers," ordered into a hierarchy of "capacity," creating and receiving wealth. The phalanstery of Charles Fourier and Robert Owen's cooperative community of New Lanark, Scotland, illustrates in different ways the reformist and radical—and undeniably Promethean—dimension of these plans for a new organization of labor. Similarly, Friedrich List, inspired by Alexander Hamilton's 1791 *Report on Manufacturers* and his time in the United States, proposed scientific and political approaches to industrial modernization appropriate to young nations, including the establishment of a customs union.[26]

Nonetheless, while engineers such as Gaspard Coriolis (*Du calcul de l'effet des machines*, 1829) focused on the intersection of the physical and the economic in developing their new science of work and human, animal, and mechanical outputs, while Charles Babbage worked to improve both his calculating machine and his theories on the factory (*Economy of Machinery and Manufactures*, 1832), the first worries arose concerning a system that increased cadences and yields of production, but at the cost of an impoverishment and even a degradation of workers. In successive editions of his *Traité d'économie politique* (1803), Jean-Baptiste Say tried, in vain, to downplay the words of Pierre-Édouard Lemontey, who critiqued Adam Smith's argument concerning the benefits of the division of labor into many specialized but repetitive tasks in pin-making. Lemontey characterized this impoverishment of work as a new hell to which the "worker-machine" was condemned: "The being whose existence the arts of efficiency has reduced to a single gesture seems to descend into the ambiguous class of the polyp, without an apparent head and which seems to live only by its arms."[27] And these concerns were brought up by workers themselves, skilled and literate artisans for the most part, who in their first periodicals evoked this world, supposedly marvellous in the future, but completely irrational and frightening at present: "In Louisiana a machine was just invented that, under steam power, digs the earth, picks it up, and moves it aside. Thus men that live like machines can be mechanically buried."[28] A bit later, Karl Marx and Friedrich Engels presented an accounting of the problems caused by the division of labor and mechanization in an economic system founded on the private ownership of the means of production in their *Manifesto of the Communist Party*. For Marx and Engels, this new industrial world of capitalism was a historical stage in which the private appropriation of capital by some excluded the mass of workers and accelerated their loss of skills and autonomy. The passage from small workshops to "the great factory of the industrial capitalist" turned workers into "slaves" of the bourgeoisie and of the machine.[29] The capitalist paid the workers a wage, becoming rich by accumulating the difference between the use value and the exchange value of their work. His power also allowed him to alienate the worker from both his social and his natural worlds.

The new industrial society of the nineteenth century expanded the number of wage earners, a group previously limited to small segments of society. In Europe, this new class of wage earners was paid a minimal amount—just enough to permit the survival of the worker and his family—and lacked legal guarantees regulating his work situation. Debates concerning the line between free and forced labor were particularly important among nineteenth-century economists. In theory, forced labor was abolished during this period; the *corvée* (days of labor imposed by a landowner on peasants) disappeared in France with the Revolution of 1789, and progressively in other countries, even if serfdom was not abolished until 1861 in tsarist Russia. However, historians have shown that the strict separation between free and forced labor was relative and far from impermeable. Thus in the Anglo-Saxon world most wage earners were similar to domestic servants, possessing few rights. In France, the worker's passbook (*livret*), instituted under Napoleon, remained in effect until 1890. Outside of Europe, the frontier between free and forced labor remained fluid and ambiguous, as "temporary servitude fell within the scope of contracts that were considered free and voluntary from a legal standpoint."[30]

Slave labor was increasingly denounced by abolitionists, and disappeared in 1833 in the British Empire, in 1848 in the French Empire, but only in 1865 in the United States and 1898 in the Spanish Empire. In the political economy of work, slaves had effectively become counterproductive and a brake on the forward march of progress, even if Jean-Baptiste Say still insisted on the profitability of slavery at the beginning of the century. While liberal economists denounced slavery as an attack on individual liberty, they were also careful to defend the property rights of slave owners and the profitability of economic activity based on slavery (see Figure 1.4).[31] Along with many abolitionists, they feared that freed slaves would desert the plantations for uncultivated and unclaimed territory, where they would live in indolence and autarky, potentially weakening the local labor market. The abolition of slavery by the UK in 1833 effectively resulted in a loss of labor on the sugar plantations in important British colonies. But how to convince former slaves to work on the plantations? To respond to this problem, the British—followed by the other important colonial powers—put in place at mid-century a system of indentured labor by which workers from Asia and Africa were recruited to the colonies and contracted to work for low wages in order to support their families, who remained at home.[32] In exchange for the cost of transportation and the promise of a meager wage, workers signed a contract that obliged them to work on the plantation for a set number of years before they could return home or, in some cases, remain, but as free laborers. Between 1834 and 1920, 1.5 million Indian workers were contracted under this system and sent to British colonies, notably to Mauritius and the Antilles. In the French colonies, 118,000 indentured workers were recruited to Réunion, 42,000 to Guadeloupe, and 25,000 to Martinique. Over the course of the century, 75,000 Chinese indentured workers, sometimes pejoratively known as "coolies," were sent to Malaysia, Sumatra, and Cuba to work in terrible conditions far from the view of European economists.

This new form of forced labor expanded massively in the second half of the nineteenth century, largely justified by liberal economists on the basis of racist arguments that

FIGURE 1.4 Slaves working with an early cotton gin, 1869. Photo: MPI / Getty Images.

assumed the indolence of "inferior" races and the supremacy of whites. At century's end, a liberal economist such as Paul-Leroy Beaulieu could justify colonial exploitation in the name of Europe's civilizing mission; without the intervention of the organized and industrious peoples of Europe, he argued, the colonies would remain undeveloped and inefficient, left to "decrepit" races and incapable of "spontaneous development."[33] Far from disappearing, forced labor was redefined over the course of the century; the model of the free worker celebrated by economists was continuously in competition with new juridical and social forms of subordination.

SOLUTIONS TO THE ALIENATION OF LABOR

While liberal theoreticians portrayed work as something that could be exchanged in a supposedly free market, several other thinkers and theorists sought solutions to the problem of alienated labor. The end of the Old Regime and the triumph of the principle of a free labor market effectively inaugurated a period of turbulence and intense conflicts in Europe. Industrialization had seemed to give birth to a monster—pauperism—and a massive severing of social bonds. How to reestablish social peace and integrate the new industrial proletariat? In addition to a paternalism that sought to organize the world of work by means of a system of moral obligations, diverse currents of socialism that emerged around 1830 in France and Great Britain, and then in the German states, tended instead to imagine a harmonious and free world of work, made possible by fair provisions and good regulations (see Figure 1.5).

FIGURE 1.5 The town of New Lanark, Scotland, c. 1825. Photo: SSPL / Getty Images.

Formulated as early as 1808 by Charles Fourier in his first book, *La théorie des quatre mouvements*, and revisited more systematically by Victor Considerant and Louis Blanc in the 1830s, the principle of the "right to work" spread widely throughout working populations on the eve of the 1848 revolutions.[34] According to Fourier, the right to work was "the most essential" of human rights, that without which, "the others are but derisory."[35] With his discussion of the right to work, Fourier made the unrealized principles of the French Revolution and of the theories that preceded it the fulcrum of his social critique. But it was especially in the heady intellectual mix of the 1830s, when socialist approaches multiplied, that the theme of the right to work was seriously discussed. A graduate of France's polytechnic university, Victor Considerant, leader of the École sociétaire dedicated to disseminating Fourier's ideas, countered the demands of radicals and democrats for the right to vote by stating, "We say to the people that the most important right is the *Right to work*."[36] In his *Organisation du travail* (1839), Louis Blanc popularized this idea, arguing that the state should guarantee the right to work and provide a minimum salary by means of what he called social workshops, or producers' cooperatives managed by workers.

As manufactures and factories became more common, centralizing and deskilling the work process, Paul Lafargue responded to Louis Blanc with his *Droit à la paresse* (*Right to laziness*; 1880), while in 1877 Robert Louis Stevenson published *An Apology for Idlers* (1877). In these works also, the question of control over one's time, life, and also work was central. Earlier in the century, the Fourierists had been virtually alone in insisting on the value of "attractive labor," rather than on the utilitarian or moral dimensions of work.[37] By means of an organization based on passionate attractions, the phalanstery would create a new society where "to work is to live; to live pleasurably, is to work according to the natural impulses of one's will."[38] In actual communities, such as the Familistère de Guise envisioned and later organized by Jean-Baptiste Godin, the challenge of implementing attractive labor would be partially abandoned. But the idea was taken up and interpreted in various ways by artisans, mindful of not wanting to give up on their knowledge and skills, and therefore attached to the system of dispersed manufacturing and the economy of the workshop.[39] In Lyon, with its many workshops dedicated to silk manufacturing, artisans paid particular attention to the Fourierist validation of work as creative, autonomous, and pleasurable. Pierre Charnier, a former weaver and one of the most important heads of a Lyon workshop who was also a founder of mutualism and member of the weavers' council of *prud'hommes*, wrote "the silk manufacturing of Lyon is like a very large and unique garden with an inexhaustible water supply to meet all sorts of needs, divided into sections, where the cultivation of each section has as many free gardeners as plants and flowers."[40]

After the 1848 revolutions and the repression that followed, socialist ideas and projects were transformed, reborn, and developed in diverse forms. Marxism, purporting to be a "scientific" form of socialism and founded on the analysis of capitalism and how it would eventually be overtaken by the class struggle and the passage to collective ownership of the means of production, tended little by little to become the dominant school of thought, but without ever completely crowding out others. At the end of the nineteenth century, globally, socialist ideas were organized into hierarchical, structured political parties, whether they were called socialist, social-democratic, or labor parties. Generally divided between reforming and revolutionary branches, these parties would henceforth work to gain control of the state apparatus in order to reform work and its organization.

FROM THE REJECTION OF ROUTINES TO AN OBSESSION WITH PRODUCTIVITY

While nineteenth-century economists were primarily interested in industrial labor, that of the factory and the workshop, throughout the century most work and most workers were located in the countryside, in the agricultural sector. Aside from in England and Belgium, the number of agricultural laborers did not diminish over the course of the century but grew. In France, the high point for the number of agricultural workers was the 1860s; in China the rural population grew from 300 million to 450 million over the course of the century, while in Egypt it grew from 3 million to 15 million. British industrialization and the rise of factory work was only possible because elites controlled significant peasant populations in Scotland, Ireland, India, and Africa that could furnish the factories with the raw materials they needed. The new industrial workers of Europe and the United States, celebrated for their productivity, came from the most mobile segments of the peasantry. However, unlike urban workers who early on developed rich forms of social and political organization, the peasantry remained dispersed and poor, scorned as traditional and backward, little seen or heard, and lacking both spokespeople and outlets in which they could speak. As difficult and poorly paid as factory work was, it seemed increasingly attractive to the pauperized masses of the countryside when compared with the difficulty of agricultural work, and the misery and debt that invariably accompanied each bad harvest. Over the course of the nineteenth century, agricultural work was repeatedly subject to crises caused in part by imperialism and the development of international commerce, and which gave rise to famines that devastated Ireland in the 1840s, India in the 1870s, and China and Africa in the 1890s.

In *Le peuple* (The People), Jules Michelet denounced the "slavery of the peasant," and criticized the "economists [who] use the term *labourer* to mean the [industrial] *worker*, thereby forgetting twenty-four million agricultural labourers."[41] On the other hand, Marx compared the peasants to "a bag of potatoes" to denounce their passive acceptance of their own exploitation.[42] But other notes were sounded as well; in the preface to her *La mare au diable* (The Devil's Pool; 1846), George Sand chose to ignore the association of the peasantry with suffering, hard work, and death in order to suggest how agricultural labor could give rise to hope, life, and the promise of social, moral, and political progress. As these examples suggest, peasant labor was perceived and described in ambiguous and ambivalent terms, and peasants were alternately denounced as ignorant brutes or praised as virtuous and holy. In an 1882 painting of a farm in Picardy—an important grain-producing region—the painter Lhermitte depicted a peasant boss handing out wages to day laborers. This painting is an excellent example of the French Third Republic's interest in agrarian policy and its concern with protecting and integrating peasant labor into the republic, all while distancing it from revolutionary upheavals. Every detail of this monumental canvas communicates the dignity of work: the young man facing the boss in the background accepts his pay while keeping his hand on his scythe, while the face of the old harvester, sitting on a bench, shows his fatigue. However, while such images idealized agricultural labor, agronomists and economists were more likely to highlight the archaic culture of the peasants, with their passion for land that discouraged them from making profitable investments, and their pathological caution that kept them from adopting new practices based on scientific research, including modern technologies that they viewed with suspicion. Aside from a few authors such as Sismondi, political economists were rarely interested in an agricultural labor considered overwhelmingly backward.

If agricultural work seemed to incarnate stability, order, and prudence, industrial work increasingly symbolized the alliance between science and progress, the growing obsession for productivity, and rationalization. While agricultural labor seemed uncontrollable because dispersed, factory work became the target of a number of rationalizing utopias. From the 1780s through the 1830s, the physical aspects of work were increasingly understood in relation to mechanization.[43] At the same time, a growing insistence on disciplining and controlling the workforce and its activity was evident. Recruitment, training and qualification of workers, and methods of remuneration were all means by which these physical requirements could be put in place, as was control over the organization of production. Manufacturers, engineers, and economists couched their projects for mechanization in terms of creating a disciplined and moral workforce. However, in a great many sectors of the economy, workers defended their traditions and their customary rights through a political economy from below. Nineteenth-century workshops were far from the orderly vision of manufacturing promoted by engineers and economists, as discipline of and control over the workforce was fragile. Even in the large centralized spinning factories, male and female spinners were long considered independent contractors.[44] And workers never failed to assert their prerogatives and to claim control over their work, as we see in debates in workers' councils or in the long persistence of practices such as taking scraps from the workplace (embezzlement), which remained important in a number of trades in England, France, and Germany. Taking scraps of wool, silk, and cotton, as well as woodchips, was considered to be a worker's right and a legitimate form of compensation. Despite a growing criminalization of this practice, and the vehement denunciations of economists and manufacturers, it remained central to workers' experience during this period.

In the immediate aftermath of the French Revolution, manufacturers and economists unceasingly denounced workers' "spirit of liberty." Prerevolutionary institutions and law had limited negotiations between individuals; after the revolution, workers had been given "free rein to discuss as equals."[45] Manufacturers' complaints concerning what they called workers' "insubordination" were abundant. Thus, in Rouen in 1804, employers denounced the freedom of weavers and their habit of changing workplaces when they didn't like the price they were offered for their work. This practice remained common in numerous trades at least through the 1860s; we see it with workers in paper manufacturing who demanded their sovereignty and their right to authority in the name of the "laws of their trade" and of their "small republic"; we also see it among the powerful cloth-shearers in wool manufacturing as in Aix-la-Chapelle or Verviers.

However, over the course of the century, the discourse of rationalization intensified until it became an obsession. First in the United States, in order to increase work productivity and make up for a lack of qualified workers in the country, the engineer Frederick Winslow Taylor developed a new, supposedly more scientific, management of work based on the division of the work process into small, easily learnable tasks. "Taylorism" was rapidly adopted in the United States, although its acceptance was slower and more progressive across the Atlantic, even if the First World War and its total mobilization of society accelerated the process. In 1900, Henri Le Chatelier developed an authoritarian version of Taylorism, in which the worker was seen as a simple cog that must be regulated in order to obtain maximum output. These visions of the social and political organization of work were influenced by a scientific imaginary of efficiency and the concern with optimizing the output of every worker. Following Anson Rabinbach, it is necessary to emphasize the importance of the metaphor of the "human motor" in the science of work at the century's end, as for example with the studies of Étienne-Jules Marey on the dynamism of the body at work. Thus was put in place a veritable obsession with improving the labor force as a fundamental imperative of contemporary, productivist societies.[46] Nonetheless, the positive determination to measure outputs also led to results that were socially more interesting. If Taylor and his followers in Europe basically sought to take control of workers' skills away from them in order to subjugate them to the paternalism of employers, another science of work was emerging, one that was attentive to the fact that human labor, part of the equation by which productivity was measured, required attention and protection. As engineers tried to measure human fatigue in the workplace, legislation protecting the worker's body emerged.

CHAPTER TWO

Picturing Work

SUSAN HINER

When everything had been sold, twelve francs seventy-five centimes remained, that served to pay for Mademoiselle Bovary's going to her grandmother. The good woman died the same year; old Rouault was paralysed, and it was an aunt who took charge of her. She is poor, and sends her to a cotton-factory to earn a living.
—Gustave Flaubert, *Madame Bovary*[1]

In the final paragraphs of Flaubert's 1857 masterpiece, *Madame Bovary*, the reader learns the cruel fate of Emma's daughter Berthe. Contrary to her mother's upward trajectory from farmer's daughter to petit-bourgeois housewife turned shopaholic fashionista, Berthe Bovary's path exemplifies the downward spiral of a family caught in the clutches of modernity. Ruined by fashion's rapid and widespread diffusion, commodities' new disposability, and readily available credit, Emma Bovary plunges her daughter back into the laboring class she herself had escaped just a generation before. Now penniless, Berthe, christened in memory of an unknown aristocrat whose name Emma overheard at the only ball she ever attended, would end up working in one of Normandy's many cotton mills.

Both flax and cotton were significant industries in Europe, providing the raw materials for luxury goods produced in Paris and elsewhere. Historian Jean-Pierre Chaline asserts that "in Rouen and district there were some 2 million cotton spindles at the end of the 1840s ... [which] produced 20 million kilogrammes of yarn."[2] Flax, used to make linen goods, had long been a mainstay of the region as well, along with the spinning of wool. These and other textile industries, such as silk weaving, were also located in French industrial centers such as Lille, Mulhouse, and, of course, Lyon, three times the epicenter of textile workers' protests over wages and the economic heart of luxury production in France since Louis XIV. During the period of industrialization, the introduction of machines—such as the spinning jenny and later the sewing machine—would lead to production on a mass scale, keeping pace with new forms of consumption ushered in by institutions such as the department store.[3] In the mid-nineteenth century, little Berthe would not be working in an artisan's cottage, but rather in a water- or even steam-powered factory, a mill designed for spinning raw cotton into yarn, likely resembling the interior of the Manchester mill pictured in Figure 2.1; indeed, greater Rouen was known as "the Manchester of France."[4]

This image, like many such pictures appearing in newspapers in the nineteenth century that gave visual form to the printed word, emphasizes vastness, uniformity, and mechanization. The receding horizon of the interior space is distant, creating the impression of a cavernous expanse, and the vertical timbers and archways repeat systematically to

FIGURE 2.1 Dean Mills cotton mill, Manchester, England, 1851. © Chronicle / Alamy Stock Photo.

the rear and continue beyond the frame of the image on the left. This same verticality is replicated on the upper floor, where balcony rails enclose the workers. The mechanized spools and spindles echo in infinite regress the vertical movement, as do the workers themselves, primarily female, who stand at their tasks before the giant spinning machines. These repeated vertical lines reinforce the notion of mechanized uniformity, just as the upright workers mimic the machines at which they work. Although there are distinct overtones of incarceration here, the image nevertheless strives to present a picture of rationalized, efficient work. This is its purpose as an illustration accompanying a printed text extolling the mill. The female workers appear well groomed, each wearing a dress, smock, and hairstyle typical of the mid-nineteenth century. In spite of the male overseer at the far right of the image, the two women in the foreground are conversing while one adjusts her chignon, suggesting an atmosphere of community in the midst of efficient production. Productivity itself is signalled by the tightly filled and stacked baskets in the left foreground.

Like many other examples of industrial imagery produced for mass distribution in Britain, Europe, and America, the Dean Mills cotton mill print proclaims clean, harmonious, efficient labor, and the volume of output corroborates the efficacy that is contiguous with pleasing working conditions. It accompanies an article describing Dean Mills, near Manchester, England, which Prince Albert had recently visited. Although the image is ambiguous—the potential dangers of millwork are signalled by the woman's gesture of getting her hair out of the way of the machinery—both the image and the article seem to function as self-congratulatory illustrations of industrial advancement. What the image does not illustrate is that women factory workers were "paid less than half the salary [of men]," which men "resented because it made women more desirable workers."[5] Further, representations of female factory workers were rare, not only because such work was deemed dangerous and exploitative, but also because it took a woman "away from her role as sustainer of the family and transformed her into a social being."[6] It was thus more common to find women represented working in agriculture, where they remained a signifier of the "timeless, nurturing realm of Nature."[7] European visual culture, especially with respect to women, served up contradictory messages: sometimes idealizing workers' lives and offering either nostalgic or optimistic views of nineteenth-century labor and, at others, critiquing the dangers or misery of their plight.

My invocation of Flaubert's Berthe Bovary suggests possible trajectories for workers like her, trajectories that we will consider through the images examined in this chapter. Workers, whether idealized, sentimentalized, or critiqued, populated nineteenth-century visual culture, from popular illustration to high art, from newspaper prints to photographs. And no matter its form—print, painting, or photograph—the image is never neutral, never free of an ideological position, and this is especially true with respect to images of work picturing women. This chapter explores representations of work, focusing primarily on fashion work by women in Paris in the long nineteenth century and gesturing to the broader European context and to other industries. Because the garment industry (including textiles) was one of the most rapidly accelerating economies of the nineteenth century in continental Europe, England, and North America, it offers a wide range of visual representations that illuminate how work—especially female labor—was perceived and presented in nineteenth-century culture.[8]

PICTURING WORK IN THE LONG NINETEENTH CENTURY

In an important essay on the image of the working woman, Linda Nochlin presents "the issue of the status of the working classes" and "the position of women" as two of the most vexed subjects of nineteenth-century social history.[9] Indeed, visual evidence demonstrates an intensified focus on women workers over the course of the long nineteenth century, evolving from a tendency to eroticize or sentimentalize women in the world of work to an increased awareness and tolerance of their role as laborers. As Michelle Facos explains, "artists devoted increasing attention to urban subjects after 1840 ... [and] looked with greater intensity at the working class, the group which grew the fastest and epitomized the working world."[10] Greater populations of women entering the workforce produced increased anxiety around shifting gender and social roles; by century's end, however, some degree of acceptance of women in the workplace took hold, a shift reflected in visual culture.[11] By the early twentieth century, images of women working in factories were increasingly common. Before turning to the specific focus of this chapter, however, I will consider the context and functions of picturing work more generally in the period 1800–1920.

Several key themes emerge in the representation of work in nineteenth-century European art. Commentators often classify work pictures according to three principal categories: rural agricultural work, (sub)urban industrial work, and the self-conscious labor of art itself. In French and British art, we find pastoral scenes of the harvest that frequently idealize workers and their surroundings through nostalgic portrayals of vast, fertile fields and agricultural workers—mostly men—engaged in manual labor. For English painter John Linnell, "harvest was a timeless practice that lay beyond historical process," and his paintings indulged a wistful rural fantasy featuring wholesome peasants and rolling fields unspoiled by industry or machinery.[12] Similarly, artists like Jules Breton in France offered sentimental harvest scenes depicting sunlit fields and bales of hay—a "rosy vision of toil in the fields."[13] Setting and product supersede the experience of labor itself, and in both contexts the reality of agricultural innovation is absent, as is the displacement of workers by machines, which was the legacy of the nineteenth century more globally. This is not to say that agricultural paintings were not socially engaged; indeed, Gustave Courbet's *Stone Breakers* of 1849 pays tribute to the backbreaking toil of the anonymous laborer, and Jean-François Millet's 1857 *The Gleaners* asks viewers to contemplate the physical agony of repeated bending only to recover the paltry leftover grains that could not be sold at market.

What these and other works also proposed was a gendered division of labor, one that was not necessarily historically accurate, but as Martin Danahay asserts, was necessary to reinforce "Victorian ideologies of work."[14] Madeleine Reberioux, likewise, articulates a similar division in French agricultural painting, in which men are the reapers and women the gleaners.[15] Ideologies such as the now questionable notion of "separate spheres" were widespread in bourgeois evocations of gender relations and work environments throughout Europe and America. It is thus not surprising that depictions of women laboring would differ vastly from those of men, whose bodies were portrayed as sinewy, muscular, and powerful. Women, even working women, were rarely portrayed doing intense manual labor, and their bodies thus conveyed different meanings and cultural expectations. Indeed, as Danahay asserts, "'manliness' was emphasized in this period to exclude women from the category of 'work' and promote the image of the male as breadwinner."[16] Agricultural work, on the other hand, reinforced the ideological connection of the nurturing woman to nature; in short, it promoted motherhood as female identity.

In industrial or urban scenes, a similar gender division prevails. Common among such images are scenes of the iron foundry, the steel mill, or the blacksmith's shop, as we find in Goya's 1817 *The Forge*, George Gassie's 1862 *Le Forgeron*, or Adolph von Menzel's 1872 *The Rolling Mill*. Darkness and energy overwhelm such images, with muscular male bodies turned to the fire or wielding their anvils, engaged in what appears to be difficult and dangerous manual labor. This gritty, hazardous world of heroic masculine industry contrasts with the loom scene in Figure 2.1, where hygiene, order, and safety prevailed in a predominantly female workspace. When working women were represented as engaged in manual labor, as in representations of French *moulineuses* or British coal haulers, they tended to be defeminized, with attention drawn less to the strength of their bodies than to the difficulty, indeed the danger, of the labor. Danahay contends that "an ideological redefinition of work along gender lines ... was carried out in artistic representations," and thus working-class labor was frequently encoded as masculine, while bourgeois leisure was often encoded as feminine.[17] Both Danahay and Ballinger cite the example of Ford Maddox Brown's painting *Work* (begun in 1852) as a key example of this gendered division of labor.[18]

Some artists, however, challenged these gendered assumptions, and particularly in French art of the second half of the nineteenth century, realistic images of women toiling begin to emerge, and the effacement or ideological restriction of women's labor was increasingly contested. As a reaction to the distant historicizing of classical art and the idealism of Romanticism so prevalent in the first decades of the nineteenth century, realism in art and literature opened new perspectives on what *counted* as art and what subjects were worthy of representation. Work thus became more visible as an appropriate subject of social and aesthetic commentary, and, eventually, especially by the time of the First World War, women working could be pictured without idealization.

Female urban workers not working in factories, but rather in workshops in the needle trades, fall outside of these two broad categories of agricultural or factory work. France was the center of both art and fashion in the nineteenth century, and these two phenomena intersect in the representation of women working in the fashion industry. I focus on the needle trades and the broader industry of fashion work here because this was one of the few industries dominated by women in the nineteenth century throughout the western world, and yet, frequently, representations of their work are either sentimental or erotic; both gestures deflect from work and impose ideologies. Focusing on some of the key features of visual representations of this kind of work, the ideological messages underpinning these representations, and the relationship of these work pictures to cultural shifts during this long nineteenth century, this chapter seeks to decode the visual rhetoric of some of the most iconic depictions of women workers in nineteenth-century France. These discussions will point to broader trends across the western world.

In prints in particular, we discover rich, under-studied sources for a cultural history of work with respect to the social construction of women in the workplace. As we shall see, visual depictions of women working often erase their actual work and suggest instead the consumption of the worker herself. Male workers, on the other hand, are typically portrayed laboring, as in William Bell Scott's 1861 *Iron and Coal* or in Millet's 1850 *Sower* in which outsized male limbs are pictured in movement and the subjectivity of the worker is not foregrounded. Danahay persuasively argues that such a gender dichotomy also placed male workers in aesthetic, nonmanual fields—writers, for example—in a precariously feminized position. At the same time, however, women pictured working challenged the image of nineteenth-century femininity and thus posed a threat to the gendered order of things. Let us now turn to a brief history of the pictorial tradition of representing urban workers in western Europe before considering in greater detail the female worker in the nineteenth century.

ILLUSTRATING URBAN WORKERS

Illustrating work and workers in European cities reaches at least as far back as the early sixteenth century to the genre of the illustrated street vendor, which, while having received little critical attention, offers a valuable pictorial history of the urban worker.[19] In London, an oral culture of street vending dates to medieval times and was memorialized in the poetry of John Lydgate. From the seventeenth century on, illustrations of these itinerant workers became commonplace, and by the late eighteenth and early nineteenth centuries, British artists Francis Wheatley, William Marshall Craig, and Thomas Rowlandson offered versions of the *Cries of London* that staged working-class vendors and service providers engaged in public performance.[20] In France, the illustrated genre of the "cris de Paris" emerged in the sixteenth century, although urban street vendors were present much earlier.[21]

In some incarnations idealizing and in others caricaturizing, this genre presented a series of images of street vendors, male and female, usually portrayed in isolation, their trademark "cries" printed beneath their stylized images. In Figure 2.2 we find Madame de Chiffon, hawking "used stockings, used shoes, used clothes," and Madame de Bouquets, who cries, "Ladies, beautiful roses, buy some beautiful roses!" In France, the genre is also referred to as that of "*les petits métiers*," or itinerant traders, and it offered "snapshots" of workers of the popular class, identifiable by their cries but also by their costumes and trappings.²² The *chiffonière*, for example, is loaded up with multiple hats and piles of used clothing draped over her arms; likewise, the *bouquetière* holds a wide basket of flowers. The purpose of these illustrations was to present a pictorial explanation

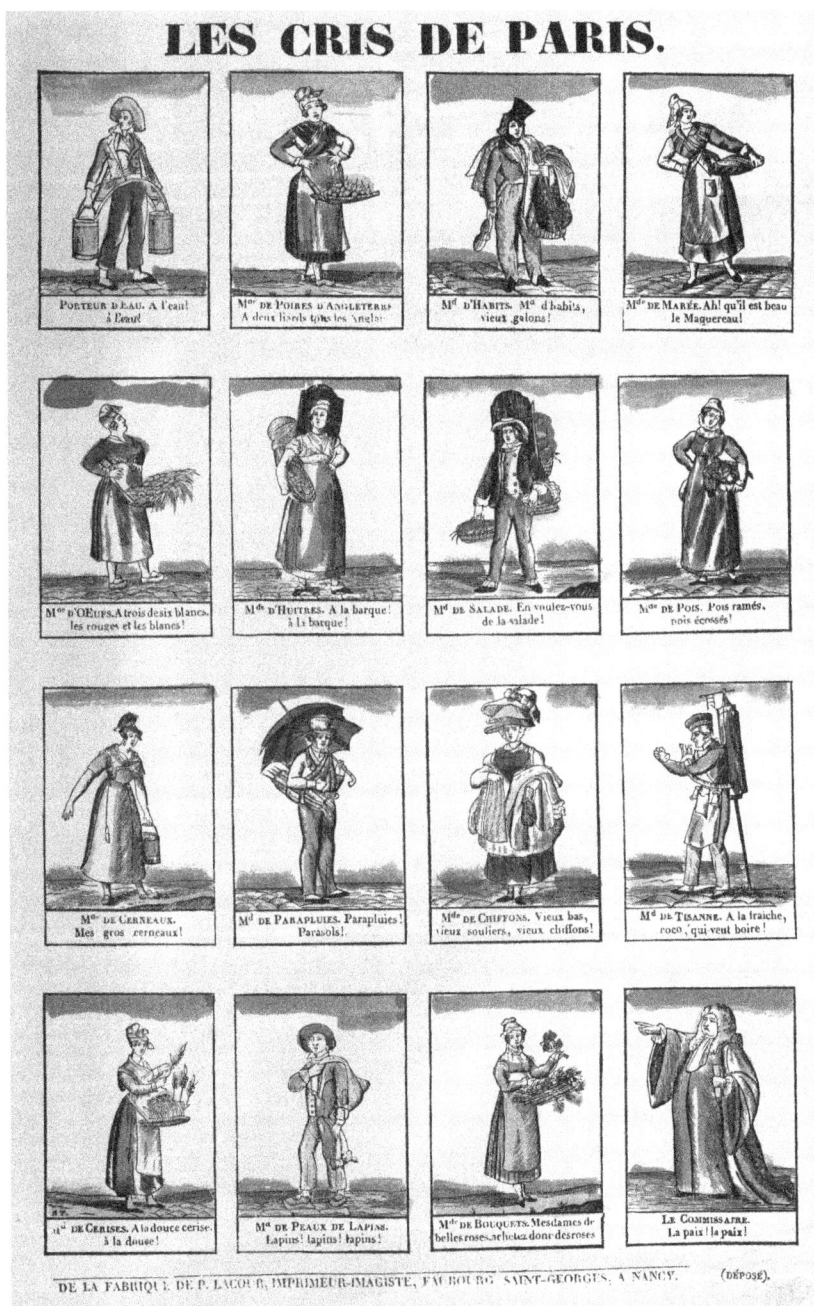

FIGURE 2.2 P. Lacour, *Les cris de Paris*, 1831. © INTERFOTO / Alamy Stock Photo.

of a linguistic system— "*Cris de Paris*"—and to render visually intelligible what might sound cacophonous and chaotic in a crowded urban landscape.[23] As such, they offered a picturesque panorama of the city and its working-class inhabitants.[24]

But these prints also contributed to a normalization of perceptions of workers, who appear contented and healthy, not miserable and famished. They were particularly popular in the nineteenth century, when authors like Balzac and later illustrators such as Eugène Atget were nostalgically documenting the disappearance of old Paris in their works.[25] Vincent Milliot argues that these stereotyped figures served to "tame these working people," who might otherwise seem threatening in an urban center with a growing population of workers.[26] By reducing them to stereotyped features, these pictures circumscribe workers within palatable behaviors and appearances, and their identity, decontextualized from particular settings, is tied purely to their function.

Costume was crucial in coding the social types represented in the *cris de Paris* prints. As Robert Massin has indicated, "If the cry is a distinctive characteristic of most roving tradespeople, there is another equally important one that also permits distinguishing trades practices in the street: dress."[27] By the time of the French Revolution many prints featured female figures with "beautiful white kerchiefs" and "very dainty shoes," fashionable accessories whose function was purportedly to conceal but which in fact drew attention to low-cut gowns and glimpses of legs.[28] A similar tendency seems true for the *Cries of London*, where we also find beguiling, young female street vendors dressed, if not as provocatively as their French counterparts, nonetheless in charming gowns posed with one foot forward to reveal a slim ankle. By merging fashion illustration with social depictions, these prints, many produced for elite buyers, were already engaged in the idealization, and thus mythologizing, of working women.[29]

EROTICIZING WORKING WOMEN

In the early nineteenth century, images of women workers multiplied, in no small measure due to the expansion of the fashion press, whose early illustrators, including Gavarni, Grandville, and Numa, were known for producing conventional fashion plates as well as other kinds of images of women. Laundresses were particularly rich subjects for illustration throughout the nineteenth century, romanticized in works by printmakers and artists from Daumier to Bonnard. But so too was the *grisette*, a folkloric figure popularized in literary works by Honoré de Balzac and Alfred de Musset. *Grisette* was a catch-all term for an unmarried working-class woman, generally employed in the fashion trades, and named originally for the gray-colored cloth of her neat but inexpensive dress.[30] The term *grisette* first appears in the seventeenth century, and the figure herself was mythologized by literature and visual culture during the first half of the nineteenth century. She was lovingly caricatured by lithographer Henry Monnier, who produced three different series entitled "Les Grisettes" in the late 1820s. According to Beatrice Farwell, "Monnier's *grisette* is characterized by a round face and tiny waist and feet. She often wears a frilly white cap and, if she is a milliner's assistant, carries a hatbox."[31] In Monnier's representations, the working girl is rarely pictured working. Rather, she entertains bourgeois suitors, chats with her girlfriends about these suitors, receives gifts, and takes walks, typically wearing an exaggeratedly large hat, black satin *escarpins* (flimsy, open shoes), and a skirt just short enough to reveal her shapely ankle. The iconography surrounding the *grisette* thus was varied—playing at times on her fashionability, and her aspirational elegance, and at others on her good-natured humility, and, of course, frequently featured the companionship of men. The *grisette*, while a specifically Parisian type, achieved international acclaim thanks to travel guides that presented her as one of many Paris "attractions."³²

But not all illustrations that contributed to the mythology of the female fashion worker in nineteenth-century France were caricatures. In 1824 Pierre de la Mésangère's *Le Journal des Dames et des Modes* published an illustrated series of women workers, entitled "Costumes des Ouvrières de Paris." Drawn by Louis-Marie Lanté and engraved by his frequent collaborator Georges-Jacques Gatine, this series necessarily focuses on clothing, for the women are mostly engaged in work that revolves around the fashion industry, and they are gracefully posed and dressed in smart attire. Mercer, *modiste*, feather worker, and straw hat vendor, as well as maid, flower merchant, and cook are but some of the occupations represented in this detailed series of forty-seven images.³³ If female fashion workers, and ancillary fashion workers such as laundresses and pressers, seem over-represented in this series, this is in part because the prints were produced for publication in a high-end fashion periodical, but also, most likely, because the new expansion of the fashion press in the nineteenth century worked in tandem with an expanding fashion economy. For along with these advancements in the press, the nineteenth century also introduced a new economic model of fashion as an ever-shifting phenomenon, and there was now a relaxation in the ancient guild system that had previously given a monopoly of fashion work to men.³⁴ In France by the end of the eighteenth century, the tailors' guild, for example, had lost some of its control to the seamstresses, who were now empowered to form their own guild; more important, the *modistes* would specialize within the seamstresses' guild to become the elite fashion creators and trendsetters of the nineteenth century.³⁵

The *repasseuse* pictured in Figure 2.3, as in the other representations of Parisian female workers in Lanté's series, is elegant and fashionable in a high-waisted blue dress and neat fichu covering her bosom. Although her hands are busy with ironing what appear to be handkerchiefs and lace collars or ties at her tidy table, the viewer's eye is drawn less to her work and more to her appearance. Her hairstyle is elaborate, with a double part, side ringlets, and high chignon, and her tiny, narrow feet, shod in dainty black flats, peep out from the decorative hem of her dress. The caption, which reads simply "Paris. Repasseuse," universalizes this kind of work, similar to the vignettes of the *Cris de Paris*, and suggests that this woman is exemplary of all female pressers in the capital. Work is thus romanticized and mythologized as this stylish, blushing lady makes what was without a doubt exhausting, monotonous labor look graceful and pleasant. All of Lanté's forty-seven images in this series portray work in this way; in fact, even a worker associated with food preparation, the oyster woman, against all probability wears a lace collar and fashionable shawl.

While, unlike in Monnier's series, labor is signalled (in the case of the presser by the iron, table, and articles of clothing to press), it is not actually acknowledged as labor. As Anne Higonnet has argued, like the *Cris de Paris* prints before them, this visual classifying of labor, decontextualized from its real conditions, while seeming to "individualize labour, in fact objectified it as costume and accessories"; indeed, she continues, "we know nothing of her working conditions or her relationships to her employers."³⁶ Rather, the *métier* print becomes a vehicle for illustrating pleasing females and fashionable dress. Images such as Lanté's deflected potential anxieties about working women entering the marketplace as both producers and consumers and the changing social roles that came with new economies. Furthermore, they conceal some of the realities of such labor, in favor of

FIGURE 2.3 Louis-Marie Lanté, *Paris. Repasseuse,* 1824. © Florilegius / Alamy Stock Photo.

a lovely typology that mythologizes the female worker as attractively productive. Lurking behind these visually pleasing portraits of contented workers in the most fashionable of nineteenth-century cities is the perceived social disruption inherent in their potential to move beyond their station and pass out of their class, thanks to the very elegance—whether goods or practices—they produce and/or sell.

Women workers also began to appear more regularly in nineteenth-century print culture as a result of the influx of women into the public spaces of work. Workshops regularly functioned as stores and often had wide windows and sometimes even opened onto the street. Shop windows that allowed for the viewing of female workers were already common, as Nina Kushner points out, in the late eighteenth century: "A prospective patron did not have to cross the threshold of a shop to see the women working inside. These shops were fronted by big glass windows in which the *marchande* [female merchant] showcased her fashions."[37] This increased visibility of women on the job, coupled with greater access by the lower classes to clothing and accessories previously reserved for elites, inevitably led to anxieties that would be reflected in visual culture. According to Valerie Steele, women-run boutiques (dress shops, hat shops, corset shops, etc.) also housed *ateliers* (workshops) where the goods were produced.[38] Indeed, the *atelier* was a favorite subject of illustrators, for it provided them opportunities to picture groups of young women at work—often engaged in conversation, dressed fetchingly, and apparently unaware they are being watched. The implied voyeurism in such scenes confirms that these were images produced for a male public. They were a pretext for depicting seductive, working-class women, and very rarely did they actually illustrate work or the work process.

While the Lanté series presented demure female figures, whose eyes are invariably either lowered to their work product or directed away at an invisible client, many prints featuring female fashion workers openly eroticized them. These images draw a direct, if not explicitly stated, connection between licit and venal work and they muddle the distinction between female workers as producers and as consumable objects. Such is clearly the case for Charles Philipon's corset vendor, one of a series entitled *Têtes de femmes* depicting charming Parisian working women.[39] Unlike the Lanté series, where the entire figure of the worker was represented along with token tools and products, in Philipon's series we find women workers, such as this *corsetière*, portrayed from the waist up (Figure 2.4). Here, focus falls on the expression of the worker; and, as with other women depicted in this series, the artist accords as much attention to her seductive charms as to her handiwork. Production and consumption thus become blurred in this schema. The elegance of the corset merchant, whose voluptuous feminine form is mirrored in the corset that sits on the counter directly in front of her torso, is signalled by the details of her dress and hairstyle. Her coy glance is hardly modest; rather, she looks directly at the viewer, perhaps inviting a purchase, and certainly inviting a comparison of the freestanding undergarment on the table with her own curvy feminine form. The image thus suggests an imaginary vision of this worker in *déshabillé*, as the foregrounded undergarment seems to merge with the dress behind it. As Steele emphasizes, in nineteenth-century visual culture, "the corset assumed the role of surrogate for the body; it also functioned as a sign of undressing and making love."[40] The *marchande*'s fashionability—sloping shoulders covered in gauzy film, ballooning mutton sleeves, and tiny waist—emphasizes as much the requisite "good taste" of the fashion worker as the desirability of her product; and like the elegant product she makes and sells, she too incarnates consumable elegance.

Like so many other representations of women workers in the first half of the nineteenth century, including advertisements, this image of a *corsetière* embodies what Judith Coffin has identified as a set of conventions inherited from eighteenth-century imagery:

Unlike representations of male labor, which focused on the worker and the work process, those of female labor centered instead on commerce and sales and on women as vendors or beautiful objects. The "artistry" of working "girls" was the closest any came to acknowledging skill. Intimate conversations, gossip and rumors, and flaunting workshop rules and discipline were represented as the core of seamstresses' "work culture."[41]

In spite of the fact that women were working, in workshops and in factories, and that machines were being introduced into the work world, Coffin suggests, the cultural imagery used to signify working women remained highly gendered throughout the nineteenth century in both France and beyond.[42] Thus, Philipon's corset maker is also its vendor, and the difficult, and less picturesque, labor of sewing stiff fabric and melding the form is obscured by the *corsetière*'s charming sales pitch.

The captions that Philipon attributes to each of the images in his *Têtes de femmes* series express his taste for satire, for each adjective he uses to qualify the female workers puns on some quality associated with the cultural identity of the worker or her product.

FIGURE 2.4 Charles Philipon, *L'utile marchande de corsets*, 1830. © INTERFOTO / Alamy Stock Photo.

The "agaçante modiste" plays on the double meaning of *agaçant*, meaning both irritating and teasing. Philipon's *modiste* is particularly seductive with exposed bosom and flirtatious look; and the hat she designs, with its outsized ribbons and bows, incarnates coquettishness. Likewise, the "fraîche écaillère" refers both to the freshness of the oysters (with their aphrodisiac connotations) and to the pretty charms of the oyster woman; the "gentille blanchisseuse," with her frilly cap, frank gaze, and exposed bosom, is both pretty *and* kind, that is, willing to give favors freely.

In the case of the corset maker, like her product, she is "utile," meaning both useful and necessary. And indeed, in order to achieve the tiny wasp waist and the fashionable hourglass figure that was (and remains) the standard of idealized femininity, a structuring undergarment was required to literally construct a feminized form and emphasize secondary sexual characteristics such as breasts and buttocks. But what does it mean for the worker herself to be "necessary," and for whom? She is necessary for her female client because she provides the requisite tool for creating the desired feminine silhouette; but for the male viewer, for whom these prints were most likely created, her utility is of a different nature. "Necessary" women, or "les femmes comme il en faut," (women that one needs) was a euphemism for prostitutes, and thus the adjective with which Philipon qualifies this worker confirms through a witticism what the image already implies—that fashion workers were dangerously similar to prostitutes.

The potential for slippage into prostitution was an integral feature of the cultural imagery depicting garment workers. And this was not just myth, for workers in the garment trades typically did not earn much and, because fashion operated seasonally, did not work year-round. Thus, "many working-class women sporadically turned to prostitution to survive. Meanwhile, middle-class men tended to regard poor women as legitimate sexual prey."[43] There is indeed a sense in which working women become sexual prey precisely through the imagery that defines them. Images such as Philipon's allowed illustrators to engage in mythmaking and cultural production; sexuality could be suggested, if not overtly displayed, and the urban working woman thus fulfils the erotic fantasy of a male viewer that his modest middle-class wife must not. In her study of women in Degas's paintings, Eunice Lipton offers a cogent explanation for the sexualization of such workers, which she calls "ideological distortion," suggesting that this surplus of erotic imagery reflected social anxieties regarding "the vast increase of workers in Paris in general and the many complicated ways in which the working poor were entering middle-class life. Working class women seemed to be everywhere: employed in cafés, restaurants, all kinds of boutiques, and department stores; traipsing the streets between work and home: enjoying themselves in cafés, café-concerts, and dance balls."[44] One way of defusing the potential "danger" of a prominent female working class was to sexualize, and thus objectify, them. Moreover, foregrounding the erotic, such images and other social commentary could ignore actual working conditions: "it neutralized middle-class fear and guilt towards workers, and it rationalized exploitation."[45]

SENTIMENTALIZING WORKING WOMEN

While women working in the French needle trades were eroticized through representation, in Britain, the image of the seamstress, and others working in similar trades, was frequently sentimentalized. Indeed, the seamstress in Britain became "a working-class paradigm," as Lynn Alexander demonstrates, illustrated in prints and painting over a sixty-year period.[46] Anna Blunden's 1854 image of a wan seamstress pleading to the heavens for relief as she

FIGURE 2.5 Victorian women sewing, 1888. Photo: whitemay via Getty Images.

works on a man's shirt in her garret apartment is one of many similar images inaugurated with Richard Redgrave's iconic 1846 painting *The Sempstress*. In this and so many other illustrations in the same vein, the pathetic figure of the seamstress calls attention to her plight and serves to sentimentalize the working woman more broadly who ought to be protected by a wage-earning man (see Figure 2.5). Distinct from a factory worker, she works alone and performs a task—sewing—that would have been universal to all nineteenth-century European women and carried heavy domestic overtones. But the fact that she is working means that she is now divorced from her domestic role in a traditional family: the figure of the seamstress could thus express empathy for the working class while simultaneously encapsulating social anxieties about working women and the potentially damaging effect of their work on the institution of family.

French artists also displayed empathy for workers as interest in portraying urban workers in high art rose in the second half of the nineteenth century, sparked by a turn to realism as a result of social and political upheavals. As Linda Nochlin writes, "after the 1848 Revolution, the worker becomes the dominant image in Realist art, partaking of both the grandeur of myth and the concreteness of reality."[47] In this context, Daumier's laundress of the 1850s bears little resemblance to Philipon's "gentille blanchisseuse." Rejecting the mythologizing, folkloric prints of the early nineteenth century that owed so much to earlier stereotypes of female workers, Daumier captures the burden of manual labor even as he frankly asserts the double duty women often performed as workers and mothers. The "difficult, delicate, and painful job" of a laundress in the city aptly justifies the title Daumier gives his painting, *The Burden* (Figure 2.6):

> From early dawn, washerwomen pull their cart loaded with clean linen, arriving in the city to reach their clients—their "regulars"—who check quantity and quality, turn over the dirty linen to clean … and this every ten days. That same evening, the linens are soaked together for the night, which mixes up the dirt. The next morning, they

are placed in a basin, covered with a big cloth on which ashes are placed. Hot water is poured from time to time to make the potassium carbonate percolate slowly to the bottom of the basin; salinated water is brought to pour again over the ashes to increase the concentration, this is repeated.[48]

The description expresses the demanding physical dimension to this labor: heavy loads transported in carts, or on backs, from the outskirts of the city to the bourgeois dwellers

FIGURE 2.6 Honoré Daumier, *The Burden*, or *Laundress*, 1850–3. © Peter Barritt / Alamy Stock Photo.

at the center and back again, repetitious monotony of physical gestures of lifting and pouring, and exposure to chemicals, heat, and steam.

Daumier's portrayal captures the impact of such work on the body of the laundress. For unlike the female bodies in the flirtatious images of the past, this woman's body is visibly laboring: her neck and shoulder contorted under the heavy sack of washing, and her body bent in order to move forward under such a weight. And unlike the studied *décolletage* of Philipon's female workers, the breast of Daumier's laundress is prominently thrust forward, as a reminder of her maternal identity rather than as a seductive feminine form. She is exposed to the elements (and likely to a predatory male gaze) on the urban streets: the wind whips her skirts, as well as her child's little form. The two figures seem to fight even to walk against the headwinds that suggest all of the untold struggles of working-class women—insufficient wages, physical injury, hunger. Daumier is clearly concerned with the moral dimensions of work, but not those lurking under the surface of the popular, eroticizing images of working women from the first half of the century. Rather, the moral message here proclaims the virtue and the distress of the hardworking woman. It should also be noted that Daumier reserved a particularly caustic disdain for middle-class working women, who in his *Bas-bleus* series are repeatedly pictured abandoning their husbands and children to pursue careers in the public sphere.[49]

Unlike the popular print culture we have been exploring, high art had, until mid-century, mostly depicted (male) workers as idealized rural, agricultural laborers.[50] The impressionists, however, would regularly picture scenes of urban labor, but without attaching the sort of obvious social commentary that we see with Daumier's laundress. The so-called "painter of modern life," Constantin Guys, praised by Baudelaire for his capacity to capture the essence of urban modernity in his fluid, transitory scenes of Paris, often took prostitutes as his subject. Meanwhile, alongside their celebrated representations of carefree bourgeois life, impressionists such as Caillebotte, Manet, and Degas painted masterpieces depicting the world of work with subjects now familiar to us, such as beer maids, dancers, prostitutes, and milliners.[51] Nochlin pointed out that much of the classic critical work on the impressionists' themes centered on an exploration of their contribution to the representation of bourgeois leisure. But, she continues, "middle- and upper-class men's leisure is sustained and enlivened by the labour of women: entertainment and service workers like those represented by Manet."[52] Nochlin rightly suggests that these art works ask us to see paintings such as Edouard Manet's *Bar at the Folies Bergères* or Edgar Degas's dancers as "representations of work" as much as of nineteenth-century leisure. And the reason they have not been substantially treated as such is because the worker is a female who is simultaneously constructed as consumable "by a male viewer."[53]

Degas did, of course, portray women as workers. His remarkable series of women workers include dancers, prostitutes, milliners, and laundresses. Zola's *L'Assommoir*, published in the same period as Degas's laundress series, offers a literary window into the world of the Parisian laundress with his character Gervaise. David Baguley helps to complete the sociohistoric context of a worker such as Gervaise, one of a "vast population of female workers" who were:

> exploited not only for their labour but also for their sexuality. The harsh conditions of the laundress, her pittance of a wage, her enforced recourse to drink and prostitution, are ignored in titillating representations of her sensuality; half-undressed in the steamy heat of her shop, admitted to the intimacy of the bachelor's quarters, sexually accessible, clean and fresh, exposing underwear and flesh, objects of fantasy and fetishism.[54]

Degas's laundresses, in contrast, are portrayed laboring, just as his decidedly unerotic prostitutes are pictured in ways that emphasize that prostitution is indeed work. The deliberate deglamorizing of women in these images was a stark reminder of the literal transactions of prostitution and the arduous, monotonous, behind-the-scenes labor of performance, service, and fashion work.

In his *Les repasseuses* (*Women Ironing*) (Figure 2.7), part of a series begun in 1876, Degas offers a scene radically opposed to that of Lanté's lovely female presser. There are two workers pictured here, both laboring in what appears to be an unkempt, steamy workroom. Contrasting with the open space of the prints examined above, one woman is bent over in the act of ironing, pressing hard with both hands, while the other opens her mouth in a wide yawn, expressing the boredom and exhaustion associated with her daily activity. Neither woman's body is eroticized or idealized: both wear traditional garments—kerchief and apron—and the atmosphere of the space is cloudy, the surface of the painting almost blurry.[55]

Art historians Eunice Lipton and Marni Kessler have offered rich readings of this painting and others in the series in the context of earlier representations of laundresses in high and popular art and in terms of sociocultural conditions. While Kessler focuses on the painting's suggestion of the "consequences of their unhealthy work and living

FIGURE 2.7 Edgar Degas, *Les repasseuses* (*Women Ironing*), 1884–6. Credit: Peter Barritt / Alamy Stock Photo.

environments," Lipton emphasizes the repeated signs of the "drudgery of the laundresses' work life."[56] These signs include the wine bottle, grasped by the yawning laundress (it has been well documented that laundresses and other workers were encouraged by their employers to drink as they worked), but also the bent figure and stretched arms. "Through a delimited and explicitly vocational repertory of gestures, Degas has captured for our eyes the repetitious and ritualistic aspect of ironing."[57] Unlike most representations of women workers in the nineteenth century in popular art, which, as we have seen, focused on either idealizing or eroticizing (or both) their subjects, Degas's painting, similar to his ballet and millinery works, seems rather to offer up an authentic view into female work culture in the modern city.

FROM *GRISETTE* TO *CATHERINETTE*: THE EMERGENCE OF THE WORKING GIRL

In the late nineteenth century, urban industry expanded dramatically across Europe and North America, and provincial women entered the workforce in droves.[58] In turn-of-the-century Paris, unmarried women working in the clothing industry were known as *catherinettes* after a folklore ritual associated with coming of age. It had been understood as an entry point into traditional gender roles and sexuality. But it was transformed in the *ateliers* of the metropolis, becoming instead a celebratory initiation to a work community.[59] A defining image of the working girl, the *catherinette* was now acknowledged for her work and celebrated annually in a parade through the streets of Paris. In this photograph (Figure 2.8), and others like it, we discover new ways of representing women working. Depicting a group of *modistes* and/or seamstresses dressed in their handcrafted headpieces, photographs such as this one show us women workers who have some measure of control

FIGURE 2.8 Group of *catherinettes*, 1908. Courtesy of Bibliothèque nationale de France.

over their own representation. It presents a community of women not necessarily or exclusively available for male consumption but rather existing for themselves and for the historical record. These women are taking the street politically and forcefully, even if all in good fun, and they serve up a stark contrast to the eroticized fashion workers of the early prints, which sought to evoke desire, and the universal and sentimental image of the seamstress evoking pity.

Similarly, in early-twentieth-century Britain, Sylvia Pankhurst painted a series of works cataloguing urban women workers across Britain, of which there were approximately five million in 1907, according to Kristina Huneault.[60] Like some of the late-century paintings of working-class women examined above, Pankhurst's paintings acknowledge the hardship of labor even as they celebrate it. Most important, like the photographs of Parisian *catherinettes*, they challenge an ideology that enforced boundaries on the feminine that did not include work. The onset of the First World War in 1914 ushered in a rise, if not necessarily in female employment, in the visibility of women working.[61] Across Europe and in North America, the war brought women into the munitions factories, into the fields, into the mines, and into the streets, and photography, the newly popularized form of representation, could broadcast and normalize images of women working that would have been unimaginable just a few decades earlier. Similarly, poster campaigns feature women working in unexpected industrial settings and performing dangerous tasks previously reserved for male workers. In a reprise of the nineteenth-century industrial imagery of the blacksmith's shop or the steel mill, here we find women neatly dressed in aprons and kerchiefs, but also wearing trousers and clogs, turned towards fire and steam to produce what appear to be munitions (Figure 2.9). The heroism traditionally associated with the strong male worker has now been transferred to women, who are pictured in the act of laboring, faces turned away from the viewer, bodies in action.

The images examined here have more to say about the belief systems and cultural perceptions surrounding female work and workers in nineteenth-century France than about the actual working conditions of workers themselves. Some illustrations, as we have seen, were nonetheless engaged in representing more faithfully working conditions and work processes: Daumier and Degas make such an attempt. Here we do not see romanticized and mythologized female working types; rather, we find images of backbreaking and sometimes dangerous labor. These images offer a glimpse into the harsh reality of manual and service labor in nineteenth-century France, a reality so often disavowed in the visual culture from this period.

The idea with which this chapter opened—of a ghostly Berthe Bovary packed off to the textile mill—cannot be fixed into a stable image, yet it can open a wealth of possible pictures for how working women entered the economy of fashion in nineteenth-century France and other related economies across Europe and America. Did she remain a textile worker, as Flaubert implies, working before vast machines in a Norman factory town, far from the workshops of Paris? Or did she, like so many provincial girls with some sewing skills, move on to the capital to work her way through an *atelier*, perhaps remaining at the bottom—as a delivery girl or one of many anonymous seamstresses or embroiderers, the so-called *petites mains* (little hands) of the workshop—or rising to the top to become the proprietress of a shop? By essentially erasing Berthe's identity at the story's end, Flaubert closes his novel about the false promise of modernity's progress with the dehumanizing prospects that mechanization would bring. Unlike Flaubert's linguistic abstraction, however, the images picturing work I have considered here document evolving cultural views regarding work, workers, and the workplace.

FIGURE 2.9 Women war workers, 1918. Credit: Chronicle / Alamy Stock Photo.

These images reveal that the visibility of women workers was controlled and deployed to reinforce gender roles. But with labor changes, and concomitant shifts in gender perceptions, the role of women in productive economies in the new century would become less threatening.⁶² Through a critical analysis of images that places them in the context of their production and their reception, we may uncover some of the ideological messages contained within the illustration of work and workers in nineteenth-century France and, more broadly, in the West. Such careful, contextualized readings of visual materials offer a nuanced narrative about working-class women, bringing Berthe Bovary and those she represents back into our sights.

CHAPTER THREE

Work and Workplaces

CASEY HARISON

Work and workplaces probably saw as much change during the age of empire (1800–1920) as any period in the human past. Much of the change had to do with two developments: the Industrial Revolution and the "new regime" of capitalism. Many traditional skills, trades, and places of work gave way under the relentless advance of industry and capitalism during the age of empire. Workers in textile mills, iron foundries, cotton fields and other workplaces became more and more tied to a generalized and global system of production as Atlantic nations exploited their own resources and those of faraway places. At the same time, rising wealth among the upper classes expanded the need for service workers and domestic servants. Work and workplaces changed in significant ways after 1800, contrasting with the "old regime" that went before it and leaving patterns we live with today.

This chapter focuses on skilled and unskilled work done by persons who labored with their hands, the physical places where they performed that labor, and the cultural changes that occurred over time at the workplace. Factory workers, domestic servants, agricultural laborers and the places where they worked—not bankers, merchants, clerks, or engineers and the places where they worked—are our subjects. Geographically, most of the examples are from western Europe and Russia, but with details from the Americas, too. The age of empire was especially an Atlantic phenomenon, but Japan also participated. Nearly the entire world was impacted, willingly or not.[1] The chapter reviews topics related to the structure of work before examining in more detail the lives of men, women, and children, and the cultural changes they experienced at the workplace during the age of empire.

STRUCTURAL SHIFTS AND PLACES OF WORK

As with any historical "age," there were elements of both change and continuity in the age of empire—in work and workplaces, as in other spheres of life. But as historians have long argued, there likely was more change, and less continuity, in this age than others. Most of this had to do with the development of modern industry and capitalism. Over time and in some places, industry and capitalism contributed to longer, better lives though with great costs: the expansion, often through violence, of empires; the exploitation of non-renewable natural resources; and sometimes the degrading of life—including work and workplaces—for those groups not in position to prosper during the advent of industry and capitalism. During the age of empire, the negative impact on the working classes of the Atlantic world mostly outweighed the positive.[2]

Many, though not all, workplaces were greatly changed during the age of empire. From the perspective of workers and their advocates, certain persistent problems attended the rise of industry and capitalism. These included the growth of pay by item produced—whether shoes, clothing, or cigars—rather than a wage for a full day's labor; this "piece-rate" encouraged divisive competition and pushed workers to labor at excessive speeds and for long hours. The growth of subcontracting left workers at the mercy of sometimes unscrupulous bosses—*tâcherons* (taskmasters), as French building workers called them. In the age of empire, employers and governments mostly operated together to control workers: sometimes by requiring them to use internal passports; regulating and spying on them at the workplace and in the boarding houses where the poorer among them lived; and passing laws that forbade them to organize or strike. Traditional skills came under pressure during the age of empire as the old hierarchy of master, journeymen, and apprentice was undermined or done away with in many trades. The desire of employers to maximize profit led to the emergence of the hated "sweated" trades, often in textile or clothing production, and to which women and children were particularly susceptible.[3]

Over time, structural shifts produced important changes in the workplace. Between 1800 and 1920, urban populations swelled. Manchester, England, grew from under 50,000 in 1800 to almost 300,000 in 1920; Berlin from under 200,000 to over 2 million; and Paris from just over 600,000 to almost 2.9 million in the same era. More and more of the laboring classes lived as part of a permanent urban workforce, or as migrants in cramped single rooms or dormitories for part of the year before going back home to the native village for a few months. Across the Atlantic world by the end of the age of empire, the workplace for most of the laboring class had shifted from the rural field or cottage to the urban factory or large workshop.

A crucial development for workers during the age of empire was the introduction of new technology into the workplace. Factories and mills where production was mostly accomplished through large machines tended by humans, or manufactories where numerous workers were employed but where production was still done by hand, had existed before, but now they became larger. Big machines in big buildings and an increased scale of production was a startling difference from the small-scale—indeed, "human"-scale—artisanal production of workplaces of the past.[4] Industry and capitalism dramatically altered the workspace of factory, mill, and home (see Figure 3.1).

Still, it would be incorrect to emphasize too singularly the changes that took place between 1800 and 1920. As in all eras, long-established patterns and practices persisted. As in all eras, there was some mix of continuity and change in work and workplaces. One continuing pattern in the first decades of the age of empire was the prevalence of the "cottage trades" or "putting-out" system in areas of production such as shoemaking. The cottage trades saw middlemen supply materials to workers at rural homes that were turned into finished products to be sold at market. The system persisted because rural labor typically cost less than labor in cities.[5] In western Europe and North America, the cottage trades faded as workers moved to the cities, as the items made at home were produced in factories, and as rural home-work shifted to the apartments and furnished rooms of cities, contributing to the growth of sweated labor in, for instance, the production of clothing by women and children using sewing machines. Cottage trades would persist in Asia, Africa, and Latin America into the twentieth century, but by the turn of the century in the Atlantic world this form of production seemed archaic and inefficient.

In the age of empire, there also persisted an even older system: the servile labor of slaves, peons, sharecroppers, tenant farmers, and serfs, whose work was mostly agricultural and

FIGURE 3.1 Inside the Krupp Factory, 1905. Photo: Albert Harlingue / Roger Viollet / Getty Images.

whose places of work were the rural fields, plantations, and estates that produced crops such as tobacco and sugar that were integral to global capitalism (see Figure 3.2). By 1800, there were hints of the end of servile labor in the Atlantic world. The French Revolution promised emancipation to slaves in France's Caribbean colonies, though in the end Haitians had to free themselves. The American Revolution likewise promised liberty, though not to black slaves in the South. But even as slavery was gradually abolished in the Atlantic world, for a long time there was little real change for agricultural workers and their workplaces: after attaining their freedom, former slaves in Haiti, Louisiana, and Brazil typically became tenant farmers, still tied to the land, still using physical labor to tend the crops of wealthier landowners, still owing payment in money or kind to local notables, and still removed from the benefits of modernity like schooling and health care. Servile labor was a mainstay of agricultural life in many sections of the Atlantic world beyond the age of empire.[6]

If we were to think of labor happening only in rural fields, factories, and mills, we would be missing a large segment of the working population. Many, perhaps most workers in the age of empire moved between jobs fairly frequently, and so the road or street could be a workplace, too. This was clearly the case for porters and prostitutes. Those near the bottom of the laboring world, casual or day laborers, were another mobile part of the workforce. These were typically persons who had not acquired the skills that might land them jobs with wages that could support themselves and a family, or who may have had infirmities or emotional or psychological difficulties that made it impossible for them to do anything but menial work. These were persons working for meager wages, periodically out of a job, and sometimes dependent on charity for food,

FIGURE 3.2 Picking cotton, United States, 1878. Photo: Prisma / UIG / Getty Images.

clothing, and shelter. Their workplaces were the construction sites where ditches were dug, the abattoirs where animals were slaughtered and carcasses processed, or the streets where used goods were peddled to the poor. By the middle of the nineteenth century, governments across the Atlantic world were passing laws and professionalizing police forces in order to control this section of the laboring poor. Still for many persons, casual or intermittent labor, vagrancy, or begging remained part of the life course.

AT THE WORKPLACE

During the age of empire, work and workplace helped shape one's consciousness. Bruce Laurie, describing the working people of Philadelphia in the nineteenth century, writes that "working-class culture and consciousness do not simply happen or develop in a vacuum. Instead, culture and consciousness are made and remade by the interplay of living and working conditions and what individuals bring to communities and workshops from prior experiences."[7] Indeed as the workplace shifted from the cottage or small workshop to the textile mill or steel factory, older forms of working-class culture changed and new forms emerged.

The majority of European and American workers and workplaces were rural and outdoors in 1800, but by 1920 the majority were urban and indoor. This was truly a significant change in the human experience. For male workers during the age of empire, the indoor workspace might be a mill, factory, or artisan workshop; outdoors, it could be a building site or *chantier*, to use the French term, rural field or the streets where porters, cab drivers, and "ragpickers" plied their trades. The workspace could be close to where workers lived or it could be far. Sometimes factory workers lived in dormitories or sometimes they had to walk a distance to get to the job; the stonemason Martin Nadaud recalled spending two hours going and coming to some of the Parisian building sites where he worked.[8] Working out-of-doors was often seasonal; this was true of agricultural labor, as well as construction, which often drew migrants who walked or took trains to cities in March and returned to provincial villages during the "dead season" of December through February.

Many of the traditional jobs were done outdoors; many of the newer jobs indoors. Working-class memoirists always noted factory work as loud, hot, smelly, and often hazardous. Slaughterhouses were invariably described as awful workplaces. Sewers in nineteenth-century cities undergoing urban renewal like London and Paris were rebuilt, cleaned, and maintained by armies of workers. Like factories, sewers confined workers in an interior, sometimes claustrophobic space, where gasses accumulated that were potentially toxic.[9]

Workshops, which had dominated urban production before the Industrial Revolution, were typically smaller and more intimate. Modern factory production replaced artisanal production more quickly in places such as Manchester, Birmingham, and London in England than Paris and Lyon in France. Honoré de Balzac's *Eugénie Grandet*, a novel published in 1833 and set in the French provincial town of Saumur, provides a description of an artisan workshop:

> They do business in the ground floors of the houses in this street, but you could not call these low-ceiling rooms, innocent of glass window and display case, cavernous, dark, bare within and without, shops. Lovers of the medieval would recognize in them our ancestors' workshops in all their primitive simplicity ... Air and daylight filter into the damp cavern behind through the upper part of the door, or through the space left between the ceiling and the low wall which forms the shop-front, when the solid shutters, set at elbow level and held in place by heavy iron bolts, are removed every morning. This wall serves as a place on which to set out goods, as an indication of the nature of the business carried on.[10]

Working in a small shop was not necessarily better than a factory. The artisanal workplace of Norbert Truquin, a nineteenth-century proletarian was tiny. "Nothing," he recalled was "more brutalizing than work in confined quarters."[11]

Historian Alfred Kelly writes that in the nineteenth century when railroad construction helped drive industrialization, "brute strength" remained as important at the workplace as new skills or technology.[12] This was as true for the *fortes* moving heavy goods on the docks of Nantes and Bordeaux in France as for the black and white roustabouts lifting cotton bales on the wharfs of New Orleans.[13] Émile Zola, whose *L'Assommoir* (1877) was virtually sociological in its descriptions of the workspaces of Paris, described the requirement of physical strength for men working at an iron forge and lifting 20-pound hammers all day long.[14]

Injuries at the workplace were common in certain industries and trades. The French woodworker Jacques Étienne Bédé remembered injuries occurring as workers dragged large wooden beams up and down stairs to finish them; in one case, the threat of injury led to a strike.[15] The building trades, particularly that of roofer, were notoriously dangerous. In Zola's *L'Assommoir* the downward spiral of the character Coupeau begins when he suffers the typical roofer's mishap: falling from his workplace, the roof. Over the course of a long career working out of doors on Parisian construction sites, Martin Nadaud saw many men injured and unable to return to work. Nadaud himself broke both arms in a fall at a site in 1831, though he was able to recover and return to the job.[16] Labor in the countryside was no less dangerous; the French peasant Émile Guillaumin's leg was broken when a bull trampled him in 1861.[17] These were dangers associated with traditional trades, but the hazards of modern factory work were notable too. One of the most catastrophic industrial tragedies of the age of empire took place at the Triangle Shirtwaist Factory fire in New York City in 1911 when almost one hundred and fifty persons—mostly young women—died when they could not escape the burning building because the doors had been locked by the owners.[18]

As the age of empire progressed, the often deplorable state of work and workplaces was both impossible to ignore and a continuing concern, not only for workers and their supporters, but for those in the upper classes who worried that these conditions would breed unrest—strikes, rebellion, even revolution. Governments did little in the first half of the nineteenth century, but became more responsive in the second half of the century, partly as a result of the widening of the vote, which led to the founding of political parties such as the Social Democrats in Germany and the Labour Party in Great Britain that worked on behalf of workers. In Germany, the conservative chancellor Otto von Bismarck enacted important reforms in an attempt to stifle political unrest. Strikes and trade unions were legalized, and laws prohibiting "conspiracy" against laissez-faire undone. By 1900 compensation for injuries suffered on the job, shorter working hours, and regular workweeks, with the "weekend" period of rest, were becoming more common. Municipal and national governments now sent inspectors to factories, building sites, and other workplaces to ensure that laws reducing job-related hazards were being followed.[19]

Eating meals provided a much-needed break during the workday. Workers looked forward to meals, even when consumed at the workplace. The working-class diet during the age of empire relied heavily on alcohol, grains, and root vegetables, supplemented by meat and dairy products. There were, of course, regional and national differences in diet. For instance, in Germany, the main foods for workers included dark bread, potatoes, and beer. There was some change over time, as calorie and protein intake grew among European and North American populations after mid-century. But for others like the Russian working class, a diet heavily dependent on grains remained mostly unchanged.

The work schedule and conditions of the workplace determined the routine of eating. Here is Franz Rehbein's recollection from nineteenth-century rural Pomerania in Germany:

> The work goes continuously, with at most one short pause for lubrication, until noon. Then we quickly wolf down lunch; we've barely swallowed the last bite when the back-to-work whistle sounds. You don't even have time to wash your spoon; you can only lick it off, or, if you really have time to, wipe it on the corner of your dusty smock. At four o'clock there is a snack break, and as for quitting time, well, only the machine master knows when that will be. So it goes day after day.[20]

For the weaver Ernst Schuchardt in nineteenth-century Saxony, lunch was mostly root vegetables—turnips, potatoes, cabbage, carrots—and sometimes a thin slice of meat. There was an hour break for lunch, during which the foreman watched workers.[21] The French reformer Flora Tristan observed that the friendly bargemen she travelled with on the rivers of central France in the early 1840s ate boiled eggs, radishes, and bread, and that they and their masters had their meals together.[22]

According to upper-class observers such as the Welsh industrialist and reformer Robert Owen, alcohol consumption was a problem for male workers—by the end of the nineteenth century, a big problem.[23] Workers were aware of the high rate of alcohol consumption, but were less likely to see it as somehow subtracting from the productivity of labor. For many, alcohol provided a way to sooth the physical pain of the workday. Franz Rehbein, the farm worker in Pomerania, had schnapps in the morning to warm up and give him some energy for a long day in the fields.[24] The habit of workers missing the Monday workday after drinking heavily on Sundays was virtually universal in the age of empire. The Russian factory worker Sëmen Kanatchikov remembered these "Blue Mondays" as part of the routine of working-class life in late-nineteenth-century Moscow.[25] Employers complained endlessly about Blue Monday, but workers thought of it as unexceptional.

Rivalries or animosities among workers based on ethnicity, tradition, or gender were a source of division at the workplace, and a condition against which class solidarity struggled to gain ground. Males could resent female workers in workspaces deemed "masculine" by tradition or prejudice. Building sites, for instance, were almost always dominated by men; historian Michelle Perrot described the nineteenth-century French *chantier* as "masculine" and "xenophobic."[26]

Some ethnic or religious groups and their workspaces were essentially ghettoized. Visiting London in 1840, Flora Tristan was appalled by conditions in the working-class Irish and Jewish quarters of the city. She estimated St. Giles had two hundred thousand Irish proletarians, most of them laboring for meager pay as porters. Their workplaces were streets that were a "cesspool" of filth and fumes. Jews in the clothing trades along "Petticoat Lane" were treated as "pariahs." Tristan left London—the model industrial modern city and a hint of the future—"terror-stricken" by the terrible things she had seen.[27]

The best-known traditional rivalry of the age of empire was probably that of the many sects of *compagnonnage* in France. Dating from the medieval period, *compagnonnages* were confraternities of workers within a single trade that combined technical education, mentorship, and community. *Compagnons* had to undergo demeaning and sometimes dangerous acts of initiation to be admitted to a trade's sect. These sects, to which only men belonged, were notorious for the brawls they engaged in and for their efforts to control production of goods. The workspaces of the *compagnon*'s Tour de France (a period spent working in different cities throughout the country) included the *chantiers* of carpenters and the small shops of butchers—workplaces that were segregated by sect, trade, and gender.[28]

But one did not have to belong to a *compagnonnage* to witness exclusion at the workplace. There were also prejudices based on whether one was brought up in the country or the city, whether one spoke urban cockney or rural dialect, or if one happened to be of an ethnicity or religion that was in the minority. In France, Martin Nadaud spoke the patois, or local dialect, of his region and felt prejudice at the worksite for doing so. At the same time, he recognized the endless prejudices against building workers who came to Paris from Belgium or the German-speaking sections of eastern France.[29] The Russian worker Sëmen Kanatchikov spent time at factories in Moscow and St. Petersburg and was typical in automatically identifying others—German, Finns, Estonians, and so on—by their ethnicity.[30] Peasants distrusted city folk and city folk denigrated the "bumpkins" who arrived in town looking for work and driving down wages. Nonetheless, by the second half of the nineteenth century, workplace solidarity started to overcome difference—this was one of the goals and eventual successes of labor movements in Germany, England, France, Belgium, the United States, and elsewhere.

A quality that almost always emerges in the memoirs of workers, male and female, is pride and dignity. Workers could admire and take pride in the modern world they helped create. Here is the observation of Sëmen Kanatchikov on the iron foundry at St. Petersburg where he worked at the turn of the century:

> Workers would look with a loving glance at its massive iron body as they passed by. As for me, I began to be gripped by the poetry of the large metal factory, with its mighty metallic roar, the puffing of its steam-driven machines, its columns of high pipes, its rising clouds of black smoke that sullied the clear blue sky. Unconsciously, I was being drawn to the factory, with its stern poetry of labour, a poetry that was growing dearer and closer to me than the quiet, peaceful, lazy poetry of our drowsy village life.[31]

The French peasant Émile Guillaumin was proud of the crops he produced and the animals he raised.[32] The sewer workers of Paris, whose workplace seemed so strange and toxic, carried themselves with such pride that one would not dare make light of their livelihood.[33] Workers deeply desired recognition of their productivity and creativity, and often felt this was not forthcoming at the workplace or in the larger society. Through their labor, building workers such as Martin Nadaud transformed the workplace into a timeless and beautiful structure. Nadaud wondered how Parisians could pass the great buildings he and other stonemasons had labored on without stopping to gaze in wonder. Other workers chafed at mundane slights. Franz Bergg, an apprentice server working at restaurants in Elbing, Germany, remembered the indignity of having to work for tips. The maid Doris Viersbeck working for families in Hamburg, Germany, bristled at having to bathe the family's dog.[34] Breton maids in Paris resented being given demeaning nicknames and treated as "rustics."[35]

Structural changes in the economy and society brought on by the development of industry and capitalism led to cultural change at the workplace—the assembly line replacing the artisan bench, mass production replacing the "masterpiece" or culminating work of the artisan who had learned all the skills of his trade—and left many workers feeling that labor had lost its true meaning. This was more and more the case as industrial labor replaced artisanal labor. Yet workers inside and outside of the factory faced the challenge of the stultifying sameness of the workplace. For Karl Marx, one of the great analysts of historical change, this was a predictable characteristic in this age of "alienation." Repetitive labor—cigars rolled, blouses sewn, automobiles assembled—especially occurred with the adoption of assembly-line production around the turn of the century. But domestic service, which kept young women indoors for hours on end, could be no less dispiriting.[36] One of the most eloquent expressions of the drudgery of the era comes from the French joiner Gabriel Gauny, whose workplace of the 1830s was the artisans' shop. For Gauny, his workspace was "worse than a prison." The most hated part of the working day for Gauny was the "last hour." This was "the most terrible hour … Expectant waiting exaggerates its duration tenfold. Weary boredom, the horrible occupation of producers condemned to labours whose long duration evokes disgust, torments the limbs and spirit of the worker … Evening falls, and his soul wears itself out counting the minutes." Like the captive Jews in Babylon, thought Gauny, the worker becomes an "insurgent slave." "There is only one single attraction in work," wrote the introspective Gauny, "the moral feeling of satisfaction that a man experiences in carrying out his duty."[37] Under modern capitalism, any workplace, rural field, factory, or traditional workshop could be an unsatisfying space pregnant with disaffection or even rebellion.

WOMEN'S WORK AND THE WORKPLACE

Work for women during the age of empire was typically unskilled and less well-paid than for men, and their workplaces were often in settings outside of the factory: at home producing garments on a sewing machine, in the houses of well-off families doing domestic service, or in taverns working as servers or barmaids. In the second half of the nineteenth century, urban women laboring at home or in the factory might also serve as the primary caregivers for families. A difference between the age of empire and other "ages" is that this double burden saw women employed in new forms of work. This movement into the modern workforce was eventually joined to the winning of political rights, so that by 1920 women in some parts of the world were moving from a secondary rank to full citizenship. Emilie Carles, born in 1920 to a peasant family in the French Alps, acquired an education and became a teacher for local children, eventually gained the vote, and became an activist for political and environmental causes. As she knew, these were accomplishments that were impossible for earlier generations of women.[38] Still, the political and economic advances of Emilie Carles and other women happened mostly after 1920. The road to greater equality was long and arduous, and in many places and for most of the nineteenth century the lives of working women did not change substantially from that of their mothers or grandmothers. This was especially true in the countryside where gender divisions remained more static than in the cities.

By the turn of the twentieth century, there were a substantial number of working women in the Atlantic world. A 1907 census showed that 36 percent of all German women—mostly from the working class—labored in jobs outside of the home. This figure did not even include the enormous number of domestic servants or the prostitutes working in the larger cities.[39] Over 18 percent of industrial workers in 1907 were women, up from 13 percent a generation earlier.[40] The lack of opportunities for skilled labor was an important detail in the lives of women. Indeed, it was more than this: skilled work—which promised better working conditions and pay—was simply inconceivable for many women in the age of empire. Mary Jo Haynes describes this in terms of a "life course" that did not typically include plans to learn a trade: "Finding an occupation does not appear as a patterned or planned aspect of the female life course ... As they appear in the memoirs, boys at least had an image of their occupational future against which to measure what actually happened to them ... But for girls even the model was elusive."[41] Many women migrated from countryside to city to work as a maid or in the factory. Adelheid Popp went from a job as a maid at age fifteen to factory work in Vienna. The factory was a shock: "Everything displeased me—the dirty, sticky work; the unpleasant glass dust; the crowd of people; the crude tone; and the whole way that the girls and even married women behaved." To Popp's eyes, everyone appeared malnourished.[42] Here as in so many working places, women were the targets of sexual harassment.

Doris Viersbeck, a cook and maid in late-nineteenth-century Hamburg, Germany, faced travails typical of her situation: dealing with the endless crises of the family she worked for; enduring long hours and the expectation from family members that she was always "on call"; little privacy or free time (see Figure 3.3). Viersbeck rarely got to bed before midnight and was always exhausted.[43] It was not uncommon for maids like Viersbeck to be the target of sexual advances by the fathers and sons of the families for which they worked; the pregnant maid driven from her job was a not entirely incorrect stereotype of the day. For "Frau Hoffman," a maid in East Prussia, children born to servants outside of marriage (she had two herself) was the norm.[44]

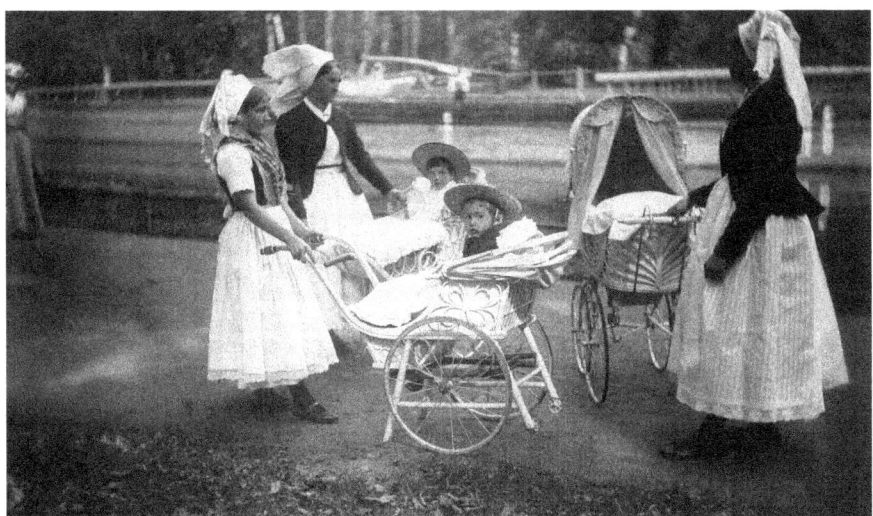

FIGURE 3.3 Nannies of the Spreewald region, c. 1903. Photo: ullstein bild / ullstein bild via Getty Images.

Jeanne Bouvier was typical of many working females during the age of empire. Born in 1865 to a farm family in the French department of Isère, as a girl she tended cows. Then at age eleven she went to work in a silk factory and two years later entered domestic service, first in the French city of Vienne and then in Paris. Eventually Bouvier became a skilled seamstress. Bouvier went to work at such a young age because her family was poor and because laws against child labor were rarely enforced. Workplace conditions were awful:

> At the factory, they served soup in the morning and evening, but what soup! It was so bad that the dogs refused to eat it. We were also given a place to sleep, but in deplorable conditions. The beds were made of four planks nailed together, a sack of wood shavings as a mattress, barely any bedspread, and sheets that were almost never washed. The dormitory was an attic without a ceiling. The roof tiles were directly above our heads, and if we sat on our beds, our heads would touch them.[45]

Bouvier left for Paris at age fourteen, and her first jobs there as a maid were not good, but then she went to work for a doctor's family and was treated better. In Paris, she lived in *garnis* (furnished rooms) and survived on bread and milk. Like others, she was desperate to learn a skilled trade—in her case, as with many women, sewing—that would earn her more money and better living conditions. As she perfected her sewing skills, life for Jeanne Bouvier slowly got better.

Qualitative assessments of women's work like those in the many novels of Émile Zola set in France in the second half of the nineteenth century attest to the conditions described in the memoirs of working women. The character Gervaise in *L'Assommoir* works in degrading and sometimes violent conditions at a washhouse in the industrial section of northern Paris.

> It was an immense shed with a flat roof, exposed beams supported by cast-iron pillars, and enclosed by clear glass windows. A wan daylight penetrated the hot steam hanging

like a milky fog ... Everywhere a heavy moisture rained down, laden with the smell of soap, a persistent, stale, dank aroma sharpened at times by a whiff of bleach. A row of women stretched along the washing-boards down each side of the central passage; their arms were bare up to the shoulders, dresses turned down at the neck, skirts caught up, showing their coloured stockings and heavy laced boots. They were all banging furiously, laughing, leaning back to bawl through the din, bending forwards into their washtubs, a foul-mouthed, rough, ungainly-looking lot, sopping wet as though they had been rained on, with red, steaming flesh.[46]

Gervaise's dream was to own her own laundry shop, and in the novel she eventually does, though happiness, prosperity, and good health remain elusive; for Zola, this was the lot in life of the working class.

Ottilie Baader, a seamstress working in Berlin at the end of the nineteenth century, recalled, "My life has been all work."[47] At first, Baader worked at a factory, but the introduction of the sewing machine brought for her, as for tens of thousands of women across the Atlantic world, a revolution in work (Figure 3.4). Now she was at home in a tiny apartment in front of a sewing machine from six in the morning to midnight, while also caring for an ailing father. *Confection*—the making of ready-made clothes to be sold at stores—had begun to replace tailoring in the first half of the nineteenth century and the introduction of the sewing machine hastened the process. Unregulated or "clandestine" homework like this escaped the eyes of labor inspectors who at the end of the century were just starting to visit workplaces.[48] This was sweated labor of a different kind; as Judith Coffin writes, the "factory had come to the home."[49] By 1900, there were an estimated eight hundred thousand female and male homeworkers in France alone. Still, homework was not simply a bad or a good thing. Many women preferred the workshop to home because friends and conversation could be found there, even as others felt oppressed in the factory and freer at home where they could also mind children.[50]

FIGURE 3.4 Cheshire clothing factory, 1908. Photo: Past Pix / SSPL / Getty Images.

Not all women going from countryside to city went to factories or the sewing machine. As we have seen, many went into domestic service, working in the households of wealthy families. Certain areas of the French countryside were a conduit for domestic servants. The young Breton woman coming from western France to work as a maid or wet-nurse in the home of an upper-class Parisian family was common by the end of the nineteenth century. Once a job was secured, the young Bretons typically had "no contract, no regular working hours, and virtually no right to privacy ... [their] rights depended almost exclusively on the inclination of their employers."[51] By 1914, there may have been fourteen thousand female Breton domestics working in Paris.[52] This migration of "pariahs" was accompanied by demeaning stereotypes. And yet many of these women seemed happier working in the homes of wealthy Parisians than remaining in the comparatively poor villages and towns of their native Brittany.

The female service workers whose numbers increased between 1800 and 1920 had to deal with not only low wages and sometimes unpleasant working conditions, but also the unwanted advances of customers, bosses, and fellow workers. An anonymous nineteenth-century German barmaid described in Alfred Kelly's *The German Worker* moved from one job to another, looking for improved conditions and pay. For her, some taverns were better places to work than others, but wherever she went she was considered "'fair game' for any man with money."[53] Working in bars taught her to smoke and drink, with consequences for her health. Prostitution claimed many young women coming from the countryside who did not go into domestic service or work in taverns or factories. Most prostitutes worked illegally and in the shadow economy, though in certain places prostitution was regulated.[54] In Paris, there were gradations of *maisons de tolérance* (legal bordellos), from those with comfortable beds and rugs on the floors to the seedy brothels used by soldiers and sailors, and even worse places that might simply be the back of a room or shed.[55] Flora Tristan, the reformer and early socialist, was appalled by the great number of prostitutes she saw "swarm[-ing]" the streets of London when she visited in the 1840s. She thought most of the clients were young males from the upper classes, and attributed the situation to the extremes of wealth that existed in English society.[56]

Not everything about women's work and workplaces was new. Age-old trades such as washing clothes at public fountains persisted in some places. When Tristan visited the southern French city of Nîmes in 1844, she was captivated by the sight of three hundred to four hundred washerwomen standing in dirty water, slapping clothes on the stones hour after long hour at an ancient fountain built by the Romans.[57] It was hard work that seemed never to have changed. Such was the case, too, for women in rural Russia, even after serfdom was abolished in 1861. When Russian men and women migrated to work in cities such as Moscow, St. Petersburg, and Jaroslavl their lives changed dramatically, but as the social investigator Olga Semyonova Tian-Shanskaia discovered in the 1890s, tradition continued to govern women's lives in the Russian *mir* (village). Women tended cows and chickens, while also raising the family and performing traditional cottage trades such as sewing, lace-making, and fulling felt boots. Homeless old women (and men) sometimes resorted to begging.[58]

These were the mundane jobs of women during the age of empire. But during crises like wars or revolutions, women could take up extraordinary occupations, including the *cantinières* and *ambulancières* who served the Paris Commune during the spring of 1871, feeding and caring for soldiers, and the *ravannas* ("camp followers") following in the wake of the Peruvian armies who caught the eye of Tristan.[59] Here, workplaces were the fields where armies moved and fought.

CHILDREN'S WORK AND THE WORKPLACE

During the age of empire, children worked at many of the same jobs and in the same places as adults. As the historian Jürgen Kocka writes, child labor only "turned into a scandal when it became work outside the household and family—factory work."[60] Children were paid less and were less able to protest or resist than adults, and so like working women they were susceptible to some of the worst excesses of industrialization (see Figure 3.5). The vivid, unhappy images of children's lives in the writings of Charles Dickens in the first half of the nineteenth century were all too true in the age of empire, and contrast with the concurrent Victorian idealization of childhood. When governments and the middle-class public began to look at child labor, they were appalled by what they saw. What we know about the working lives of children during the age of empire often comes from the observations of writers like Dickens, sympathetic reformers, government officials, mostly after about 1850, and from literate working-class adults writing their memoirs and looking back on their own, typically miserable experiences as children.

The problem of child labor became apparent early in the age of empire. Robert Owen, the industrialist and future utopian reformer, was troubled by the child labor he saw in the factories he managed and partly because of this became one of the great critics of the era. Owen founded a model factory at New Lanark, Scotland, and then a well-known social experiment at New Harmony, Indiana, United States.[61] For Owen, it was both heartbreaking and bad economics to have children working in the mills:

> It is not to be supposed that children ... could remain, with the intervals of meals only, from six in the morning until seven in the evening, in constant employment, on their feet, within cotton mills, and afterwards acquire much proficiency in education. And so it proved; for many of them became dwarfs in body and mind, and some of them were deformed.[62]

As he attempted to prove at New Lanark, an ethical form of factory production could be created that was also financially lucrative. In *A New View of Society* (1813), Owen argued

FIGURE 3.5 Children pushing a coal wagon, 1869. Photo: Grafissimo via Getty Images.

that a solution to the problem of child labor was to provide a "rational" education that could also render children's labor "useful." And so at his New Lanark mill, Owen created the "New Institution" to provide a place for children to learn, play, and acquire working skills suitable to their age.[63]

New Lanark was the exception. Elsewhere, poor working conditions for children were the rule. In northern France in 1841 Norbert Truquin, unskilled and illiterate for much of his life, was sent at age eight by his father to work in the shop of a wool-comber:

> [The] workshop measured three and a half meters long by three meters wide, not counting the coal cellar that was my bedroom. This room was lighted by a four-pane window which gave onto a corridor that was two meters wide and that led to an interior courtyard. Immediately opposite, a wall three meters high prevented the sun's rays from entering and warming up this hovel.[64]

Truquin worked in the hot, dirty space from 4:00 a.m. until 10:00 p.m. In the memoir he wrote after gaining literacy, he noted "it is not hard to imagine how unhealthy this work is for the child. *Nacteurs*, as these unfortunate children are called, have a wizened look and are for the most part rather brutish." Truquin was beaten and physically abused. His clothes became worn. When the master got sick, the boy had to act as his nurse—a duty Truquin hated. And so even as a child, he changed jobs frequently. For a time, Truquin made bricks in a yard. This was exhausting labor at which whole families were employed. At age thirteen, he was working at a slaughterhouse. There, his job was to break animal bones that were boiled and turned into "boneblack." He also cleaned up the courtyards of the slaughterhouse: "Nothing," he remembered, "could be more sinister." From there, Truquin went to work in a mill, which he thought was not as bad as other places; there was at least more order and cleanliness, and some camaraderie among workers. But if the bosses heard a complaint the worker was dismissed.[65]

In Russia, as the nineteenth century waned, village children lived and worked much as they always had. When Olga Semyonova Tian-Shanskaia visited a village near Moscow in the 1890s, she found children performing age-old tasks around the barnyard. Girls tended calves and watched younger children, while boys plowed, mowed, transported sheaves, and looked after horses. Boys might also perform day labor for a landowner "to pay off a debt incurred by a father."[66] In the *mir*, children sometimes were pushed into begging.[67] In France, too, agricultural work in the nineteenth century was much as it had always been and child labor was part of this. Émile Guillaumin, raised in the French countryside, was minding pigs at age nine. This was hard, dirty, sometimes perilous work handling animals larger than himself. Guillaumin did this until he was fifteen, at which time he moved on to "men's work," planting and harvesting crops.[68]

As a boy, the German Ludwig Turek worked at a job his father secured for him at an iron foundry. The experience at the foundry was seared into Turek's brain:

> On days when they poured iron it was like being in hell. It was no rarity to work overtime until two in the morning. And even so you had to be there on time the next morning. Anyone can imagine how brutal the exploitation was under such circumstances. I later worked in similar hellholes, and I know that nobody can stand it for too long.[69]

Turek became a revolutionary in 1919 and then a member of the German Communist Party. He traced his political radicalization to the abuses he suffered working as a child and from the rough encounters he had with police as a boy in the streets of Hamburg and Bremen.

Agricol Perdiguier, a French worker who wrote a famous memoir of his experiences as a *compagnon* on the Tour de France, was born in the countryside, where his first job was collecting manure. Later he learned joining in his brother's workshop and then was apprenticed at age sixteen to a master's shop in the southern city of Avignon.[70] Here he acquired traditional skills learned in an essentially preindustrial setting which he perfected as he moved from city to city. Similar if less time-bound skills were acquired by young German workers during a *Wanderjahre* (journeyman year) and by Russian workers organized in formal or informal *artels* (cooperatives).[71] Perdiguier advanced to the stage of journeyman even as it was becoming clear that the tradition of *compagnonnage* could hardly compete with new forms of production in the age of empire. *Compagnonnage* would not survive the century. Indeed, everywhere apprenticeship had lost the meaning it had under the guilds. As Sean Wilentz notes of the American experience in the first half of the nineteenth century, "apprentices" were in fact usually just poorly paid child labor.[72]

Many of the individual stories of working children are heartrending, but that of Fritz Paul, a cigar maker from Germany, is particularly hard to consider. Raised in the countryside, Paul left his family at age eleven to work for a nearby farmer. He rose every day at 3:30 a.m. to feed the pigs and tend sheep. He slept in the stalls with the animals. The workplace conditions were terrible, and his foot became infected and had to be amputated. He was twelve years old. Fitted with a prosthetic, Paul was no longer able to do farm work and so apprenticed at a cigar factory, where he contracted tuberculosis.[73] Still, this was an improvement over the farm. At the cigar factory working with other children and women, Paul slowly advanced his skills by moving from wrapping to rolling cigars. Tobacco, a warm-weather crop like cotton, spices, cacao, tea, and coffee, was emblematic of the age of empire: appealing to middle-class consumers in the northern latitudes, but transformed from raw material to finished product by working-class hands. In the case of Fritz Paul and so many others like him, empire in the form of a tropical product—tobacco—joined with the relentless, sometimes ruthless dynamism of capitalism to bring children into workplaces where their labor was exploited, leading to lives that were stunted and breeding resentment against the system.

Between the start of the age of empire in 1800 and its end in 1920, the distance between worker and master or boss at the workplace widened physically, politically, and culturally perhaps more than it ever had in the human past. The modern workplace saw workers identify themselves as something new and vital to modern production, with interests tied to the larger polity, but also sometimes in opposition to those in control and to the system of production itself. This did not mean that the modern workplace was a uniform thing. As we have seen in the lives of working men, women, and children in the factories, mills, apartments, and rural fields of Europe and the Atlantic world, it was not. The end of the age of empire was marked by the catastrophe of the Great War when workers using the tools of modern industry were marshalled by their nations to fight against each other. It also saw workers draw upon their experiences at the modern workplace, on the battlefields of Europe, in the voting booth, and among revolutionary crowds to enter yet another "age" in the history of working-class culture.

CHAPTER FOUR

Workplace Culture

VICTORIA E. THOMPSON

During the period 1800–1920, new methods of production (including but not limited to mechanization), new ways of organizing production (as in factories), and innovations in the sale and distribution of goods existed alongside traditional methods of making and selling all sorts of objects. While the experience of some workers remained largely shaped by craft traditions, others were socialized into the new world of the factory. And these were only two of the various workplaces of the age of empire: the farm and plantation, the market stall and boutique, the dock, the street, and the sewer were all workplaces. This chapter, however, focuses largely on manufacturing. Yet even limiting our discussion of workplace culture to manufacturing, one must talk of workplace cultures in the plural; the culture of the small, artisanal workshop of 1820 was vastly different from the culture of the mechanized factory of the 1890s.

At the same time, continuities existed. Traditional practices and values that governed the workplace in the early nineteenth century were passed down from parent to child and from master to apprentice. As skilled workers who were steeped in these cultural traditions became the leaders of working-class organizations and movements, they brought many of these practices and values with them. This is not to say that traditions passed down from one generation to the other intact; new circumstances and new exigencies meant that traditions were constantly reinvented as needed. Nonetheless, this chapter will argue for a measure of cultural continuity that is notable, particularly in the emphasis on sociability and community in working-class life.

Just as workplace culture varied from work site to work site, it also expanded beyond the place of employment to encompass other areas of working-class life. One's identity as a worker was shaped not only by the work one did to earn a living, but also by family, neighborhood, and leisure. As these topics are addressed in other chapters in this volume, this chapter will only touch on them fleetingly. However, it is important to remember that workplace culture was connected with other realms of workers' social and intellectual lives, and traditions and rituals that governed the workplace, as well as those that sought to transform it, partook of the larger cultural tendencies of the period.

Traditions and rituals are part of workplace culture. Every work environment has its own culture: a set of explicit and implicit rules that govern workers' interactions, a hierarchy granting some power over others, practices that mark important moments in the work cycle, and means of rewarding some and punishing others. Workplace cultures can be nourishing or abusive, and in many cases rules and rituals that empower some oppress others. Work sites in the age of empire were governed by such rules and practices. Some are easier than others to identify; we know the most about artisan cultures in part because of historians' interest in artisans and in part because many artisans were educated and wrote about their experiences of work. For other types of workers—early factory workers, for example—we need to read between the lines of what others wrote about them. Fortunately for the historian, workplace culture was of great interest to observers, who worried incessantly about the corrupting potential of the workplace, and sought ways to control and "improve" workers. Workers themselves also participated in efforts to transform workplace culture, in ways that sometimes corresponded to the goals of their employers, and at other times clashed with these goals.

THE PERSISTENCE OF TRADITION: ARTISANAL PRACTICES AND VALUES

In his study of artisans in early modern Europe, James Farr situated the "highwater mark of corporatism" in the late seventeenth and early eighteenth centuries.[1] Corporatism is the idea that society should be organized into groups or bodies (*corps*) and assumes that individuals subsume their own interests to those of the group. The rise of individualism and laissez-faire in the eighteenth century made corporatism suspect, and called the guild system into question. Workers' politicization in the era of the French Revolution further challenged the guild system, as many feared that corporate bodies served as incubators of sedition. In France, the d'Allarde Law of March 1791 abolished the guilds and replaced masters' privileges with a tax; it was followed by the Le Chapelier Law outlawing all trade organizations and workers' "'coalitions' under penalty of fines and imprisonment."[2] In 1799 and 1800 the British Parliament passed the Combination Acts, which did away with trade organizations' ability to set wages and working conditions. In both countries, work was henceforth to be governed by a contract between the individual worker and his or her employer. In the German territories, the corporate system persisted until mid-century, but economic crisis in the 1830s and 1840s, followed by a wave of industrialization in the 1860s and 1870s, undermined corporatism and led to the adoption of laissez-faire employment practices.[3]

Historians have generally seen the first half of the nineteenth century as a period when artisanal culture was in decline, although some of the factors behind this decline, including new production practices such as the putting-out system or the use of subcontractors, as well as mechanization, had been transforming a variety of trades from at least the mid-eighteenth century. While the legal changes discussed above undermined the ability of masters to control entry to their trade and the quality of the work product, workers' organizations were tolerated or even encouraged in much of Europe. These organizations preserved much of the traditional culture of the corporate system. Values that were central to corporatism, such as the importance of hierarchy and community, also structured more modern work sites, including the factory. Thus, James Farr argues that while "by 1870 everywhere in Europe corporatism had been largely dismantled ... Part of the artisan's response ... was a *de facto* continuation of collectivist expressions, even though they were deprived of any basis in law."[4] During the age of empire, corporatist traditions were paradoxically both under attack and strengthened, and in either case transformed.

Traditionally, the corporate system ensured the quality of goods produced, the implementation of work rates and conditions that both masters and workers considered reasonable, and a measure of discipline over workers by means of a hierarchical organization of masters, journeymen, and apprentices. Masters employed journeymen and apprentices, often providing food and lodging. In 1830 in Lyon, center of the French silk industry, seven thousand master weavers employed roughly twenty-five thousand "journeymen, apprentices and female assistants" in workshops that were most often also their homes.[5] Journeymen were responsible for teaching apprentices the skills and knowledge of their craft: what they referred to as its "mystery." Journeymen also sought to develop their skills as they worked towards the completion of a "masterpiece" that would allow them to accede to the top ranks of the craft; part of this training was a system of "tramping," or moving from workshop to workshop in different towns and cities, what in France was known as the "Tour de France" and in German territories the "wanderpflicht."[6] Mobility allowed journeymen to make contacts with others in their trade, and provided them with a measure of leverage against masters. This mobility was facilitated by a network of fellow journeymen, united in associations. Journeymen formed associations in Great Britain, France, Germany, and the Low Countries. Journeymen's associations collected dues used to support the tramping system, to help workers survive in case of work stoppages, and to pay for funerals and festivities. Paying dues and participating in group activities—whether drinking in the pub or marching through the city to celebrate the craft's patron saint—were ritualized means of creating community and fostering identity as a member of a particular trade. Journeymen's associations also transcended individual trades: in France, the *compagnonnage* "Enfants de Maître Jacques" (Children of Master James) encompassed twenty trades. Associations such as this fostered identities based on common bonds between workers. They could also reinforce other sources of identity such as religion, as we see with the French organizations imbued with Catholic beliefs and traditions, or the organization of Jewish cigar makers in Hamburg whose funds were used in part to support those sitting shiva in mourning of a family member.[7]

At the beginning of the nineteenth century, it was becoming difficult for journeymen to make the transition to master. Through their associations, journeymen organized work stoppages to enforce wage schedules and prevent other workers and masters from engaging in practices that would undercut agreed-upon wages. These functions of journeymen's associations were ritualized. In France, journeymen who sought to implement a wage schedule (*tarif*) (Figure 4.1) would go from workshop to workshop, negotiating with masters. While they were there, the workers in the shop would stop work, an extra incentive for the master to come to a quick agreement. If no agreement was reached, workers took their tools and left.[8] Journeymen also enforced agreed upon wage schedules, as the Parisian hatters attempted to do in 1830, entering workshops where hats were being made at a lower cost (and workers thus paid lower wages) to "destroy ... tools and equipment."[9] In the economic crises of the first half of the nineteenth century, as masters also saw their incomes and status erode, the two groups increasingly joined together in common cause. This was particularly true in a city like Paris, where the line between small masters and workers was often blurry. As Achille Leroux wrote in the 1830s: "There are a great many men who exist between the master and the worker ... they work for masters and are treated as workers by these men, and in turn they are treated as masters by the men that they employ."[10] The participation of masters in journeymen's actions created a larger sense of belonging to a working class whose members were united by common concerns and common values, a transition clearly underway by the 1840s.

In the traditional corporate system, apprenticeships were governed by a written agreement by which the apprentice would remain in the master's shop for a given period of time in exchange for learning a trade. Apprenticeship had long been regulated through state-supported statutes. In England, the 1563 Statute of Artificers and Apprentices

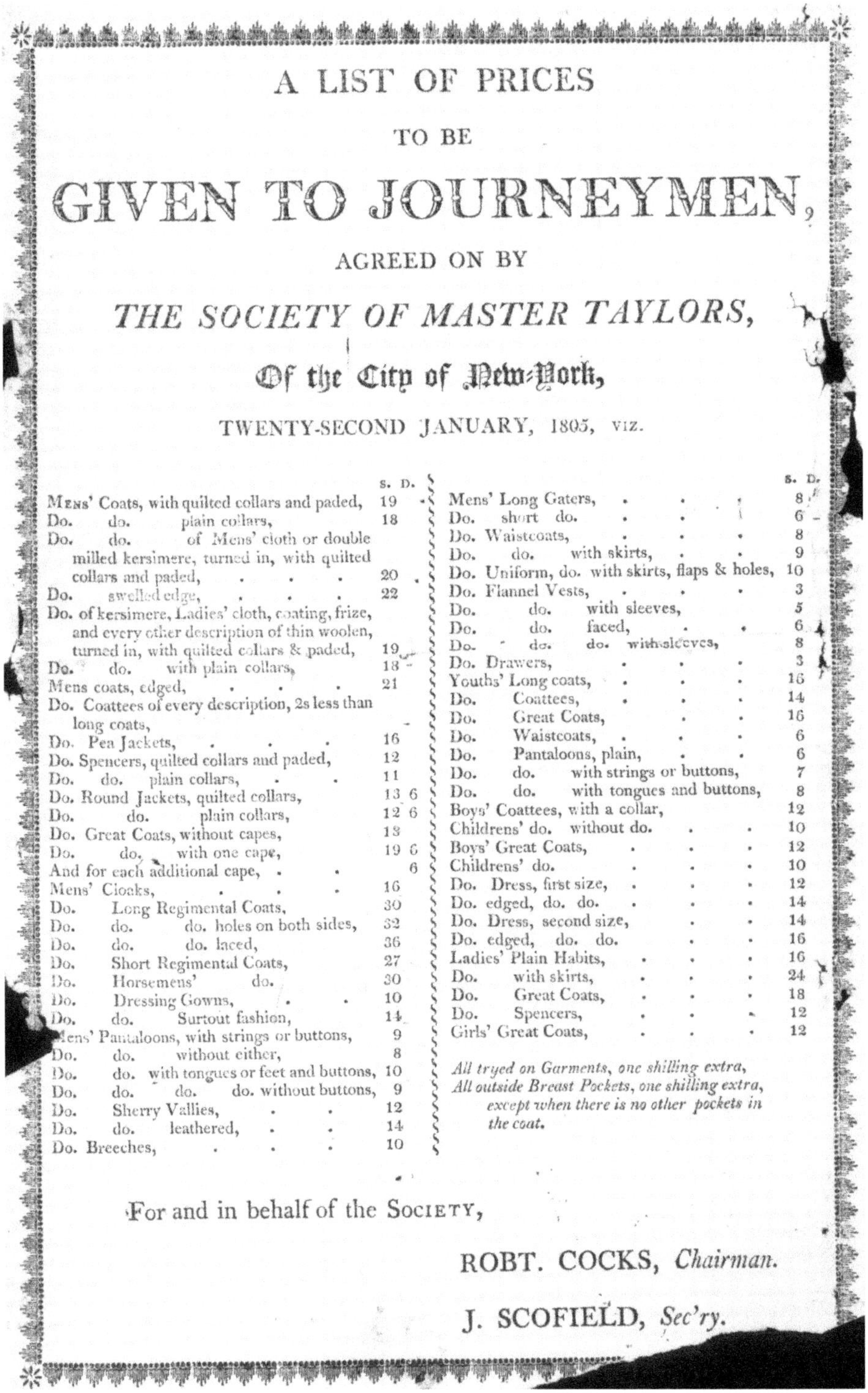

A LIST OF PRICES

TO BE

GIVEN TO JOURNEYMEN,

AGREED ON BY

THE SOCIETY OF MASTER TAYLORS,

Of the City of New-York,

TWENTY-SECOND JANUARY, 1805, VIZ.

	S.	D.
Mens' Coats, with quilted collars and paded,	19	
Do. do. plain collars,	18	
Do. do. of Mens' cloth or double milled kersimere, turned in, with quilted collars and paded,	20	
Do. swelled edge,	22	
Do. of kersimere, Ladies' cloth, coating, frize, and every other description of thin woolen, turned in, with quilted collars & paded,	19	
Do. do. with plain collars,	18	
Mens coats, edged,	21	
Do. Coattees of every description, 2s less than long coats,		
Do. Pea Jackets,	16	
Do. Spencers, quilted collars and paded,	12	
Do. do. plain collars,	11	
Do. Round Jackets, quilted collars,	13	6
Do. do. plain collars,	12	6
Do. Great Coats, without capes,	13	
Do. do. with one cape,	19	6
And for each additional cape,		6
Mens' Cloaks,	16	
Do. Long Regimental Coats,	30	
Do. do. do. holes on both sides,	32	
Do. do. do. laced,	36	
Do. Short Regimental Coats,	27	
Do. Horsemens' do.	30	
Do. Dressing Gowns,	10	
Do. do. Surtout fashion,	14	
Mens' Pantaloons, with strings or buttons,	9	
Do. do. without either,	8	
Do. do. with tongues or feet and buttons,	10	
Do. do. do. do. without buttons,	9	
Do. Sherry Vallies,	12	
Do. do. leathered,	14	
Do. Breeches,	10	

	S.	D.
Mens' Long Gaters,		8
Do. short do.		6
Do. Waistcoats,		8
Do. do. with skirts,		9
Do. Uniform, do. with skirts, flaps & holes,		10
Do. Flannel Vests,		3
Do. do. with sleeves,		5
Do. do. faced,		6
Do. do. do. with sleeves,		8
Do. Drawers,		3
Youths' Long coats,		16
Do. Coattees,		14
Do. Great Coats,		16
Do. Waistcoats,		6
Do. Pantaloons, plain,		6
Do. do. with strings or buttons,		7
Do. do. with tongues and buttons,		8
Boys' Coattees, with a collar,		12
Childrens' do. without do.		10
Boys' Great Coats,		12
Childrens' do.		10
Do. Dress, first size,		12
Do. edged, do. do.		14
Do. Dress, second size,		14
Do. edged, do. do.		16
Ladies' Plain Habits,		16
Do. with skirts,		24
Do. Great Coats,		18
Do. Spencers,		12
Girls' Great Coats,		12

All tryed on Garments, one shilling extra,
All outside Breast Pockets, one shilling extra, except when there is no other pockets in the coat.

For and in behalf of the SOCIETY,

ROBT. COCKS, *Chairman.*

J. SCOFIELD, *Sec'ry.*

FIGURE 4.1 Clothing prices set by master tailors, New York City, 1805. Photo: MPI / Getty Images.

obligated all artisans to complete a seven-year apprenticeship. In the German territories apprenticeships were set at three or four years, followed by another few years of compulsory tramping, and a waiting period or *Mutjahre*.[11] These rules allowed masters to control entry to the trade and assure work quality; states and municipalities supported the authority of masters as a tool of social control. Even after laws were passed outlawing workers' corporations in France and Great Britain, apprenticeships remained common. In Paris, 5 percent of adolescents in the workforce had a written apprenticeship agreement as late as 1902.[12] While this reflects a minority of workers employed who were under the minimum age limit for full-time work (thirteen years as of 1892), it also indicates the persistence of the apprenticeship system, especially when we take into consideration that in some trades, especially those in which significant numbers of women worked, such as market vending and hosiery, apprenticeship was largely an informal system.[13]

James Farr has noted that work not only served as a means of survival, but was also "a sign of social place."[14] In the corporate system rules and rituals established and maintained a clear hierarchy. When William Lovett became an apprentice cabinet maker, the journeymen emphasized his lower status by demanding that he buy drinks for whomever taught him a new skill. Apprentices had to learn the hierarchies of their trades; in Sturt's wheelwright's shop:

> The body-makers are the wealthiest of all and compose among themselves a species of aristocracy to which the other workmen look up with feelings half of respect, half of jealousy. They feel their importance and treat the others with various consideration: carriage makers are entitled to a species of condescending familiarity; trimmers are considered too good to be despised; a foreman of painters they may treat with respect, but working painters can at most be favoured with a nod.[15]

Making a mistake could mean fines or a beating.

Apprentices had to learn the rules of the workshop, and also be willing to break them. In England, journeymen tailors expected apprentices to "smoke, smuggle liqueur into the workshop and take part in the sale of sewing-silk from the employer's stock"; they also had to keep an eye out and warn journeymen who were smoking or drinking that the foreman or master was approaching. Apprentices were expected to contribute part of their wages to a fund for buying drinks and to participate in punishing those who worked too fast or at night.[16] These practices built community that was also manifested in rivalries between different journeymen's associations, as in 1826 when an agreement between rival *compagnonnages* in the Paris construction trades was breached and violence broke out.[17] Workers' organizations also manifested their identity in public festivities, as in the case of the Parisian hatters, who "required the workers to participate in common rituals of solidarity: banquets, funerals for members, masses and processions in honour of the patron saint." These "ritual enactments of brotherhood," as William Sewell characterized them, created a strong sense of community that was enhanced by family and neighborhood connections.[18]

The apprenticeship system was such a central part of artisanal culture that workers protected it fiercely, and replicated its structure even in the absence of a formal organization. William Lovett's first, and unsuccessful, apprenticeship was as a rope maker. He was subsequently hired by a local carpenter, but when the carpenter's apprentices threatened their master with legal action, "exasperated to find that a rope maker could find employment as a carpenter," he was let go.[19] Lovett went to London, where he had no luck finding work in the ropeyards. When he met some carpenters from his home region who were also looking for work, they proposed an arrangement that created among them a relationship mirroring traditional craft hierarchies:

> they readily agreed that I should go round with them to seek for some [employment]; and that if we were fortunate enough to get work together in some building, I should do what I could of the roughest part of it, and should allow them half-a-crown each weekly, in consideration of my not having served any time in the business. To this proposition I readily consented, as I was anxious to learn the trade, and the following morning we went round together.[20]

He later worked out a similar arrangement with another carpenter that he met at his lodgings. Lovett continued to encounter difficulties because of his apprenticeship as a rope maker. After having worked for a cabinet maker in a shop where he was paid low wages for piece work, he found employment at what he described as a "cabinet manufactory" (Figure 4.2). When the other workers learned that he had not served a proper apprenticeship, they threatened to harass him until he left the shop. However, he called a shop meeting to plead his case, an event that had its own rituals:

> To call a meeting of this description the first requisite was to send for a quantity of drink (generally a gallon of ale), and then to strike your hammer and holdfast together, which, making a bell-like sound, is a summons causing all in the shop to assemble around your bench. A chairman is then appointed, and you are called upon to state your business.[21]

After hearing his story, his fellow workers allowed him to stay on at the shop; thus, Lovett became an apprentice, working in a series of workshops until he gained the experience to be admitted to the Cabinet Makers' Society.

FIGURE 4.2 Victorian carpenters at work. Photo: whitemay via Getty Images.

Lovett convinced his fellow workers to accept him by appealing "to their sense of justice," asking whether it was fair that because he had been apprenticed in a trade where no employment was to be found, he should forever be banned from learning another. E. P. Thompson has argued that values such as "'justice', 'independence', security, or family-economy were at stake" in most work-related conflicts in the 1830s, rather than "straight-forward 'bread-and-butter' issues."[22] While Thompson may overstate the case, it is clear that the question of wages was often inextricably linked with these other values that permeated artisanal culture. For example, the ability of masters to control access to the trades through apprenticeship ensured both their independence and their control over wages. In the tailoring industry, the rise of *confection* houses—manufacturers of ready-to-wear clothing employing relatively unskilled workers doing specific tasks according to a new division of labor—brought down wages for all tailors, journeymen and masters alike.[23] Similarly, mechanization, as in spinning and weaving, often brought with it a lack of control over entry to the trade, as unskilled workers were hired to take on tasks that required little training. In Lyon, entrepreneurs set up factories in convents, where girls from the countryside were paid low wages and supervised by nuns.[24] In the English countryside, textile mills similarly hired women and children at lower wages to do unskilled work. Unlike apprentices, whose entry into the craft was sanctioned by a master and whose training included the skills, knowledge, and traditions of his craft, workers in textile mills and other industrial concerns located outside of cities brought the culture of the countryside and the family to the workplace.

WORKPLACE CULTURES AND ECONOMIC TRANSFORMATION

Coal mines and textile factories drew on the population of the surrounding countryside for their workforce. In 1826, a new mining company in Decazeville, France, sought to exploit the region's coal more efficiently. Three-quarters of the mine workers were peasants, who worked only on a seasonal basis as they remained committed to tending their small farms.[25] Similarly, in rural areas around Moscow before 1861, peasant serfs worked in large factories (as well as in their homes) in the textile industry for most of the year, tending to agricultural tasks during the summer.[26] Local traditions and relationships shaped workplace culture in these cases, as did family structure. In the Yorkshire and Lancashire textile factories in the 1840s, up to one-half of the women workers were employed in the same concerns as their husbands.[27] Just as in traditional peasant culture girls and women were expected to be subordinate to husbands and fathers, so too were women subordinate to men in the factories. According to Deborah Valenze, "women were noted for their willingness to work, even into the evening hours, when male workers expected a regularly scheduled break ... Unlike their male counterparts, they seldom questioned the orders of factory managers and overlookers, and they were much less likely to be involved in unions."[28] In small factories in Russia, women workers were sometimes charged with doing the laundry and cleaning the homes of owners and stewards.[29] Historians have noted that with few other options for employment, women could not afford to make trouble, but in fact women did engage in work stoppages and other acts of resistance, often in concert with male family members. Nonetheless, traditional peasant culture and the emerging bourgeois culture of domesticity combined to encourage women's greater acceptance of the demands and rules of the workplace.

Although in many cases workers came to textile factories from the countryside, workplace hierarchies quickly emerged. In worsted spinning and weaving, most workers learned the job while in the factory. As Karl Ittmann noted, the "lack of a pre-existing craft tradition [left] the field wide open for the creation of hierarchies of work in what were essentially new occupations." With no formal structure of apprentices–journeymen–masters, hierarchies based on gender, age, and ethnicity emerged. In English worsted mills, the work that women, children, and Irish men did was the most "labour intensive and rote."[30] Among weavers and spinners, English men took charge of tending to and supervising machinery, jobs that came to be defined as "skilled" in opposition to the "unskilled" labor of the machine operatives. Once established, hierarchies were maintained by recruitment practices in which skilled workers gave preference in hiring to family members. While a young son of a skilled worker could expect to become a skilled worker himself, hierarchies based on gender and ethnicity were fixed, with no chance of moving up through the ranks.

Hierarchies were sometimes maintained through violence and harassment. In spinning and weaving, overlookers were charged with supervising both the machines and the workers, and were one of the few groups of workers in the mills who underwent formal training. Overlookers sometimes used violence to enforce discipline, as in the case of an overlooker who beat a Bradford boy to death in 1857.[31] Overlookers also used their power to sexually harass female employees. Sexual harassment, like other forms of violence within the mills, was a constant aspect of workplace culture that remained "a mainly secretive problem."[32]

Workplaces were also shaped by a culture of precarity. In the first half of the nineteenth century, workplaces were undergoing significant transformations. Laws abolishing masters' corporations in France and Great Britain accelerated a process already underway in the eighteenth century by which lower-paid workers produced lower-quality goods for an expanding consumer market, as was dramatically evident in trades such as tailoring, shoemaking, and textile production. Mechanization also brought down wages, as did the expansion of subcontracting in a variety of trades. These changes were encouraged by the economic crises of the first half of the nineteenth century, and exacerbated the impact of these crises on workers. E. P. Thompson has described the unemployment of the period from 1820 to 1850 as "cataclysmic."[33] This thirty-year period was one of repeated economic crises, the consequences of which were dire for workers. In Marseille, France, the Chamber of Commerce reported that in the late 1840s tailors, suffering from changes in the organization of production due to the rise of ready-to-wear clothing, worked only about one hundred and fifty days a year, as opposed to three hundred in most trades.[34] An 1827 account of conditions among skilled weavers in Lancashire, who faced massive unemployment as mechanized mills became the norm, is chilling. Upon visiting the home of a weaver, a member of the Select Committee on Emigration saw:

> on one side of the fire a very old man, apparently dying, on the other side a young man about eighteen with a child on his knee, whose mother had just died and been buried … We went upstairs, and, under some rags, we found another young man, the widower; and on turning down the rags, which he was unable to remove himself, we found another man who was dying, and who did die in the course of the day. I have no doubt that the family were actually starving at the time.[35]

To under- and unemployment were added changes in the workplace initiated by employers. In northern France, mechanization was often seen as the answer to the economic crisis of 1827 to 1831, and so that none of the money invested in new machinery would be wasted, workers who talked, smoked, played games, or engaged in other activities that would take them away from their work were fined.[36] In the mines of the Loire valley in France, company owners responded to the economic crisis of the 1840s by lengthening the work day and increasing the expected output per day, leading to a rise in accidents.[37] In the cities, masters tried to eke out a living as their profits fell by employing lower-paid piece workers or putting work out to men and women working from their homes, "behaving less and less according to the artisanal expectations of their trade."[38] Many masters also became sweated laborers themselves. Economic precarity was thus accompanied by unwanted and unwelcome attacks on the traditions and customs of the workplace that added to a sense of crisis among skilled workers in particular, who felt the loss to their status and identity the hardest.

WORKERS' ORGANIZATIONS AND THE CULTURE OF ASSOCIATION

Skilled workers took the lead in organizing and resistance. As we have seen already, journeymen's organizations provided a means by which workers could protest falling wages and declining working conditions. These organizations often overlapped with mutual aid or friendly societies, organized by workers to help pay for costs associated with accidents, unemployment, or death. Mutual aid was a central component of corporatism, as workers pooled their resources to help each other in and outside of the workplace (see Figure 4.3). Even in trades not organized into corporations, mutual aid was a core value and practice. The merchants who sold used clothes in Paris's Temple Market, for example, protested police attempts to limit their sociability in 1843 by declaring in a petition that

FIGURE 4.3 A journeyman arrives at a fellow felt maker's workshop, 1820. Photo: Hulton Archive / Getty Images.

they had "all and at every instant need for each other in their commerce."[39] What Fabrice Laroulandie has termed a "spirit of solidarity" was common in many trades, and was perpetuated in the mutual aid and friendly societies that proliferated during the 1820s.[40] These societies provided workers in need with financial support, but they also served as a basis for organizing work stoppages. Mutual aid societies grew in number during the first half of the nineteenth century. In Paris, 120 were registered with authorities in 1820; that number grew to 262 by 1846, with doubtless more that were not registered. In London, mutual aid societies had at least 650,000 members in 1793 and 925,000 in 1815.[41] Mutual aid societies also existed in Russia; the first such society in the city of Odessa was founded by printers in 1816.[42] In the United States, mutual aid societies were often formed by immigrants who looked to other members of their ethnic and/or religious community for help, as was the case of the Hebrew Mutual Benefit Society, organized in 1826 by members of a New York City synagogue.[43]

Mutual aid societies extended the culture of the workplace beyond the workplace, as workers met in synagogues and churches, in pubs and at wine merchants. Other types of organizations similarly shaped and were shaped by workplace values. In the first half of the nineteenth century, skilled craftsmen in England joined educational societies, including Mechanics' Institutes, where they attended public lectures and had access to books from the library. These were organized by middle-class benefactors wishing to spread their own culture of self-improvement to the working classes. Workers also organized their own associations, some of which were encouraged by employers, as in Essex, England, when silk workers were allowed to set up a "Literary Institute" at the company's expense, open only to working men, after they expressed discomfort with the middle-class norms that reigned at the Mechanics' Institute.[44] Skilled workers advocated for workers' education, wrote newspapers and pamphlets, and participated in utopian socialist movements such as Owenism and Saint-Simonianism. They became politically active through Chartism in England and in the upheavals of 1848 on the continent. Through these practices, workers both maintained and transformed the traditional emphasis on communal bonds uniting members of a trade into a broader ethic of association that crossed trade lines.

The concept of association structured attempts during these years to remake workplace culture. In the French working-class press, artisans opposed their values of association and mutual aid with what they saw as a bourgeois ethic of everyman for himself.[45] They argued that new means of organizing production made it impossible for family members to stay together; instead, each family member went off to his or her own workplace, resulting, they warned, in a dangerous isolation of the individual. Many workers proposed that male workers be paid wages high enough to allow their wives and children to stay out of the factories, what became known as the "male breadwinner model." Others argued that both men and women should work, but that they should do so in communal settings. Robert Owen and Charles Fourier both envisioned model industrial communities where workers could maintain strong familial and social bonds. The Saint-Simonians experimented with abolishing the traditional family in favor of both love and work relationships based on personal preferences. Proponents of producers' cooperatives argued that if workers owned the means of production, they would be able to look out for each other through profit-sharing plans. In all of its guises, association was a response to transformations in the workplace that were experienced as attacks on workers' values and experiences: experiences not only of producing and wage earning, but of family relations and sociability as well.

MORALITY AND ROMANCE IN THE WORKPLACE

That workers' communities were being undermined did not escape the attention of proponents of mechanization and new means of organizing labor, but these changes were often interpreted differently. Sociability, which was at the heart of many workers' visions of association, was sometimes seen by employers as evidence of a dangerous dissolution of hierarchy and distinction. For French observers, the term *pêle-mêle* (pell-mell, or without any clear order) was used to capture this supposed lack of structure to working-class life. As Louis René Villermé wrote in 1840, factories "where ordinarily many workers are brought together *pêle-mêle*, are schools of drunkenness and libertinage."[46] The Catholic *L'Ouvrier* (*The Worker*) used the same language, warning parents that textile manufacturers "brought together in an inevitable *pêle-mêle* men, women, children, young girls and young boys; from which it follows that immorality reigns among these sad populations." Parents would be better off, they advised, sending a child into a traditional craft, where they would find "less danger of demoralization."[47]

Although as we have seen all workplaces had their own culture that established hierarchies, shaped patterns of sociability, and influenced workers' sense of themselves, observers who were alarmed by industrialization worried that newer sorts of workplaces such as factories were peopled by men and women lacking any sort of culture whatsoever. In his 1842 *Notes of a Tour in the Manufacturing Districts of Lancashire*, W. Cook Taylor warned that the "manufacturing population is not new in its formation alone: it is new in its habits of thoughts and action, which have been formed by the circumstances of its condition, with little instruction and less guidance from external sources."[48] The default work culture that emerged in this context was seen as one of bad habits. An 1844 description of the working classes in France and England blamed mill workers for their own poverty, decrying their "lack of sobriety and of [good] conduct."[49] These bad habits were believed to be contagious. As part of an 1851 inquiry into the troubled embroidery industry in France, the mayor of Gorze stated, "the daily small gatherings of female workers outside their doors can contribute to bad habits, because they spend long hours telling each other about their relations with boys, and thus each perverts the other."[50] These young women worked out of their homes; observers worried that the possibilities of "perversion" were much worse when men and women worked side by side in the textile mills or underground in the mines. Villermé expressed his outrage that factory owners:

> mix the sexes [in one place] when *ordinarily* you could so easily separate them. Aren't you aware of the loose talk that this mix provokes, the lessons in bad morals that result ... and the stirring passions that you are encouraging as soon as the senses are awakened?[51]

Villermé worried about the "dangerous falls [from virtue], almost inevitable," that he believed young girls in these factories were subject to, and as we have seen, sexual harassment was part of workplace culture.[52] Workplaces were also locations where romance could bloom, and consensual sexual relationships begin. In Germany, a survey by the textile employers' association found that in 1913, 38 percent of pregnant women who worked in textile factories were not married, although many women married their partners after becoming pregnant.[53] Yet sexuality was considered a tremendous danger in the workplace: factory owners fired single women who became pregnant, and went to great lengths to make sure that all nonwork spaces, including courtyards, cafeterias, and restrooms, were segregated by sex. The owner of a cotton manufactory in Germany had his 1885 rules concerning relationships between men and women drafted by a priest:

> All mutual dealings between [male and female workers] during their free time is forbidden. Violations, as well as frivolous interactions, that breach Christian morality, even outside of the factory, between young people of both sexes, will be met with a warning from the workers' committee, and if this is ineffective, a notice of termination.[54]

Yet separating the sexes was no guarantee that women would be safe from sexual harassment, especially since they were subject to the authority of male supervisors. A woman factory worker in St. Petersburg in 1901 reported that when the women left the factory, they were searched to make sure that they had not stolen anything. These searches were done by male stewards in the presence of other men, and were experienced as physical and psychological assaults. As this woman worker wrote, "during the search … they would toss out remarks of such content that I cannot bring myself to repeat them"; she described the experience as a "vulgar humiliation of my person."[55]

While middle-class observers worried most dramatically about factories and mines, sociability—among members of the same sex and between men and women—was a central aspect of all workplace cultures. Artisans, like the embroidery workers of Gorze working out of their homes who gathered on the doorsteps to gossip, left the workshop to visit the café or pub or talk with neighbors. In Bradford, England, handloom weavers gathered at noon to spend "an hour talking about pig-feeding, hen-raising, and bird-catching, and now and then would have very hot disputes about free grace."[56] Employers in textile mills passed regulations prohibiting games and talking, as did police authorities in Paris who in 1865 outlawed "brawls, quarrels, rows, cries, songs or games of any sort" in any of the city's public markets.[57] Yet the capital's street-sellers continued to serve as centers of working-class sociability, people around whom neighborhood residents could gather to exchange news and information.

What some saw as the unregulated and unstructured sociability of working-class life led to a belief that it might be a good idea to reinstate the guilds. In France during the empire and Restoration (1804–30), those who supported restoring the guilds argued they would create "discipline and order."[58] For these same reasons, government authorities tolerated journeymen's associations, which they believed could help check the spread of revolutionary ideology among workers.[59] Yet to reestablish the guilds would mean placing limitations on the principle of laissez-faire, which in the minds of some would be tantamount to renouncing progress. The rhetorical question posed by Théodore Fix in 1846 captured this perspective:

> What would we have done with the principle of the division of labour, with the most ingenious machines and with the immense capital accumulated by this generation of labour, if we had remained imprisoned in the circle of corporations, masterships, and confraternities, if we still had to battle the privileges of soil and of birth and with all these obstacles that would compromise genius and paralyze the impact of the most beautiful discoveries, the most useful inventions?[60]

Yet while many favored individual contracts as the primary means by which workers associated with employers, they worried that the new economy might unleash individual passions.

PATERNALISM

If traditional craft culture could not save the workers from immorality, and associationist and socialist solutions were not acceptable to middle-class observers, paternalism offered another means of shaping workplace culture. Paternalism is the name given to a set of practices adopted by employers that aimed at changing worker behavior and increasing worker dependency on the employer. As a belief system, paternalism was closely allied with the culture of domesticity, with its celebration of a strong father figure. It was, as Patrick Joyce has argued, an "expression and validation of a sense of superiority, of being master in one's own factory, just as in one's own home."[61] The belief that workers were like badly brought-up children, neglected by their own parents and thus in need of instruction from their social "superiors" drove paternalist policy, which was fundamentally optimistic concerning the ability of workers to change. Both paternalism and laissez-faire were driven by a belief in progress, as is evident in the praise that the London *Morning Chronicle* heaped at mid-century on the cotton town of Ashton-under-Lyne, outside of Manchester, where "nine-tenths of the town owes its existence immediately to the power-loom, and, in nearly all that large proportion, the houses are more comfortable, the streets more open and better drained" than in other towns, due to the efforts of mill owners to house their workers in comfortable and sanitary conditions. Contrasting the newer parts of Ashton with the "old filthy, and undrained parts of the town" where the handloom weavers—"a handful of miserable old men"—barely survive, the author equates employer largesse with progress and mechanization.[62]

Paternalism also had its practical side. Paternalist policies tied workers to the factory site by providing them with subsidized housing, medical care, schools, and even food. These benefits kept employer costs more stable than fluctuating wages might, and made it harder for workers to leave their jobs. Retaining workers was crucial: as industries mechanized, young workers from agricultural backgrounds had to be trained in the skills and rhythms of factory life. Unskilled positions in the textile mills might require less than a month of training, but many textile workers might not reach "full proficiency" for a few years, not least because of the speed of machines and the concentration necessary to operate them.[63] Dietrich Mühlberg reminds us that operating machinery "called for deep concentration, simultaneous attention to various details, rapid evaluation of observations, quick decision-making, split-second control reactions."[64] By the late nineteenth century, power looms in England and Germany had shuttles that crossed the warp between seventy and two hundred times a minute; yet even in the 1840s, operating a mechanized loom was a new, and challenging, experience for workers from rural backgrounds.[65] Furthermore, with mechanization came new jobs, such as those of "puddlers ... hammermen or pressers" in machine building and metallurgy, requiring skills that could not be passed down gradually on the job by an older generation of workers.[66]

Paternalist policies thus also included increased supervision and training. In Paris in the 1850s and 1860s employers in the printing trade and in the manufacture of artificial flowers instituted in-house training programs to ensure workers learned skills as well as the rules and rhythms of the workspace.[67] In textile mills and other factories, employers used foremen or overlookers to supervise workers on the shop floor. Workers gradually lost the ability to hire assistants or repair machines, and written rules governed worker and foreman alike. Rules forbade smoking, drinking, games, and socializing on the shop floor, as workers needed to be focused on their jobs to produce efficiently and maximize the employers' return on the investments made on mechanization. Of course, learning a trade always involves accustoming oneself to disciplines that may have previously been unfamiliar; in handloom-weaver families, parents used songs and games to teach children "the patience required for sedentary yet tiring work."[68] Yet in the factory, new disciplines of the body and mind were part of a larger environment in which comings and goings, break times, and rhythms of work were outside of the worker's control. In this context, it is not surprising that German workers who left home workshops to work in the factory equated the move with being sent to prison.[69] At the same time, the very real danger involved in working with powerful machines often encouraged workers to accept the new modes of factory discipline for their own safety.[70]

Paternalism weakened traditional cultures inherited from the field or home workshop, while also creating new workplace cultures. Worker housing that provided separate bedrooms for parents and children, policies that released women from work early so that they could care for their homes, and moral tracts that celebrated a certain model of family life encouraged the adoption of middle-class notions of domesticity.[71] Social committees organized "trips, mill socials (at which the mill band would play), and sports days."[72] The birth or marriage of the employer's child, or the election of the mill owner to political office was celebrated with food and music by the whole community of factory workers and their families. Building schools and churches, and then wielding influence over the lessons and sermons imparted therein, encouraged workers to view their employer as a beneficent superior, but also provided locales where workers could socialize and form their own relationships.

Employers did not envision the benefits of their paternalist policies as a form of charity; rent for housing was deducted from wages, as were dues for mutual aid societies and school fees. This helped keep costs down, while also rendering paternalism more in line with laissez-faire beliefs; it was possible to argue that workers were helping themselves improve under the guiding hand of a caring father figure. Yet paternalism had its limits. Women and immigrant and unskilled workers were often not able to afford the deductions in wages that would have allowed them to live in company housing or be part of a mutual aid society.[73] In larger cities, workers did not need to depend on employers for self-help societies or for leisure activities, and thus paternalism was less effective there than in more rural, isolated areas.[74] And while a factory band or dinner might provide opportunities for enjoyment, at the end of the day, wages were what mattered. As one worker stated, "our master thinks to put us off with a plate of beef and a glass of beer, but he will find himself mistaken. What we want is more wages, and we will have it."[75]

STRIKES, POLITICS, AND WAR

While paternalist policies sought to render workers docile, moral, and efficient, even in the most heavily disciplined factories, workers had their own idea of what was right and their own means of advocating for the values of justice and fairness that E. P. Thompson and others have argued were central to artisanal culture. In one German town in 1910, workers went on strike to defend those who were late when the transportation system broke down, arguing that they shouldn't be penalized for lateness when it was through no fault of their own.[76] Growing acceptance of the routines of factory life did not mean decreased protest on the part of workers. Whereas on the eve of the First World War the factory had become "part of the familiar universe" of many French workers,[77] the number of strikers increased more than sixfold between 1893 and 1920.[78] In Great Britain, the number of strikes rose from just under 400 in 1908 to nearly 1,500 in 1913.[79] In part, this increase was due to the growing acceptance of trade unions, which some employers saw as a valuable tool in managing conflicts between workers and management. Yet the growth in union membership, and the creation of national and international organizations designed to coordinate workers' efforts to increase their wages and improve their working conditions, created the conditions for large-scale strikes (see Figure 4.4).

Like other aspects of the workplace, the strike was shaped by tradition and ritual. In Vienne, France, in 1819, workers opposed the introduction of a mechanized wool cropper when they came together as a community to destroy the machine, singing and drinking as they did so.[80] In 1900 in Troyes, France, when textile workers went on strike shopkeepers donated bread and wine and rent payments were suspended.[81] Community support for strikers undermines the belief, often held by employers and politicians in the late nineteenth century, that strikes were the work of outside agitators. In fact, strikes were strongly shaped by both communal and workplace norms. In British textile mills, workers would often leave their looms or spinning jennies to assemble in the mill courtyard, where they would sing and shout slogans. Strikes borrowed from community traditions of using "rough music" to mock those who abused authority, such as in 1893 in Bradford, England, where women made an effigy of an abusive overlooker and "banged on cans and shouted."[82] German workers also employed traditional means of mocking those in authority, but also engaged in a precisely timed "withdrawal of labour," whereby at the

FIGURE 4.4 A trade union march in Manchester, 1874. Photo: Hulton Archive / Getty Images.

exact same time workers would remain at their looms but stop all work activity.[83] Strikes transformed the workplace into a site of raucous or silent dissent. Strikers sometimes sought to improve their workplace, as when German textile workers demanded soap and towels for washing and cleaner lavatories. Workers also struck to maintain the right to train younger workers, in spite of the decline of the apprenticeship system.

Differences in workplace culture sometimes created rifts among workers that undermined the effectiveness of strikes. In 1887, powerloom and handloom weavers went on strike together, but the movement soon split, as the powerloom weavers focused on improving working conditions in the factory and the handloom weavers concentrated on adjusting piece rates. As Tessie Liu argues, the different strike demands "exposed the vastly different work conditions and relation to the product and to the means of production which separated industrial workers from handloom weavers."[84] Working-class parties attempted to bridge these differences by focusing on common concerns and by promoting a heroic vision of the (primarily male) laborer. Yet nationalism, which was on the rise in the late nineteenth century, sometimes got in the way. French and immigrant Italian steel workers both went on strike in eastern France in 1905 to 1906. However, they too had different demands, and animosity between the two was fed by employer practices that excluded Italian immigrants from paternalist benefits such as single-family housing and employer prejudices that painted Italian immigrants as immoral troublemakers. French workers on strike sung the anthem of transnational working-class solidarity, the "Internationale," while also calling for immigrants to be forcibly deported.[85]

By the early twentieth century, strong working-class parties existed in Germany (the German Socialist Party or SPD, est. 1875), Great Britain (the Labour Party, est. 1900), and France (the French Section of the Workers' International or SFIO, est. 1905). With the extension of the vote to working-class men, workers' parties joined other political parties in competing for the workers' vote, and organized politics became a part of workplace culture. In the French town of Carmaux, politics became part of everyday life for glassworkers and miners, who joined workers' clubs and chose to have civil, rather than religious, marriages and burials.[86] Joining political clubs and participating in the politically informed life of the community could strengthen ties among workers. At the same time, the legalization of unions and the formation of political parties could also create divisions; in 1899 union and nonunion French metalworkers fought each other at the Le Creusot factory.[87] When politics entered the workplace, as a spinner from Bolton, England, noted, "the workpeople had to be very careful how they voted or how they spoke about politics."[88] Employers attempted to use their authority over the workforce to bring about a political outcome that they favored. In England, in Halifax, workers were sent as a group to campaign rallies, and in Keighley the Marquess of Hartington, a liberal politician, was invited to speak to the workers assembled on the factory floor.[89] Some French employers accompanied their workers to the polls on election day, and used informers to gather information on assumed troublemakers. Political divisions created new hierarchies among workers, as those who were active in unions might be either stigmatized as troublemakers or favored as intermediaries who could quell potential unrest by maintaining communication between employers and employees.

The First World War disrupted hierarchies based on skill, gender, country of origin, and political or union affiliation that had been established over the course of the nineteenth century, as able-bodied men went to war and were replaced by women and colonial subjects. The war also hastened, albeit unevenly, processes of mechanization and rationalization, while allowing employers to suspend rules governing safety in the workplace. Workers were subject to an accelerated pace of work and longer shifts. In England, the result was what Angela Woollacott characterized as "an anarchic situation in which workers in different factories around the country experienced widely different regimens."[90] At the same time, new communal bonds were formed, as between women of various class and work backgrounds who found purpose (and higher wages) in working to support the war effort.

At the outset of the war, mobilization combined with increased patriotism weakened workers' movements. But the prolonged fighting, longer work hours, a rising cost of living, and food shortages (especially in the blockaded countries of Germany and Austria–Hungary), soon led to a reprisal of strike activity, which became more pronounced at war's end. Women were active in strikes that broke out in France in 1916 and 1917. In Russia, strikers were among those who brought down the tsarist regime in February 1917. The Russian Revolution inspired workers throughout Europe, who struck in 1917 and 1918, not only to improve working conditions, but also to bring an end to the war. Strike activity continued to be significant in the immediate aftermath of the war. Yet amid a general desire to return to "normalcy" and a growing fear of communism, employers and government officials took strong measures to curtail political activity on the shop floor and to reestablish prewar hierarchies. While these efforts were not entirely successful, overall, it is possible to identify several continuities in workplace culture. In the period after the First World War, divisions in the workplace according to gender and country of origin, the gap between skilled and unskilled workers, the pressures of working with and around machines, and employer efforts to control and rationalize the work process were still present. It is also possible to identify lingering craft traditions and a strong interpenetration between the workplace and the larger community. As it had throughout the nineteenth century, workplace culture continued to be shaped by both the challenges of modernization and the legacies of tradition.

CHAPTER FIVE

Work, Skill, and Technology

FRANÇOIS JARRIGE

TRANSLATED BY VICTORIA E. THOMPSON

At the end of the eighteenth century, the development of new systems of production based on the growing use of machinery began to unsettle social relations, transform work experiences, and challenge the tradition-based knowledge of workers. New technological trajectories gradually made inroads into workshops and factories in Europe and North America, according to paths that were varied and complex. Accompanying this evolution were numerous debates intended to clarify the meaning and stakes of this process. For many, the triumph of machines was neither wished for nor truly desired, because it threatened established positions and the traditional organization of artisans.[1] Before the nineteenth century, technology and technological innovation were secondary concerns for those who thought in terms of limited—"organic" or "Smithian"—growth. Enlightenment technology therefore was little interested in expansive mechanization, but was focused instead on trade, the improvement of existing tools, and the talent of artisans.[2] Nonetheless, the frontiers between men and machines began to shift as a new project of industrial expansion took hold, contemporaneous with the advent of a new model of economic growth known as "Schumpeterian," which can be defined as an increase in production by means of autonomous technical progress, a systematic reinvestment of profits, and an unprecedented rationalization of work.[3] The question of machines and of the benefits of their multiplication emerged as economists, intellectuals, and public health experts adopted the mechanist model, seeking thereby to transform the worker's body into a docile cog and auxiliary of the system of production.[4]

In the nineteenth century, as a new relationship to time, shaped by the ideology of progress and the industrial and scientific revolutions, continued to develop, a triple evolution emerged in the relationships between work, technique, and skill. Technological innovation was increasingly considered favorably, as the motor of a history conceived of as linear and evolutionary; it was also increasingly identified with the realm of production and the growth of workers' productivity; it would henceforth reflect a conviction that a radical transformation meant to reconfigure social relations for the better by alleviating suffering and increasing wealth was possible. However, the counterweight to this evolution in thinking was doubts concerning the ways in which this process might destroy traditional trades. Many observers, such as Karl Marx, denounced the insecurity that spread along with the new capitalist mode of production that required an army of reserve industrial labor to function. As elites celebrated inventors as heroes, and were passionate about machines, the status of innovation was considerably transformed: "What was new came to be associated with security, [while] routine and tradition [were associated] with corruption. To innovate became in itself a [measure of] safety," writes historian Liliane

Hilaire-Pérez. "In this way, a new set of values emerged, where innovation was seen as order and control, inverting traditional fears that newness brought with it subversion."[5] Belief in progress through technology reshaped work and its experience, the daily gestures of labor, established knowledge, as well as the rules that governed the transmission of skills and the organization of labor.

TO MECHANIZE LABOR: A NINETEENTH-CENTURY TECHNOLOGICAL UTOPIA

Few and of little consequence before 1800, productive machines multiplied thereafter, parallel with a move to bring large numbers of workers together in a single factory. Machines were more visible, and became a topic of debate, as steam began to be used as a power source—as a complement to water wheels or horse mills—becoming a source of pride and greatness. Their promoters became veritable heroes in their own countries, whether James Watt in England or Robert Fulton in the United States.[6] One must nonetheless remember that aside from a few industrialized regions in England, the factory system and its advanced machinery, along with the division of labor, were in limited use. Most work was done by hand, using simple wooden tools that were made locally. The famous "fire-pumps" became steam engines, and were prominent symbols of large-scale mechanization. Nonetheless, numerous studies have shown that the conversion to steam power was very slow and that "living power," that is, the bodies of animals and of men, as well as, and in particular, hydraulic power, remained a persistent source of competition to steam engines. In France, the number of fixed steam engines did not equal that of machines powered by hydraulics before 1870; in 1860, water provided double the power of steam, and "coal had not yet won the game."[7] Even in Belgium, which industrialized early, in 1846 steam and combined machines powered by a central motor were in use in only 1,000 artisanal and industrial establishments, naturally those that were the largest in size, out of 114,000 factories and workshops throughout the country.[8] In that same year, 2,739 windmills, 2,633 water mills, and 1,512 horse mills were in use. Even in England, studies have shown that most work remained manual and artisanal, rather than powered by steam.[9]

Despite a slow and gradual process of mechanization, the promise of technology spread and gave rise to a technological messianism that can be found in a number of discourses. In the United States in particular, the cult of the machine expanded, nourished by a moral rhetoric that identified technology with an orderly and pacific world. In the Jackson era, in the 1830s, the country was rapidly transformed and the population grew from less than ten million in 1820 to twenty-three million in 1850. The old aristocracy of southern planters had to compete with the urban, industrial populations of the northeast. Technology was for the latter one of the pillars of the nation's future, and acclaim for the sublime and liberating machine gained ground.[10] Governor of Massachusetts Edward Everett, future president of Harvard, affirmed in an 1837 speech that "The mechanician, not the magician, is now the master of life."[11] Across the Atlantic, several authors became enthusiastic prophets of the machine age.[12] An example is John Etzler, a German immigrant to the United States, and author of an 1833 book whose title announced the advent of a "Paradise within the Reach of all Men without Labor, by Powers of Nature and Machinery."[13] Etzler, strongly influenced by the theories of French reformer Charles Fourier, saw America as the new Eden, where man, a rational being, could build a pacific, happy society thanks to machines. He was himself the author of several patents.[14]

In the United States, labor force shortages along with a reliance on technologies such as the railroad and telegraph to expand and unify the country meant that it became a mechanized territory, buoyed by a powerful technological millenarianism. As in England, the inventor became a celebrated hero, and the status of the invention was transformed by the spread of the patent model. National legislation that aimed to protect inventors by granting them a moral and sacred right over their discoveries appeared everywhere in the West, although at different times.

Parallel with the multiplication of machines that called for a reworking of the knowledge and skill of workers, was the growing prevalence of theories of the machine, that is, analytic approaches to its functioning and a body of knowledge that sought to standardize the manufacture of machines and to increase their number and their output.[15] In his 1724 *Theatrum Machinarum Generale*, German engineer Jacob Leupold was the first to compile the basic principles of mechanical engineering. He defined the machine as "an artificial arrangement by means of which one can move something with a savings of time and strength."[16] But it was especially between 1800 and 1850 that attempts to define the machine multiplied and became more nuanced. By the mid-nineteenth century, industrial mechanics became a well-defined field of knowledge, with its theories concerning motors, cogwheels, and energy transfers. Engineers and technicians tended to become autonomous authorities, attaining greater social status (although this varied by country) and establishing a monopoly over technical knowledge and skills. In Great Britain and the United States, civil engineers working in private firms dominated the field, whereas in France the profession was led by graduates of state schools, forming a "State technocracy" with significant power and authority.[17] These groups led efforts to introduce and justify mechanization. With a strong belief in meritocracy, and convinced that they were the agents of progress thanks to their mastery over the machine, engineers had a major and growing influence, far beyond the realm of business and government. The exchange of ideas among theorists, practitioners, manufacturers, and the heads of workshops, between the laboratory and the factory, tended to increase and to stimulate the rapid expansion of machines all while changing the organization of industry. The term "technology," first conceived during the Enlightenment as meaning the science of artisanal practices, was transformed in this context to increasingly denote the "science of machines," a body of knowledge that sought to optimize the productivity of machines and their capacity to increase profits, all while justifying their adoption.[18]

MACHINES AND THE EVOLUTION OF WORK: CONFLICTS AND DEBATES

Although still few in number and relatively unimpressive, productive machines began to penetrate the countryside and workshops over the course of the nineteenth century, especially in textiles or as engines, bringing in their wake protests and complaints. Machines to spin and weave, and more or less automatic shearing machines, grew in number and produced fears, debates, and even mass uprisings. Upon their introduction, the new machines were frequently called *tueuses de bras* or *casses bras* (killers or breakers of "hands," that is, workers), and workers refused to give up the skills that had become engrained in their own bodies to become mechanical automatons, or extensions of a machine. Throughout the nineteenth century, the mechanization of labor was punctuated by conflict and tension when it threatened established positions and the communitarian organization of work. The most famous of these conflicts was the English Luddite movement of 1811–12, named after the mythic General Ned Ludd, the imaginary leader of the revolt (Figure 5.1). The Luddites opposed the use of machines whose purpose was to reduce production costs and wages; for example, croppers in Yorkshire rebelled against the use of shearing machines in the process of finishing woollen cloth.[19]

On the European continent, conflict existed but was more limited. In France, textile workers in Languedoc repeatedly rose up when new shearing machines threatened the position of proud hand croppers. In an 1819 petition addressed to the mayor of Vienne, in the French department of the Isère, eight master croppers denounced "the machine, more pernicious than useful, known as the great cropper," which, according to them, would entail, "the general suppression of hands." In the same period, cotton spinners in Paris rose up against English machines that "cut the hands of all the workers." This way of expressing opposition was long-lasting, and was used by very different groups of workers. After the revolution of 1848, rabbit skinners complained of the spread of machines "that cut the hands of workers." The repeated use of *bras* (literally arms, but in this context meaning "hands") was based on a specific understanding of property: for workers, their hands were the basic property that each individual possessed, symbolizing both the work practices that had become learned physical behaviors and the knowledge of a trade acquired after a long apprenticeship. While the tools of the trade were an extension of the body, the machines of the industrial era were seen as foreign and inorganic matter.[20]

In Paris, printing workers—the very symbols of highly skilled, urban artisans—destroyed mechanical presses that had been recently imported from England during the

FIGURE 5.1 Rioting mob of Luddites, 1813. Photo: Time Life Pictures / Mansell / The LIFE Picture Collection / Getty Images.

"Three Glorious Days" of the July Revolution of 1830. They also saw these machines as "rivals that came to break our hands." They protested the implementation of dual printing practices, where high-quality editions were produced using artisanal methods, while high-circulation items were printed mechanically by underpaid workers. In the countryside, some peasant communities mobilized against mechanized grain threshers that threatened to eliminate opportunities for work during the winter; England in 1830 saw violent uprisings called "Captain Swing" riots, and in France in 1847 mechanical threshers were also destroyed, very often following bad harvests.[21]

These disorders were caused by technological mutations that reconfigured the world of work. Machines were charged with worsening workers' exploitation and proletarianization. This was especially the case with children's work, increasingly condemned and rejected even as mechanization multiplied tasks for which children could be hired, such as repairing the threads broken by spinning machines in textile factories. In the writings of authors such as Honoré de Balzac, Victor Hugo, and Alfred de Vigny, the description of large machines was part of an "industrial melancholia," that was present in many literary works of the first half of the nineteenth century. One finds this also in the works of intellectuals such as French historian Jules Michelet, who observed the gigantic size of machines in British industry when he travelled across the Channel in 1834. In the 1840s, he invented the French word *machinisme* (machinery), which he invested with a moral significance, using it to condemn the English industrial system and the new social relations it produced. In *The People* (1846), he devoted an entire chapter to the "Servitudes of the Workman dependent on Machinery." If the machine was inevitable, because it was "a most powerful agent of democratic progress, bringing within the reach of the poor numerous objects of utility" it also had its dark side, in creating a "miserable, stunted population of men-machines, who enjoy but half an existence ... who beget only for the grave."[22] Michelet's denunciation of machinery was based on its effects on workers, victims of the boredom and degradation it brought in its wake.

The new system of mechanized factories was charged with gradually transforming a man into a machine without a soul, far removed from the traditional artisan laboring in the workshop or at home: "The weaver's solitary work was far less distressing. Why? He was free to dream. The machine suffers no reserve nor absence of mind," Michelet wrote.[23] Even while allowing for a possible reappropriation of machines in a future communist society, Karl Marx and Friedrich Engels similarly observed, in 1848, that in modern industry, the worker "becomes an appendage of the machine" and that the proletarian masses are "slaves of the machine."[24] For Marx and Engels, the definition of the proletarian was based on three essential factors: he was first of all the product of the industrial organization of work, and only existed in and because of large-scale industry; he produced the surplus value that permitted the expansion of capital, and in this capacity he was the source of all economic and technological development; finally, the condition of the proletarian was one of fundamental economic insecurity. This insecurity not only was the result of business cycles, but was inherent to capitalist production itself, which required a reserve army of industrial workers to function. Proletarians were thus "a class of labourers, who live only so long as they find work, and who find work only so long as their labour increases capital. These labourers, who must sell themselves piecemeal, are a commodity, like every other article of commerce, and are consequently exposed to all the vicissitudes of competition, to all the fluctuations of the market." As a result of mechanization, they added, "the work of the proletarians has lost all individual character, and, consequently, all charm for the workman."[25]

NEW SKILLS AND AN EMANCIPATED LABOR?

Running parallel to the fears and denunciations engendered by mechanization was a proliferation of writings that sought to recover the world of the machine by imagining the worker as technician, and the machine as an appendage that would supplement the fragile and bounded body of the worker. In fact, the development of technology created new specialists: mechanics, machine builders, boiler men and stokers, and foremen, not to mention engineers who specialized in the mastery of this new world of technology. For technicians and engineers, the machine became the new iron slave that would emancipate workers by freeing them from performing dangerous tasks. To defuse worries and calm perceptions of the harmful relationship between men and machines—increasingly dangerous on a daily basis and the cause of many accidents—a new image of the machine as an extension of the worker's body developed. Machines became quasi-human, endowed with magical powers. Andreas Malm and Alf Hornborg have recently examined how the machine became a fetish in nineteenth-century England, a source of illusion and myopia, nourished by the belief in technology's modernity, but also founded on the very real depredation of natural and human environments.[26] The English chemist Andrew Ure, for example, wrote that the mechanized spinning machine was a quasi-person, imbued with an *élan vital* to become an "Iron Man." Michelet used the same type of imagery in his unfinished history of the nineteenth century in describing the factory of Watt and Boulton "excessively producing workers of iron, of copper, by which England would soon have the strength of four-hundred thousand men."[27] Another, more frequent metaphor, made machines and tools a new type of slave whose job it was to help men and support their weak bodies. On the occasion of the 1862 Universal Exposition in London, economist and former Saint-Simonian Michel Chevalier saw machines as a prolongation of the body: "tools are for man supplementary organs by means of which they can tackle an infinity of jobs." Far from brutalizing the body and spirit as some feared, machines would supplement and enhance their abilities, making possible their emancipation rather than, as the idea of proletarianization threatened, abolishing all their autonomy and liberty.[28]

Throughout the nineteenth century, the machine question was at the center of a vast debate over its possible reappropriation. How to transform the machine from an entity that threatened to incorporate man into an instrument of his emancipation? The project of social reformers who invented the "social sciences" after 1830 sought to imagine a technology that privileged autonomy and would allow for the full realization of the humanity within each person. For "socialist" thinkers, in another vision of technological innovation, the future would bring the advent of the free worker, producing a pure technician who would devote himself to intellectual work, leaving the mechanical aspects of labor to inorganic artifacts. Far from rejecting the mechanical world, these thinkers tried to reconquer it by defining the characteristics of a "romantic machine"—an alternative to that of the engineers and economists—capable of reenchanting the world and the workplace, and bringing into being a more democratic order of things.[29] This idea can be found in varying forms in the works of radicals such as Robert Owen, Charles Fourier, Etienne Cabet, and Pierre-Joseph Proudhon. For Fourier, the allocation of work according to the passions of each would hinder the rise of the worker-machine, bound to one repetitive, alienating task. With his theory of "passionate attraction," Fourier imagined that one could increase the output and efficiency of workers without recourse to the dehumanizing division of labor or mechanization, guaranteeing that workers' pleasures and passions would be satisfied.[30] His disciples took these ideas and adapted them to the factory, as in this work of propaganda that describes in detail the daily operations of the utopian community of the Phalanstery, written shortly before the revolution of 1848 by dye worker Mathieu Briancourt:

> Here, as everywhere [in the Phalanstary], machines do just about all of the tiring part of the job: the machine provides the strength, man the intelligence, and his task is limited, in manufacturing, to overseeing, directing, adjusting. You should therefore not be surprised to see several women working as pit sawyers, whose previously painful work was relegated to slaves. If you see different machines doing the identical task, it is to sustain emulation among workers, each group of which prefers a different machine to those of rival groups.[31]

The Communist Étienne Cabet similarly wrote that the progress made possible by mechanization could render workers "inventors" and "directors" of machines. In the Icarian Republic described in his *Le Voyage en Icarie* (1840), the collective owned the means of production. Far from abolishing the independent artisan, Cabet viewed mechanization as a possible means to restore artisanal autonomy by putting workers in charge of machines. Through the abolition of private property, the communist system would destroy the hierarchical relationships that the figure of the engineer embodied, and reconstitute the independence of the artisan who was menaced by the growing concentration of capital. The power of the Icarian vision and its effectiveness as propaganda lay in its ability to bring the machine to life by giving it quasi-magical attributes that would benefit the popular and working classes. But it is without a doubt Proudhon who took this dialectical reversal of the theme of the worker alienated by machines the farthest. Where many of his contemporaries saw the division of labor as an inescapable consequence of mechanization, Proudhon emphasized instead the ambivalence and complexity of these processes. For him, mechanization provided the opportunity to move away from the harmful effects of an excessive division of labor by reskilling the worker:

> the incessant appearance of machinery is the antithesis, the inverse formula, of the division of labor; it is the protest of the industrial genius against *parcellaire* (piecemeal) and homicidal labor. What is a machine, in fact? A method of reuniting divers [sic] particles of labor which division had separated. Every machine may be defined as a summary of several operations, a simplification of powers, a condensation of labor, a reduction of costs.[32]

THE DAILY HEAD-TO-HEAD WITH MACHINES

Beyond these generous and all-encompassing visions, it is obvious that a heterogeneity of situations existed, where the impact of machines on the workplace, its internal structure, and its requirements, varied considerably from trade to trade and from region to region. It was in England, then Belgium and some of the German states that the first large-scale concentrations of industry based on textile and coal could be seen; in these areas a segment, sometimes a majority, of the population—displaced artisans and journeymen, but especially uprooted peasants—would progressively form an immense class of the dispossessed, having nothing to live on but the basic physical ability to work, which brought neither appreciation nor economic security. The proletarian was he who saw his skills and knowledge annihilated by the new technologies and organization of industrial work, and his lifestyle destroyed by the rootlessness of the big city and the industrial town. In simple terms, one could say that the machine defined the proletariat. Given his low salary, the worker was effectively incapable of acquiring the means of production that industrial development rendered always more expensive, requiring the growing investment of enormous sums. The experience of the proletarian was also that of dispossession and reinforced social control. In the nineteenth century, industrialization gave rise to a growing demand for the discipline and control of the workforce and its actions.

For manufacturers, engineers, and economists, industrial mechanization was often couched in the language of disciplining and moralizing work. Claude Anthelme Costaz—member of the French Council of State and the director of the Department of *Ponts et Chaussées* (public works), in short, one of the key players in developing economic policy at the beginning of the nineteenth century—explained in 1815 that "the discovery of machines today renders the bad faith of workers powerless, because they are no longer, as before, indispensable instruments of manufacturing and one can, without trouble, replace them with new men who lack experience."[33]

The work of weavers, in Europe as in Asia, was radically transformed by mechanization. Still rare before 1880, enormous mechanical looms became common at the end of the century, provoking abundant debate. After machines that could be used in the home were improved, a machine that could weave on its own, powered by an exterior force, but for which the worker still had to change the spools was invented, followed by automatic looms that the worker only had to supervise (see Figure 5.2). An example is the Northrop

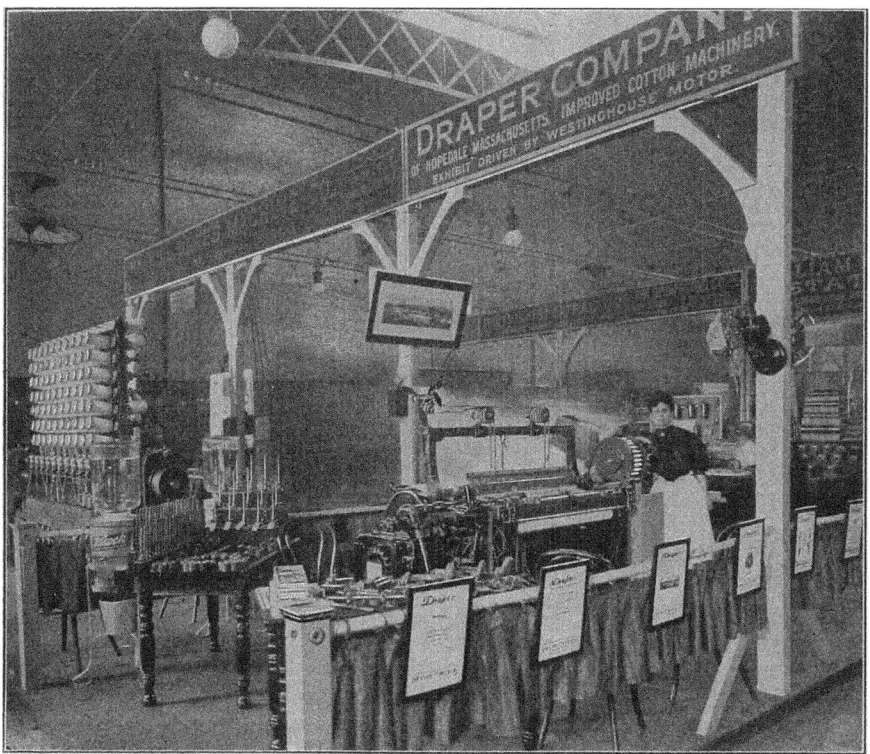

FIGURE 5.2 Labor-saving looms, Draper Corporation Catalog, 1907. Courtesy of Wikimedia.

Loom developed by James A. Northrop, a technician of British origin who lived in the United States. First displayed at the 1893 Chicago World's Fair, the machine was available for purchase the next year. Thirty thousand were put into operation in the United States between 1895 and 1900. They brought about a spectacular cost savings, because one worker could henceforth supervise sixteen—even twenty-four—looms at once. The machines could weave a variety of products, and after 1896 over eight thousand were in service in thirty-eight factories in New England.[34] This rapid adoption can be explained by the strong industrial growth of the United States and a labor shortage that favored the use of machines that did not require as many workers to operate. In Europe, on the other hand, their diffusion was much slower, and brought with it numerous protests in areas where weaving was a long-standing industry and the basis of tightly knit professional communities, with their shared culture and tradition of rebellion.

If some machines brought with them deskilling and a concentration of workers in factories, others, such as the sewing machine, had an opposite effect, reanimating home-based labor. Mechanization constantly brought about shifts in both social status and the sexual division of labor throughout the nineteenth century. In this also it is not possible to speak of one simple and universal shift, even if in general women were relegated to auxiliary or finishing tasks while men—better paid—were supervisors, managers, and ran complex machinery. If mechanization allowed women to leave the home and enter the workforce, historian Michelle Perrot observes that this did not entail "their liberation, their promotion, nor their access to technical knowledge."[35] The sewing machine, a "hybrid between a household appliance and workplace equipment, between consumption and production" was a good example of these shifts.[36] This "machine for making seams" was both an industrial product possessing complex mechanisms and an object for carrying out domestic tasks.[37] First developed in 1830, it was only in the 1850s that mass distribution could be seen on the international level, notably due to the efforts of the American firm Singer (Figure 5.3).[38] Millions of sewing machines spread throughout the world, intended to recreate the traditional system of home-based work. But in practice, the resulting sweating system led to the increased pauperization of women working from home. Far from restoring an older system of work, the spread of the sewing machine prepared women for entry into the factories in the First World War.

NEW TECHNOLOGICAL TRAJECTORIES AT THE END OF THE CENTURY AND THE EXPERIENCE OF WAR

At the end of the nineteenth century, industrial capitalism and confidence in technological progress seemed to have triumphed. Contrary opinions still existed, but they were marginalized and difficult to hear. Within the web of late-nineteenth-century reformers, mechanization was no longer questioned as it had been at the beginning of the century; it was henceforth the social conditions of its use that were discussed. The "great depression" of the 1870s through the 1890s was followed by a new period of industrial expansion. The United States and Germany were henceforth the leading economic powers, while industrialization spread to Europe's peripheries (Spain, Italy, Russia) and, more slowly, to the colonies. Aside from a few limited regions, notably in Asia, colonial territories were seen primarily as reservoirs of primary materials and of a workforce to be exploited. In the colonies, mechanization never occurred at the same pace as in the home countries. There, significant transformations did not take place until after the Second World War,

FIGURE 5.3 Singer's sewing machines, 1892. Courtesy of Bibliothèque nationale de France.

and traditional techniques remained in place much longer than in Europe. Thus, even in the mid-twentieth century, there were thirty times more handheld plows than horse-drawn ploughs in India. Small artisans and peasants had no means to obtain new technologies as extra costs accrued to them, imposed by numerous intermediaries and by the colonial administration. Certainly, large plantations that were technologically advanced and modern, financed by European capital, existed—notably sugar-cane plantations in the Antilles—but these were artificial transplants. In India as well, large industrial concentrations existed, as in the textile sector in Bombay and Calcutta, but these remained the exception.

The new technologies of the 1880s and 1890s, associated with the intensification of trade and with imperialism, transformed capitalism as well as work, and accentuated global inequalities of trade. The number of patents issued grew dramatically, while the combination of electricity, the chemical industries, and the combustion engine transformed technology. Mechanization, part of a new approach to the organization of work known as Taylorism, could be seen in factories and offices, changing the work experience. New productivity and technological schemas emerged with the development of the machine-tools industry, the growing interchangeability of parts, and continuous production.[39] Visiting the 1900 Paris Universal Exposition, symbol of this new era, the American historian Henry Adams was strongly affected by the sight of dynamos twelve-meters tall in the Gallery of Machines. The account he gives of his experience illustrates the ambivalences of the end of the century, torn between hope and doubt about large industrial technology. Far from celebrating these great objects of modernity, he expressed his fears when faced with this "sudden irruption of forces totally new," about which "no one else showed much concern."[40]

Despite worries that were not usually overtly expressed, confidence and optimism regarding technological change dominated public discourse. For economists, the harmful effects of, and on-site problems caused by, technology would be solved by the adaptation of workers to machines, the introduction of professional education, and the growing intervention of states that were taking on responsibility for social welfare. The improvement of workplace hygiene and efforts to render technical systems more secure would contribute to the acclimatization of new technology. The "belle époque" was a mixed period in this regard: work hazards and accidents continued to climb, but their magnitude was constantly attenuated and minimized. In Europe, accidents and industrial catastrophes due to technological imperfections and uncertainties seemed to reach an apogee in terms of number of victims between 1880 and 1920, before declining, or rather occurring more often in new spaces undergoing industrialization. At the end of the nineteenth century, as universal suffrage and workers' organizations were put into place, regulations and protective measures were adopted to lessen the dangers of industrial work and to avoid an increase in disputes. In most European countries, especially following the German and French laws of 1884 and 1898, legislation governing industrial accidents and hazards was adopted to make the workplace safer. The result was a socialization of technological danger through the implementation of insurance, but also an acceptance that workplace accidents were a normal, even natural, part of industrial society.[41] Even if a commitment to protecting workers was difficult to implement everywhere, resisted by both workers and employers, it decreased the primary dangers in the workplace by establishing a set of standards for cleaning, oiling, and stopping machines and requiring factories to adopt systems that could prevent the malfunctioning of machine gears.

The question of the impact of the mechanization of work reappeared once statisticians began to track unemployment. Unemployment statistics were gathered at the end of the century as part of the census, and an international conference on the issue was held in Paris in 1910.[42] If in certain official reports "the rapid transformation of machines" was mentioned as a cause of unemployment, in general mechanization was seen as a solution to crises of employment instability.[43] Economic theory, and the reformers who defined the categories of the unemployed and unemployment, generally ignored the question of machines, because for them, as Christian Topalov noted, "the progress of mechanization and the expansion of the scale of production worked together to reduce uneven employment."[44] The Englishman Alfred Marshall, like Davis R. Dewey in the United States, asserted that the use of large, expensive machinery allowed employers to regularize production and thus hiring, thereby doing away with periods of chronic unemployment. According to this perspective, it was the persistence of manual labor in small-scale industries that was the principal cause of workers' misery, while mechanized, large-scale industry created hopes for a more stable, regular employment.

In the United States, as social conflict hardened in the cities, and as the breakage of and violence against machines revealed the fractures within rural society, it was rare to find a critic of mechanization.[45] Around 1880, William Moody suggested that a remedy to the harmful effects of "machinery" would be a reduction in the workday. In England, the liberal journalist John Hobson, sworn opponent of imperialism, used statistics to discuss the negative impact of machines on employment.[46] In France, during the 1889 universal exposition, Charles Gide, one of the principal theoreticians of social economy, described the "enormous deployment of productive force, [which] betters satisfies man's pride than his true needs." He denounced the "dreaded industrial machines of our time" because "the worker sometimes leaves in their gears an arm or a leg." At the same time, he affirmed the inevitable nature of mechanization.[47] As opposed to socialist or collectivist solutions, he proposed creating consumer cooperatives of tools that would allow for the domestication of industrial overproduction in order to liberate the proletariat.

The impact of technology was also addressed within the working-class movement, increasingly organized into unions and mass political parties. In England the Trade Union Congress was founded in Manchester in 1868, in France unions were legalized in 1884, and in the United States the union movement gained force after the creation of the Knights of Labor in 1876. Union membership grew quickly—if there were only 671,000 unionized workers in France, there were respectively 2.6 and 3.4 million in Germany and in Great Britain. These organizations increasingly accepted new technology as inevitable, even investing it with new hope. The "working class," still under construction at the end of the century, identified more and more with the Promethean man, and intelligence and manual skill were celebrated less than mechanical force tamed by man. The worker "brandishing a hammer" took over working-class imagery, and work experience was increasingly described as a virile contact with the machine rather than a mastery of complex skills. Technological innovation led union leaders to demand compensation in the form of increased pay or decreased work time. As the machine became the auxiliary of the worker rather than his enemy, negotiations intended to tame the machine gained ground over violent collective protests.[48] Among the unions of skilled workers in particular, "the new technologies were accepted," according to Alain Dewerpe, and even sought out "as soon as they were seen as a means to reduce fatigue at work and to advance workers' autonomy."[49] Even the revolutionary syndicalism of the end of the century, that advocated "sabotage," henceforth respected this tool of the worker. As Eric Hobsbawm wrote, paraphrasing socialist reformers Beatrice and Sydney Webb, "in most industries the object of preventing the introduction of undesirable machines has given way, with the coming of full mechanization, to the plan to 'capture' them for workers enjoying trade union standards and conditions; while taking all practicable steps to minimise technological unemployment."[50]

After 1890, industrial concentration and mechanization increased, upsetting internal balances in the world of work.[51] While, as we have seen, weavers were in a race to increase productivity, puddlers were replaced by the invention of the Bessemer Converter and spinners became simple supervisors of the *self-acting mule*. These changes, deeply resented by many skilled workers, brought into being what historian Gérard Noiriel calls a genuine "crisis in working-class values."[52] However in most countries of the world, including those in Europe, the tools used in the work process changed slowly. Peasants still worked with wooden tools and animals; many skilled workers continued to work in small establishments where both mechanization and modern work discipline had barely been put in place. The factory itself often remained a complex universe comprised of a collection of workshops where manual labor retained a very important role.[53] Even if the percentage of workers who got their start in mechanized industry continued to grow, they were far from the majority. For these new groups, changes in methods of production became a familiar routine, even if fears and suspicions persisted. Rather than evoke an abstract figure of the industrial worker, the historian must be attentive to the plurality and diversity of work experiences. Nonetheless, "scientific management" spread gradually across national borders, bringing with it techniques designed to control time and space. What is now referred to as the "rationalization" of work has been, since the 1970s, the subject of a number of studies that demonstrate the diversity of forms these new technologies of production took, according to country, branch of industry, and enterprise. This diversity existed at the intersection of technological utopias envisioning a mastery of the world developed by engineers and the incessant sociotechnological negotiations and piece-meal accommodations initiated by workers. First preached by the American engineer Frederick Winslow Taylor at the end of the nineteenth century, the doctrine of Taylorism spread in the years that followed; his works were translated into French in the early twentieth century, and the auto manufacturer Louis Renault encountered them in 1911. Although the first attempts at Taylorism resulted in unrest—several strikes in the United States and at Renault's factory when he imported the method of timing each of the worker's tasks to maximize efficiency in 1913—overall conflicts were limited.[54]

The First World War and the reorganization of labor that occurred in the 1920s accelerated the advent of a tipping point that brought into being a new regime of industrial production founded on the intensive use of technology and the adoption of new forms of the organization of work. First in Europe, the massive mobilization of conscripts in 1914 necessitated the use of more productive technology, and the employment of women to run machines accelerated the shift towards Taylorism in industrialized countries (See Figure 5.4).[55] The interwar period was similarly a period of intense technological and organizational changes. The term "productivism" appeared at this time, used to designate an economic system in which the growth of productivity became the primary goal of industry, inaugurating a new trajectory of rationalization and automatization of work that is still with us today.

FIGURE 5.4 "Munitionnette" in a French war factory, 1917. Courtesy of Bibliothèque nationale de France.

CHAPTER SIX

Work and Mobility

UTE CHAMBERLIN

When Karl Fischer (1841–1906) took up construction work for the Halle-Kassel railroad in the 1860s, he noted that "a lot of outsiders showed up: East and West Prussians, Poles and Silesians, Pomeranians and Mecklenburgers, Brandenburgers and Saxons, Hessians and Hanoverians, also a few Austrians, South Germans and men from the Eifel."[1] Fischer's life story encapsulates working-class mobility during the industrial age in Europe. Born in a small village in Silesia, his itinerant work life began in his teens when he was employed at an industrial lubricant factory two hours away, before returning home for an apprenticeship with his father, a baker. Showing no propensity for the craft, he left home again and beginning in 1859, travelled throughout Germany doing excavation and construction work on railways, roads, tunnels, and river-dredging projects. Not only was Fischer willing to move from work site to work site and change occupations based on opportunity, he also helped build the transportation systems that would facilitate mobility for new generations of workers and further industrial development. After ten years, he arrived in the eastern part of the Ruhr region, just then on the cusp of industrial take-off. He was first employed as a construction worker for a new steel factory in Osnabrück and later became an industrial worker at the plant. Troubled by health issues, he retired in 1885 and returned to his home region to live with relatives. Fischer's story provides a first window into the circumstances that characterized the mobile character of the European workforce during the nineteenth century: the rejection of a traditional apprenticeship in favor of industrial work, a willingness to change occupations, serial mobility, a move from the countryside to the new centers of industry, and eventually return migration. However, as much as rural–urban migration during the epoch of industrialization dominates the narrative of nineteenth-century mobility, this trajectory is only one strand in an increasingly complex picture of migration and mobility that scholars have painted for the period 1800–1920. This chapter explores the evolution of migration patterns and strategies and the economic and political conditions that informed them. Agricultural crises and industrial change were disruptive forces that compelled workers to move early on in the nineteenth century, and improved transportation networks and expanding global markets provided further impetus to large-scale migration. After mid-century the nation-state began to direct and interfere in its citizens' migration decisions, until, under the impact of the Great War, transnational migration came completely under its purview. Migration decisions were always embedded in a multitude of push-and-pull factors, but as workers sought economic opportunity and improvement, their choices became increasingly controlled and curtailed by state power.

Mobility was not a new phenomenon in the nineteenth century. Since the Middle Ages, rural dwellers in western and southern Europe had taken up seasonal farm work away from home to supplement earnings and to compensate for poor harvests.[2] Rural-to-rural migration was practiced widely and continued throughout the nineteenth century. It was usually circular and regional, but transnational patterns were not uncommon; one example is Italian women who went to France and Switzerland to work in the embroidery industry.[3] In preindustrial Europe, life-cycle service was common: farm girls moved to nearby towns to take up work as domestic servants and to accumulate savings before returning to their home village to marry, male youths lived as servants in another household before returning to the family farm, and journeymen travelled for extended periods of time and significant distances to hone their craft before settling down.[4] These patterns survived into the nineteenth and early twentieth centuries. Friedrich Ebert, the socialist leader and first president of the Weimar Republic, was trained as a saddle-maker, and after his apprenticeship travelled for several years as a journeyman throughout the German Empire in the late 1880s. Rather than ushering in an altogether new age of mobility, the nineteenth century has to be considered as an era during which demographic shifts, industrial development, urbanization, and the development of new modes of transportation made possible an ever widening network of migration options in terms of distance, scale, and variety, without entirely superseding migration patterns of earlier times.

Steve Hochstadt's analysis of German migration has challenged the long-standing notion that mobility was primarily unidirectional from rural to urban areas, mostly permanent, and entirely a product of industrialization.[5] Rather, overlapping developments and variations occurred based on local or regional economic, social, political, and legal conditions that influenced a peasant or worker's decision to go somewhere else. During the nineteenth century people moved between rural communities, from villages to nearby cities, between regions, and across long distances within Europe, or left Europe altogether through overseas migration. Some decisions were made individually, others as families or even as communities, and mobility often continued over generations through chain migration or the development of regional migration traditions. In family decisions, women often had a significant say. Some moves were permanent, others circular or sequential, or a combination of all three. Ultimately, each move hinged on personal predisposition. Potential migrants' decisions depended on how eager or hesitant they were to move and how they evaluated their chances.[6] Individuals and families made the decision to pack up and leave against a backdrop of complex circumstances, but always with the hope and expectation that mobility would open up better prospects for themselves or benefit their families if they moved. Each move represented both opportunity and risk.

DISRUPTION AND MIGRATION

An investigation into nineteenth-century mobility has to begin in the countryside. At the end of the Napoleonic Wars, most people in Europe lived in rural areas. Their livelihoods were disrupted through several interrelated developments. Demographic changes had a direct impact on mobility. Up until the beginning of the Great War the European population grew at an unprecedented pace, about 43 percent before mid-century and another 50 percent after. This increase from about 187 million in 1800 to 468 million in 1913 is best understood as the result of an improved food supply, increased fertility, and falling death rates.[7] This enormous demographic pressure forced many rural dwellers into nearby towns and cities. Also important, changes in landownership, foremost the consolidation of farms brought about by enclosure, and with it a transition towards capitalist farming, generated a growing number of landless laborers who left the countryside and moved to urban areas, especially when yearlong labor contracts were increasingly substituted by seasonal ones. At the same time, demand for farm servants decreased.[8] Rural industries also experienced a decline; handloom weavers could no longer compete with urban producers and had to leave their villages to find work elsewhere. After the collapse of the local linen industry in the 1840s, scores of Flemish textile workers sought out employment in France.[9] Seasonal migrations of large groups of male workers from the same village or region were common and created hybrid work identities, for example worker-peasants who went to nearby towns for seasonal construction work, or the miner-peasants in the Saar region who commuted weekly between village and mine in the 1870s. Their mobility created an extra burden for the women, children, and elderly who were left in the village.[10] In other places, as Gay Gullickson has demonstrated for the village of Auffay in Normandy, France, women's ability to move into hitherto male-dominated occupations of weaving, agricultural work, and dressmaking delayed large-scale emigration from the area until the 1870s.[11]

Crop failures and subsequent famines often triggered migration to urban areas, as in England in 1816 when grains were ruined by bad weather. Silkworm and mulberry diseases in the 1850s and recurring Phylloxera aphid infestations in the 1870 and 1880s devastated the French silk industry and vineyards and forced small farmers to sell their land and move away.[12] The most catastrophic crop failure during the nineteenth century was the Irish famine. After several years of harvest failures caused by the potato blight, the destruction of the primary foodstuff of the Irish rural population had devastating effects; about one million died. Here the connection between the threat of starvation and mobility seems most clearly visible. Between 1841 and 1861 three million people left Ireland, a net decrease of 30 percent. About two million Irish emigrated to the United States, and about half a million to Britain.

Irish rural inhabitants had not been entirely sedentary until the potato blight struck; many had already been migrating regularly to England, Scotland, and Wales for seasonal farm work or to textile centers such as Dundee, Aberdeen, and Manchester to find employment as weavers. No legal restrictions hindered their moves. The famine also temporarily overshadowed deeper structural problems such as the decline of the rural textile industry and a general deindustrialization of the Irish countryside caused by competition from the advanced English textile industry.[13] Responses to the Irish famine highlight the importance of the cost of transportation and the impact of governmental neglect. Passage to the United States was only within reach for relatively better-off peasants. According to Cormac Ó Gráda, the failure of the British government to subsidize and regulate emigration severely curtailed the number of emigrants; only a small share of less than 10 percent had their passage paid by government, landlord, or charity. Other distinctive features of post-famine migration were the preponderance of families among the emigrants and the high mortality rate on the so-called coffin ships. Many passengers who boarded were already sick; overcrowding and a lack of adequate food and medical care only heightened the death toll.[14] Finally, it has to be noted that migration not only was a lifesaver for those who left and survived the passage to the United States, but also had an ameliorating effect on those who stayed behind; their mortality rates declined as the competition for meager resources lessened.[15] Although the Irish population never recovered the losses from the massive exodus of its people at mid-century, migration scholars caution against assuming that periods of rural hunger automatically led to permanent emigration. In some rural areas of southern Sweden during the first half of the nineteenth century the local population did not move away in large numbers during times of high grain prices because of a lack of options: there were no urbanized or industrialized areas nearby that might have offered relief, and long-term migration was prohibitively expensive.[16]

Migration moves could be complex and unfold over multiple generations. "Although, ultimately, the balance of population shifted from country-side to town, this was achieved by a complex process of interdependent moves, with industrial villages playing a key role in the transition from a pre-industrial to an industrial and urban economy."[17] In European regions where industrialization took off later, temporary or circular migration persisted longer. In Spain, the pull factor of the industrialized city was much weaker throughout the entire nineteenth century. Rural laborers—because they were unable to find year-round employment in one place—seasonally migrated to other rural regions to participate in grape and olive harvests, to large estates needing temporary laborers, or left for urban areas to work in "textiles, construction, quarrying, mining, metal working, carpentry, and woodworking."[18] It was not until the 1920s that permanent migration superseded circular migration traditions. Similarly, temporary migration remained a dominant feature in Portugal and Greece throughout the first half of the twentieth century. The diversity of rural mobility across Europe demonstrates that by the time population growth and industrialization pulled rural people into urban areas, mobile workers could draw on a wealth of experiences and traditions of migration.

WOMEN'S PATTERNS OF MIGRATION

For single women, mobility patterns had their origins in traditional life-cycle migrations. Already before industrialization and urbanization, young rural women had sought out domestic service in nearby villages and towns. In 1851, 75 percent of servants in Colchester, England, came from villages that were no more than ten miles away, making it possible to walk home on their days off.[19] The decline of rural manufacturing prompted women to seek employment in nearby urban areas. As Louise Tilly and Joan Scott have shown in their seminal study about young women from rural England and France, temporary moves to the city became permanent over time; women's ties to their families and rural area loosened, and they began to regard their wages as a way to support themselves rather than as income to be sent back to their family.[20] Once they had established themselves in the city women exercised their independence by changing occupations and seeking out opportunities in the garment trades or in the textile industries. Many Irish women for instance migrated to the centers of textile production in England and Scotland.[21] The scholarly view of women's labor migration choices continues to evolve. It has been long asserted that during the nineteenth century more women than men migrated short distances from the countryside to urban centers, but recent quantitative research suggests that women's seemingly higher propensity for this type of migration might in fact be the result of an "overrepresentation of women among the adult and elderly population in general" caused by higher male adult mortality rates and international migration.[22]

A single woman's decision to leave the countryside behind always entailed a great deal of risk. Young women were exposed to sexual exploitation by their employers and to the vagaries of unemployment, especially when they worked in seasonal trades. Rachel Fuchs's study of single working-class women in Paris during the nineteenth century vividly illustrates the sexual vulnerability of young rural women who came to Paris to work as domestic servants. Being single, poor, pregnant, and without family support drove some to infanticide and abortion, while others learned to negotiate the urban environment by enlisting the help of neighbors and appealing to private charities and public assistance programs. Women who still were connected to their rural home were sometimes able to send children back home, but these ties could be easily frayed. Take nineteen-year-old Marie Beurette, a domestic servant in Paris, who sent her first child back to her village to be cared for by her family. When she gave birth to another child, she was unable to afford the additional money that her parents needed to take care of the infant, and drowned the baby.[23]

Moving away from the village was much more difficult for Russian peasant women who were expected to continue farm work and to contribute to the family household.[24] In the absence of fathers and husbands, women were often able to improve their standing in their family and village, and could become the de facto head of household if men were gone for extended periods of time. Only a small minority of women was able to move to urban areas, as village elders often denied them the required passport. Those who found a way to leave their village were most likely in marginal positions, such as widows or older unmarried women, or women who were perceived as an economic burden to their families; some accompanied their husbands into the city. In the city, rural women's employment options were limited to domestic positions and factory work, primarily in textile industries. For Russian peasant women, mobility and independence were paired with low wages and economic uncertainty.

The nineteenth century offered middle-class women new opportunities for spatial and career mobility. Teaching became an inherently mobile occupation for women. During the early decades of the nineteenth century, when school teaching was still dominated by men, governesses not only joined the household of their charges but also travelled with their well-to-do employers. Both Emily and Charlotte Brontë left home to train and work as governesses, then moved to Brussels to continue their education and establish a school, before eventually returning to England a few years later. As women were admitted to teaching, training and placement in schools could take them to new places; many French female teachers received challenging appointments in remote village schools. In Serbia, the number of women teachers rose sharply after 1872 when they were also allowed to teach in boys' elementary schools. For their training, they had to choose between attending the only Serbian teacher training school in the town of Sombor or go to an academy in Russia. Serbian female teachers who wanted independence from family control could request transfers to other towns based on their qualifications. Other times, mobility was a means of supporting the family. After her father's death, Stana Jovanoviceva left her community and applied for a teacher's position in the town of Leskovac because it had a grammar school that her younger brothers could attend.[25]

While middle-class men also moved for work or to obtain an education, the greater restrictions that women faced in both areas often made leaving home a necessity, rather than a choice. Many Russian upper-class women who wanted to train as medical doctors enrolled at the university in Zurich. The nursing profession's pioneer Florence Nightingale went to Germany to receive training at the renowned Institute of Protestant Deaconesses at Kaiserswerth and a few years later took thirty-eight nurses with her to Crimea during

FIGURE 6.1 Medical staff and nurses in South Africa, 1901. Photo: The Print Collector / Print Collector / Getty Images.

the Crimean War. Almost half a century later, about two thousand British nurses served during the Second Anglo-Boer War (1899–1902) (Figure 6.1). Towards the end of the nineteenth century, overseas colonies came to be seen as new destinations for women's employment. Emigration societies in England, Germany, and France sponsored programs to facilitate single women's overseas voyages and to establish them as domestic servants, governesses, or nurses in their nations' colonies.[26] These programs came to an abrupt halt with the outbreak of the Great War. The nineteenth century was transformative for women's employment because new work opportunities and mobility went hand in hand.

GLOBAL MIGRATION

After mid-century, overseas migration assumed unprecedented proportions: about thirty million European migrants left for the United States and another ten million for South America between 1850 and 1913. After the American Civil War, decades of

FIGURE 6.2 Emigrants from Europe on a ship bound for New York, c. 1910. Credit: Prisma by Dukas Presseagentur GmbH / Alamy Stock Photo.

industrial growth created an enormous demand for labor in the United States. At the same time, the cost, length, and risks of the transatlantic voyage dropped dramatically with the shift from sail technology to steam power and made mass migration possible (see Figure 6.2).

Initially, British and German emigrants dominated, but they were gradually joined by Scandinavians and other northern Europeans and by the 1880s, when economic conditions improved in central Europe, by southern and eastern Europeans. Emigration from Sweden increased sharply after widespread harvest failures in 1867; eventually one million Swedes migrated to the United States. In the German states, a combination of overpopulation, the ill effects of partible inheritance, and the increase of capitalist farming drove artisan and peasant families out of Europe. Later in the nineteenth century, economic downturns prompted single agricultural and factory workers to seek a better life abroad; by the 1880s, they came mainly from Prussia's eastern provinces. Out of 4.5 million German emigrants, 4 million settled in the United States.[27] Across Europe, earlier European emigrants sustained this migrant flow. The emigrants sent information back about opportunities abroad and encouraged others to follow their example, sometimes financing the passage for family members. Successful returning emigrants also prompted members of their home community to follow suit. Often, the decision to leave Europe was not an individual's first migration move; stage migration occurred when a female migrant in Scandinavia left her village to find work in the city and there learned about work opportunities abroad. Occasionally, news about opportunities could trigger a collective emigration wave. After the end of slavery in Brazil in 1888, more than a quarter million Venetians were recruited to work on Brazilian plantations between 1891 and 1897. Russian Poles were also caught by "Brazilian fever"; about forty thousand emigrated to South America in 1892 and 1893.[28]

Overseas migrants who left early in the nineteenth century rarely returned home, but when the cost of the passage dropped, circular migration became a more feasible mobility strategy.[29] Italian migrants to Argentina were called *golondrinas* (birds of passage) because they left their villages in Italy once the harvest season was over and took off for destinations in the southern hemisphere where agricultural patterns were reversed.[30] A significant segment of migrants who had initially planned their voyage to the Americas as a permanent move did return after all. Some had accumulated enough savings or wealth or were called back to take over the family farm, others had failed to establish themselves abroad or were homesick, and some decided that the American way of life did not suit them after all. Return migration is very difficult to measure but it has been estimated that about 25–30 percent of Europeans who went to the United States eventually returned.[31]

Skilled laborers were the first to embark on the transatlantic journey because they could better afford the passage, but as prices dropped, unskilled workers were able to leave in increasingly large numbers and migration intensified from those areas in the south and east of Europe that were relatively poor. The Spanish emigrants that left for Argentina, Brazil, Cuba, and Uruguay were across the board relatively skilled and came from the most economically advanced regions.[32] While skilled workers showed the highest propensity to emigrate, unskilled workers were the largest group in absolute numbers.[33] Transatlantic migration often turned into a career move; most men who arrived in the United States unskilled eventually became skilled.[34]

The growing stream of eastern European emigrants had to cross central Europe first in order to reach the major embarkation points of Hamburg, Bremen, Liverpool, or Antwerp. The shortest route with the most reliable train connections took these transmigrants through Prussia.[35] As American immigration restrictions tightened, steamship lines had to pay the return costs for rejected immigration applicants, and Prussian authorities were concerned that the returning migrants would not be able or willing to return to their places of origins once disembarked at German ports. In 1885, Prussia began to require transmigrants to carry enough money to pay for a possible return journey as a condition for crossing Prussia's eastern borders. The Prussian government also took the unprecedented step of handing control over eastern border stations and the passage through Prussia to the Hamburg-based HAPAG shipping company. At the control stations along the eastern border, HAPAG employees inspected the migrants, disinfected their belongings, and issued certificates that would allow them to continue the journey through Germany on supervised and sealed trains and to get on a ship in Bremen or Hamburg. US immigration authorities praised these procedures because they stopped "undesirable" migrants early, long before they reached American soil. Once the HAPAG system was in place, the transit through Germany took little more than a day, and the entire journey to the United States less than three weeks.

Jewish emigrants from the Austro-Hungarian and Russian empires made up a large share of eastern migrants. The restrictions imposed on Russian Jews in the Pale of Settlement such as extremely limited access to education, paired with limitations on their free movement, made economic success all but impossible. Jewish efforts to improve their economic circumstances through emigration gained more urgency after 1891 in the aftermath of widespread expulsions throughout the Russian Empire. The story of Mary (Maryashe) Antin who emigrated to the United States at the end of the nineteenth century at age thirteen encapsulates the obstacles that eastern European Jews had to overcome to emigrate. Mary and her family lived in the Pale of Settlement in Polish Russia. Her father departed first; being without any means, his journey was financed by borrowing and with the help of a charitable organization. He made arrangements for his daughters to prepare for their later emigration: "Education would be ours for the asking, and economic independence also ... He wanted Fetchke and me to be taught some trade; so my sister was apprenticed to a dressmaker and I to a milliner." It took three years before Mary, her siblings, and her mother were able to follow, and they too had to make the journey through Prussia under HAPAG auspices. Mary noted in her diary the frightening and humiliating aspects of the various inspection procedures: at the east Prussian border they "were taken away to be steamed and smoked." At the emigrant station in Berlin they felt as if they had been "captured by robbers" when they were again subjected to an intense disinfection process. Hamburg had experienced a devastating cholera epidemic in 1891 which had been falsely blamed on migrant Jews, which is why Mary and her family were yet again put through a rough "repetition of the purifying operations" when they finally reached the port city.[36] Mary's family had to spend two weeks in prison-like quarantine until they were finally allowed to board their ship. Mary's story stands for those of many others like her: 41 percent of Russian emigrants to the United States between 1899 and 1913 were Jewish.[37]

THE POLITICS OF LABOR MIGRATION

Labor migration was tangled up in competing economic and political objectives. By 1900 Germany led the market in sugar beets and produced almost half the world's sugar. The demand for foreign labor was enormous; in 1891, 27,700 seasonal laborers worked on the sugar beet harvest, 119,000 in 1900, and an astounding 433,000 in 1914. The annual movement of seasonal workers was known as *Sachsengängerei* (Saxony-going) after one of the provinces where the crop was grown. The vast majority of these workers were ethnic Poles from Russia and Austria, but Italians, Scandinavians, White Russians, and Ruthenians also worked the crop (see Figure 6.3). Despite the need for labor, the Prussian government tightly controlled the influx of workers from eastern Europe because of a general fear of Polish national agitation. Thus, the need for labor was at odds with the political objective of limiting what was seen as dangerous Polish separatism. Beginning in 1888, Polish workers from the Russian and Austro-Hungarian empires were only allowed to work in the eastern rural provinces of the German Empire and had to leave at the end of the harvest period for seven weeks before they could return the next year.[38] Only individuals, not families, got permits, and pregnant women could be expelled. The Prussian Farm Workers' Agency worked with local agents, and "by 1913 had set up 39 border offices with large camps that could take in and process up to 10,000 people per day."[39] However, the monitoring of migration only worked imperfectly; workers crossed borders illegally, and border agents often were not able to read papers in foreign languages, and, if written in Russian Cyrillic, could not even decipher names. Border controls were gradually tightened and German-language papers were required beginning in 1909.

Early in the twentieth century, when the Russo–Japanese War was making seasonal workers from Russia scarcer, a growing number of seasonal Ruthenian workers from

FIGURE 6.3 East Prussian farmworkers (*Sachsengaenger*) in Berlin, c. 1907. Photo: ullstein bild / ullstein bild via Getty Images.

Galicia, perhaps as many as ten thousand in 1903, took their place, yet at the same time attracted new government concern, because they did not fall under the same work restrictions as ethnic Poles. State officials warned that Ruthenians' interactions with ethnic Poles had to be supervised carefully out of "national-political concerns" as they might "make common cause with Polish workers and thus strengthen politically unreliable elements."[40] Border authorities, who were often unable to distinguish between Austrian Poles and Ruthenians from Galicia, feared that ethnic Poles would pretend to be Ruthenians to circumvent labor restrictions.[41] A Ruthenian "national committee" sponsored by Greek Catholic clergy tried to promote the use of Ruthenian workers to the Prussian government. They claimed that Ruthenians felt oppressed by Poles in Galicia and that they were eager to "support the German government in their efforts to gradually push Galician Poles out of Germany." They even offered to have clergy make control visits to Ruthenians working in Germany twice a year to keep them in line and from breaking labor contracts. They claimed that Ruthenians were "inclined toward Germandom" and therefore should be encouraged to learn German and must not be supervised by Polish workers.[42] This initiative never found the approval of the German government who preferred to use their own agencies to regulate the influx of foreign labor.

After mid-century, industrial cities such as Manchester and Marseille were powerful magnets for mobile workers, but the most dramatic case of rapid urban growth fuelled by in-migration was occurring in the Ruhr valley. At the end of the nineteenth century Germany was emerging as the largest economic power in Europe and its heavy-industrial center in the Ruhr needed a steady stream of labor for its coal mines and steel mills.

Sometime before the Great War the Hungarian economist Imre Ferenczi declared that Germany had become the second-largest importer of labor after the United States. Once the supply of nearby workers from the Westphalian and Rhenish hinterland was exhausted, long-distance and transnational migrants were recruited. This demand for industrial labor was so strong that it reversed migration streams. During the eighteenth and early nineteenth century northwestern German workers, so-called "Holland migrants" or *Hollandgänger,* had gone to the Netherlands for agricultural work. When opportunities in heavy industry became plentiful, this seasonal migration stopped, and instead Dutch workers, attracted by higher wages, flocked to the Ruhr.[43] The Dutch government supported these "Prussian migrants" and provided them with information about the papers and documents the Prussian government required of transnational migrants.[44]

By far the largest group of workers arrived via east–west migration. Ethnic Poles from the eastern German provinces had already moved to Berlin and Saxony in the 1860s, and after the Franco-Prussian War of 1870–1, they began to settle in the Ruhr and Rhineland. Mine owners sent Polish-speaking agents to the eastern provinces to recruit landless peasants and workers from the Silesian mines. Often, men who were recruited from the same town of origin settled in the same mining community in the Ruhr, for instance from Rybnik to Bottrop. Almost half a million Poles from eastern Prussia lived and worked in the Ruhr before 1914. As ethnic Poles with German citizenship moved west, eastern European Poles from Russia and Austria took their place as seasonal workers.[45] Beginning in 1899, they were allowed to work in west Germany, but only in agriculture. However, because of the persistent need for labor, mines, steel mills, and other industries hired them illegally. After the First World War, the reestablishment of the Polish state prompted many Poles to leave, and the German government pressured Poles without German citizenship to return to their homelands because they feared them as a dangerous political influence. In the city of Bochum, only 200 of 3,740 Polish workers remained in 1920.[46]

Official views concerning transnational and overseas migration changed over the course of the nineteenth century, as evidence from Sweden and Norway shows. Early on in the century these governments regarded transnational emigration as a loss of valuable workers. The Swedish state used legislation to prevent the departure of servants, sailors, and skilled workers but dropped all state proscriptions against emigration by 1860 as it now seemed to be a remedy for poverty and overpopulation.[47] Over time, however, emigration became so widespread in parts of Scandinavia that it had a negative economic impact. By 1910, after Norway had lost about seven hundred thousand inhabitants through migration, the countryside had become so depopulated that farms were left abandoned. Emigration from Sweden was so immense that King Oscar II called provincial governors in 1882 to discuss the problem. In the first decade of the twentieth century anti-emigration societies in Sweden and Norway pressured their governments to stem the flow and to entice migrants to return. In response the Swedish government dropped the requirement for male returnees to complete their military service. In the long run, returning migrants often were a great success because they brought with them new skills, especially modern farming methods, which could be successfully applied at home.[48] While the Swedish government feared population loss through permanent emigration it also found ways to make transnational labor mobility work to the advantage of its economy. Sweden did not only invite foreign skilled labor to help modernize industry, but it also sent industrial workers, technicians, and engineers to foreign companies, first to England and beginning in the 1860s increasingly to the United States, to acquire new skills and techniques and to bring them back home. The Swedish government promoted this type of temporary migration through scholarships and financial assistance programs.[49]

In general, the European nation-states promoted the mobility of labor. In Italy and Germany, political unification removed bureaucratic obstacles and transformed movements between states from international into internal migration. Before unification, migrants from outside the papal states who wanted to work in Rome needed to show a passport from their place of origin to be permitted to reside in the city. This restriction disappeared after the unification of Italy was complete in 1871.[50] Nation-states also became major employers of clerks, administrative personnel, and teachers in their capitals and regional administrative centers, thus attracting new migrants to urban centers. National building projects such as roads, railroads, canals, and public works required large work crews, and often foreign teams with specialized skills were hired. Italian construction workers who had gained a reputation for tunnel building were in demand in Switzerland, where they made up the single-largest group of workers building the St. Gotthard Pass between 1872 and 1882 with about 2,600 men (see Figure 6.4). For the construction of the twenty-kilometer-long Simplon tunnel (1898–1906) about a third of Italian laborers brought along their families who moved with them as construction progressed. Canal builders in Germany recruited specialists from the Netherlands, mostly for excavation work but also as technical specialists.[51]

FIGURE 6.4 Completion of the St. Gotthard Tunnel beneath the Alps, 1880. Photo: Ann Ronan Pictures / Print Collector / Getty Images.

RESTRICTIONS ON FREE MIGRATION

While legal and political conditions in general were favorable to mobility and migration throughout the nineteenth century, there were also notable exceptions to the free flow of labor. Migrants could get rejected once they reached their desired destination (by Ellis Island immigration officials), or were limited to where they could work or how long they were allowed to stay (Ruthenians and Russian Poles in Germany), but there were also instances where would-be migrants were prevented from leaving or where workers were relocated against their will. At the beginning of the nineteenth century the Napoleonic Wars disrupted the circulation of agricultural workers; many were drafted into European armies. Overseas migration also came to a stop, and the Continental Blockade limited shipping and thus the demand for sailors.[52] After the end of the Napoleonic Wars England tried to maintain its industrial lead by prohibiting the export of skilled workers and technology.[53] Specialists such as steam engine erectors were only allowed to leave if the Board of Trade approved their request; between 1815 and 1824 only three such applications were granted. The impossibility of enforcing such restrictions led to an end to the ban on the emigration of skilled workers in 1824. Within nation-states, restrictions to the free movement of labor did not exist but individual cities could use poor relief rules to reject migrants. Between 1849 and 1854 the city of Liverpool sent back sixty-three thousand poor Irish migrants because they had to apply for poor relief in their home villages. In the 1860s, laws were changed so that migrants who had been in the city for more than one year could no longer be sent back.[54] In the German states, similar poor law regulations that required the poor to return to their home villages to receive aid were abolished between the 1840s and 1870.[55]

Restrictions on the free movement of labor existed on an entirely different scale in Russia.[56] The mobility of Russia's enserfed rural population, about fifty-five million European peasants on the eve of emancipation, was controlled by the nobles who owned their villages. Some serfs who made a living as merchants and traders were remarkably well off and allowed to move about freely, albeit only with the landowner's permission, but most serfs worked the land and were tied to their village.[57] Serf owners commonly forced peasants to work on their estates for the processing of agricultural products; until 1861 wine, vodka, and sugar production were the most significant industries. The end of serfdom and the concomitant destabilizing consequences of the system of redemption payments prompted scores of peasants to leave the countryside and to seek employment in urban centers, but this was fraught with difficulties. Those who wanted to leave had to apply for a passport, but until 1894 local village authorities could deny a request without having to provide a reason. Factories hired workers only on two days of the year, the day after Easter and October 1; if one did not have a passport on that day the opportunity was gone. By 1897 about four million workers or about 15 percent of the adult rural population had migrated to cities, primarily for jobs in metal industries, railroad construction, textile factories, and mining. At first, migration was circular as peasants returned to their villages for the harvest season. The metal industry was first in abandoning the summer break for labor contracts, and by 1893 in St. Petersburg 90 percent of workers remained in the city during the summer. Under Sergei Witte's direction the pass system was simplified and train tickets were made cheaper in 1894. In 1900, 50 percent of all inhabitants of Warsaw and 70 percent of the inhabitants of St. Petersburg and Moscow were migrants.[58] Although many workers remained in the city for years, many eventually returned to the countryside during old age. The lack of old-age pensions, the better standard of living in the countryside, and traditional village ties all played a role and return migration was supported by the Russian state, which believed that workers who went back to the countryside were less likely to engage in revolution. Christoph Schmidt has estimated that it took a family five generations after the end of serfdom to make a complete and permanent transformation from rural peasant to urban worker.[59]

Convict labor is an example of the forcible movement of workers, often across long distances. About 160,000 convicts from England, Scotland, and Ireland, mostly men, were sent to Australia as laborers between 1787 and 1863, a flow that peaked in the 1830s.[60] As the journey to Australia was too costly and long compared to the option of leaving for the Americas, the labor shortage in New South Wales and other parts of Australia could not be remedied through voluntary migration. Many of the Irish convicts had migrated to England before being apprehended, thus showing a mixed pattern of voluntary and involuntary mobility. Most of them were not hardened criminals but ordinary workers, many of them skilled, who were sent to Australia for punishment and at the same time could be used to fill an urgent need for workers. Upon arrival, convicts were assigned to private masters or to the government; the program petered out when the Australian population had grown enough to meet the need for labor. Other countries used convict labor as well. After the revolution of 1848 the French government sent about 13,500 unemployed men to Algeria as agricultural workers. The Russian government initiated the largest and longest-running forced labor program. Criminals and political exiles had been sent to Siberia since the sixteenth century, but the practice experienced its greatest expansion in the nineteenth century. Between 1800 and 1918 about 1.3 million European Russians were marched or shipped to the eastern reaches of the empire, to Siberia and beyond. Upon arrival, their degree of freedom varied; some were able to live mostly without restrictions, others were consigned to huge forced-labor projects in agriculture, railroad construction, such as the Trans-Siberian Railway, and gold or silver mines.[61]

MOBILITY AND THE GREAT WAR

The outbreak of the Great War marked a caesura in worker mobility patterns as economies abruptly shifted towards war production and states began to intervene more forcefully in the movement of workers. At first, the collapse of peacetime production led to widespread massive unemployment, but demand for workers picked up quickly in wartime industries. When able-bodied workers were recruited and volunteered for the front, women and male youths were called to fill their places. Women who had lost their peacetime jobs found employment in industries that had been closed to them before, such as metalworking and chemicals. In Russia, the number of women employed in industry rose by 38 percent over the course of the war.[62] In Germany, the national government issued a decree that suspended industrial health and safety regulations and made it possible for women and adolescents to work long hours, night shifts, and in physically dangerous jobs.[63] While industrial jobs brought women into urban areas, labor shortages in agriculture sent them to the countryside. Women tended to prefer industrial jobs over farm work and national governments had difficulties persuading women to work in the fields. In England the government organized a Women's Land Army that deployed women to regions as farm helpers. Industrial and agricultural wartime jobs for women were physically exhausting, often dangerous, and usually not well paid, but the war also provided some genuinely new career mobility opportunities for women, for instance as bus or tram operators or clerical workers.

The Great War ushered in a new phase of state intervention into the free movement of labor that would continue into the twentieth century. France and Great Britain resorted to a variety of strategies to overcome labor shortages with foreign workers. France encouraged workers from bordering countries to come to France. The Office National de la Main-d'oeuvre Agricole (ONMA) had already been set up in 1912 and operated sixteen enrolment offices near Spanish and Italian borders. Two hundred and thirty thousand Spanish workers alone came to France during the war. Algerians and colonial subjects from other north African and Southeast Asian possessions were also recruited, and German and Austro-Hungarian prisoners of war (POWs) were put to work as well (Figure 6.5). The British military employed one hundred thousand Chinese workers near the front in northern France, mostly for dispatching freight or doing construction. They were segregated from the general population and were sent back at the end of the war, as were most foreign workers in France.[64]

In Germany, manpower shortages were immense. As part of the 1916 Hindenburg Program, males between the ages of eighteen and sixty who were not serving at the front were obligated to work in war industries; the original plan to establish similar requirements for women was rejected. When the domestic supply of labor fell short, both POWs and civilian foreigners, primarily from occupied Belgium and Russian Poland, were exploited for their labor.[65] One crucial industry that was thrown into crisis because of acute and unanticipated labor shortages was coal mining in the Ruhr. In some mines 40 percent of the workforce had been recruited into the army by the end of 1914. To make matters worse, many miners left to work in the better-paying munitions industries, and foreign mine workers from Austria, Italy, and the Netherlands returned to their home countries. When mine owners were unable to compensate for the shortfall of workers with the employment of male youths, older workers, and women, POWs were

FIGURE 6.5 German POWs digging peat in France, 1918. Credit: Photo 12 / Alamy Stock Photo.

forced into work in the mines, 170,000 in all. French and Belgian POWs arrived first in February 1915; eventually Russian POWs became the single-largest group. In August 1918, POWs constituted about 16.5 percent of the total number of mine workers. The German government also used voluntary foreign workers to boost the depleted workforce, but the recruitment of Belgian workers who had lost their jobs after the German occupation had limited success. Many refused out of national pride and as an expression of resistance. By October 1916, the German government resorted to forced deportations of Belgian workers to Germany. After a wave of international protests and internal criticism the program was halted in February 1917.

The recruitment of workers from eastern Europe was much larger in scope. About seventy-five thousand workers from occupied Russian Poland were recruited, mostly for agricultural work east of the Elbe but also for mining in the west. Russian Poles had been left to their own devices after the outbreak of the war and were desperate for work; some hoped that a German victory might lead to Polish independence. When the textile industries in occupied Russia came to a standstill, perhaps half a million workers came to Germany. Over time, Russian workers became frustrated with their treatment by German employers. They were increasingly controlled in their movements; they could not switch jobs, have their families join them, or return to Russia after the end of a contract. After the proclamation of a Polish kingdom in November 1916 and then after the February Revolution in Russia, many decided to break their contracts and return home. As the war progressed the differences between voluntary and coerced labor were no longer clearly discernable.[66]

Throughout the nineteenth century European working people used geographical mobility to escape adverse or deteriorating socioeconomic circumstances at home, or in hopes of finding better occupational and earning opportunities through migration. Broader demographic and economic trends such as explosive population growth, urbanization, the expansion of large-scale commercial agriculture, and rapid industrialization facilitated such moves, encouraging both seasonal rural-to-rural and rural-to-urban migrations. Denser, faster, and cheaper transportation networks, foremost trains and steamships, increased the available options and geographic extent for temporary or permanent relocation; migrants were now able to consider and afford transnational and transoceanic moves. The overall political environment in Europe was also favorable to migration; the absence of major wars and the establishment and consolidation of nation-states provided a more stable and predictable environment for would-be migrants. Compared to the previous century, the overall picture that emerges for the 1900s is one of intensification, acceleration, and a growing complexity of work mobility patterns.

This generally favorable picture must be tempered with a consideration of the position of the individual would-be migrant. Each worker's options and opportunities varied considerably, depending on a worker's skills, family circumstances, access to information, location, and local or national political conditions. Workers exercised their agency by moving to a new place of work, but they did so within larger economic and political structures and developments that were beyond their control.[67] In Dirk Hoerder's words, labor migrants "were constrained by state systems and aided by migration systems."[68] In the late nineteenth century, national governments became restrictive in their regulation of mobile labor; workers who crossed national borders were increasingly regarded as potentially troublesome foreigners or minorities.[69] During the Great War and in its aftermath, work mobility became ever more constrained, thus setting the parameters for the twentieth century.

CHAPTER SEVEN

Work and Society

MARJORIE LEVINE-CLARK

Charles Dickens's 1854 "condition of England" novel *Hard Times* paints a vivid picture of the human alienation and environmental degradation that many saw as a result of the new industrial system. Dickens's classic description of "Coketown" emphasized the ways that factories and industrial cities transformed nature into something monstrous and unhealthy and dehumanized workers:

> It was a town of red brick, or of brick that would have been red if the smoke and ashes had allowed it; but as matters stood, it was a town of unnatural red and black like the painted face of a savage. It was a town of machinery and tall chimneys, out of which interminable serpents of smoke trailed themselves for ever and ever, and never got uncoiled. It had a black canal in it, and a river that ran purple with ill-smelling dye, and vast piles of buildings full of windows where there was a rattling and a trembling all day long, and where the piston of the steam-engine worked monotonously up and down, like the head of an elephant in a state of melancholy madness. It contained several large streets all very like one another, and many small streets still more like one another, inhabited by people equally like one another, who all went in and out at the same hours, with the same sound upon the same pavements, to do the same work, and to whom every day was the same as yesterday and to-morrow, and every year the counterpart of the last and the next.[1]

According to Dickens, industrial society reduced workers to automatons, or "hands," cogs in a system that took away all possibility for imaginative thought and individualism. The movement of workers to and from factories was like a machine itself, replicating the endless motion of the steam engine, driven by inhuman forces.

Dickens was only one of a number of social critics across Europe's long nineteenth century to bemoan the effects of urbanization and industrialization on society. City life and industrial capitalism, according to thinkers such as Jules Michelet, Elizabeth Gaskell, William Morris, Karl Marx, and Friedrich Engels destroyed family relations, damaged the health of human beings and the environment, and significantly diminished the lives of the working population. Just as factory owners, bankers, investors, and others grew fat on the new organization of work and urban financial centers, the lives of the laboring classes were cast into uncertainty.

While changes to the organization of work happened at various paces and chronologies across Europe and the United States, expressions of concern about the impact of industrialization and urbanization on society universally accompanied these changes. This chapter will explore the narrative that industrial society was a danger to workers and their environment by focusing on several key themes: public health, the working-class family, and poverty and welfare. This narrative of social disruption has been a powerful one. Even while industrialists and their allies wrote about the benefits of the new order to employers and employees alike, those decrying the negative impact of factory work and the intensified nonmechanized industries that went along with it won the discursive battle. In many ways, they won because they concentrated on the social consequences of industrialization rather than the production of wealth for employers and rise in real wages for many employees.

The chapter aims to present a picture of how people gave meaning to the changes they perceived around them. As a British historian, the chapter relies on examples from Britain, with some comparisons to France, Germany, and the United States. Most of it will be broad-brush strokes, portraying themes common to Europe and the United States. Visual and textual representations of filthy cities, polluted rivers, and dilapidated tenements in which working people lived seemed to line up pretty closely with the realities of urban experiences. Even if wages improved over the course of the century, as quantitative historians have illustrated, many workers across the West suffered from malnutrition, inadequate housing, and unemployment. They experienced the industrial order as negatively impacting their quality of life. They and those observing them also saw it as dangerous. While the working poor were not passive in the face of social transformations, and they found pleasures within the constraints under which they lived, new challenges often led the middle classes to conflate workers with the problems of industrial society itself.

Yet in trying to grasp the meanings of social disruption associated with industrial society, the voices of the working poor tend to be hushed. Very often it is the words and images of observers of workers rather than workers themselves that have survived to portray the social impact of industrialization. Investigations into the lives of the laboring classes produced thousands and thousands of pages identifying the working poor as a problem to be solved. The interest of the governing classes in the lives of workers stayed strong throughout this period, as western nations became increasingly competitive with each other through the new imperialism and industrial rivalries in the late nineteenth century. Politicians and medical and scientific thinkers worried about the health of workers relative to the efficiency of their military-industrial systems. Growing scrutiny of laborers' bodies accompanied this interest in industrial efficiency.

PUBLIC HEALTH AND LABORING POPULATIONS

In the long nineteenth century, one of the biggest problems governments and private citizens identified with industrial society was filth, both environmental and moral. The new industrial, financial, and professional middle classes defined themselves very much in comparison to the working poor, and the status of home—its physical and moral cleanliness—was a particular point of contrast.[2] While the poor struggled to survive, from the 1830s middle- and upper-class government and private reformers descended on workers' communities to observe living conditions, habits, and relationships. What they saw appalled them, and the representations they produced helped to discursively construct the urban and industrial poor. They characterized working-class living as dangerous, unhealthy, and immoral and created social panics about these living conditions. While some recognized that most sanitary problems were out of the control of individuals, and required some kind of government intervention, they also blamed workers for creating the filth around them and for adapting to animalistic lifestyles.

One of the defining characteristics of nineteenth-century western society was migration, including migration from rural villages to cities and industrial towns and migration from Europe to the New World. Huge population increases as well as the draw of work in the cities meant that too many people crowded into urban centers that could not contain them. In already-dense cities such as London and Paris, migrants settled in poor neighborhoods, expanding the slums and creating severe overcrowding (see Figure 7.1). London, which had a population of about one million in 1801, grew to over two million in 1851, and, by the end of the century was home to almost seven million people. The population of Paris, at just over half a million in 1801, increased to just under three million by 1911. Between 1790 and 1860, the population of New York City grew from 33,131 to 813,669. In the new industrial cities such as Manchester in England (which grew from about 90,000 people in 1801 to 700,000 in 1901), shoddy tenements were constructed with little or no thought for general urban planning or the quality of the living environment.[3]

Filth was everywhere: human and animal waste filled cesspools and lined streets, while industrial pollution blackened the air and left its mark on buildings and water supplies. Cholera epidemics contributed to fears about poor neighborhoods and the poor themselves as sites of contagion. According to Catherine Kudlick in her study of cholera in Paris, the 1832 outbreak revealed that:

> contagion in the form of cholera spread from the lower to the upper classes, demonstrating that the bourgeois could not remain smug in their assumption that they were immune from the disease. In a more abstract sense, the new information emerging about the lower classes itself represented a form of contagion, for it made them visible while linking them to the general decay of the capital that affected all Parisians.[4]

Cholera especially challenged ideas about the distance between the classes and the safety of the urban environment.

The extent of filth supported current understandings of disease, which focused on the concept of miasma. According to this theory, bad smells from "decomposing animal and vegetable matter" and the bad air that people breathed caused them to become sick.[5] This meant that living in overcrowded conditions with no ventilation, surrounded by excrement and garbage, was the direct cause of illness. The urban poor were, in effect, condemned to disease by their very living conditions. It was no surprise, then, that mortality was so high in the cities. Contagionist theories existed alongside the miasmatic theory of disease, but the idea that the environment and local sanitary conditions were the primary sources of illness predominated for much of the first half of the nineteenth century.[6]

Before reforms in the later nineteenth century, lack of ventilation, cellar dwelling that was constantly damp, and back-to-back housing were the norm for many working poor. Even worse, according to observers, were the lodging houses, where men, women, and children crowded together in single rooms, paying by the night to share part of a dirty mattress. While calls for sanitary and housing improvements originated in England, "the first industrial nation," they soon echoed across European and American cities. "The crowded cellars of Manchester and Liverpool," according to public health historian George Rosen, "were duplicated at Lille and Rouen."[7] Outhouses and privies were inadequate and overflowing. Night soil men, like those depicted in Henry Mayhew's *London Labour and the London Poor*, cleaned the foul cesspools produced by the lack of sanitary provisions in the cities.[8]

FIGURE 7.1 Gustave Doré, a poor neighborhood in nineteenth-century Paris. Credit: Chronicle / Alamy Stock Photo.

To middle- and upper-class observers, overcrowding led to immoral behavior. They worried especially about incest and the corruption of female sexuality that such conditions seemed to promote. To many who wrote about working-class domestic conditions, the environmental filth in which the poor lived translated into moral and bodily filth. According to the physician James Phillips Kay's (later Kay-Shuttleworth) observations of Manchester published in 1832, for example, the people could be nothing but diseased and corrupted, considering the circumstances in which they lived:

> The houses ... are uncleanly, ill provided with furniture; an air of discomfort if not squalid and loathsome wretchedness pervades them, they are often dilapidated, badly drained, damp; and the habits of their tenants are gross—they are ill-fed, ill-clothed, and uneconomical—at once spendthrifts and destitute—denying themselves the comforts of life, in order that they may wallow in the unrestrained licence of animal appetite. An intimate connexion subsists, among the poor, between the cleanliness of the street and that of the house and person.[9]

Indeed, the slippage between the filth of the physical environment and the immorality of people living in it was almost universal in reports like Kay's. A clean home was a sign of moral order, but also of gender-appropriate roles, where women did not work but rather took care of the domestic tasks, a point I will come back to in the next section.

Yet there is evidence that the working poor resisted the filth around them and tried to control their living environments. During an 1842 commission inquiry into the condition of mines in Britain, for example a "deputation of females" complained to an investigating commissioner, the physician Robert Baker, about stagnant water in their neighborhood, "which they declared was not only offensive but deadly."[10] These women did not adapt to their conditions but rather demanded change. The surgeon R. Bowie in the late 1840s testified to the London Metropolitan Sanitary Commissioners how difficult it was for the laboring poor to keep up standards of cleanliness:

> However much the poor might have desired to increase the cleanliness of their houses, they had no control over the supply of water, and they had no means of procuring receptacles for holding it. Many of them, too, were quite unable from their large families, from weakness and disease, to clean their houses; neither had they any means of draining the surface of the streets, courts, and alleys in which they reside, or cleaning the privies and cesspools in the neighbourhood, or of escaping the poisonous emanations given off from them.[11]

According to Bowie, the government needed to step in and make significant changes to the sanitary infrastructure before the poor could be expected to keep their homes clean. These examples challenged the equivalency between the filth of the environment and the immorality of the people forced to live in it.

Still, urban and industrial health seemed to compare poorly with the health of those living in rural districts. Commentators contrasted the unhealthiness of urban, industrial society with the countryside. For example, the French writer Jules Michelet explained in 1846, "The manufactory workman carries all his life a very heavy burden,—the weight of his childhood which weakened him early, and, very often, corrupted him. He is inferior to the peasant in physical strength; inferior, also, in the regularity of his morals."[12] Even more concerning, Director-General McGrigor of the Army Medical Department, submitted to the 1845 British Commission on the Health of Towns that "Of the classes of society from which soldiers are recruited, I believe it will be found that ... tradesmen and manufacturers, particularly those of large towns, are soon swept away by the fatigues and diseases of an army, and that those who have followed agricultural pursuits are the most healthy."[13] Urban, industrial workers proved ill-suited to the rigors of the military. Similarly, the American writer Jack London in his early twentieth-century exposé of London's east end, *The People of the Abyss*, wrote of the ways the city destroyed workers' ability to be productive:

> At the best, city life is an unnatural life for the human; but the city life of London is so utterly unnatural that the average workman or workwoman cannot stand it ... Moral and physical stamina are broken, and the good workman, fresh from the soil, becomes in the first city generation a poor workman; and by the second city generation, devoid of push and go and initiative, and actually unable physically to perform the labour his father did, he is well on the way to the shambles at the bottom of the Abyss.[14]

If migration to the cities continued, according to Britain's General Board of Health in 1854, "we shall shortly be in actual want of able-bodied men, for the social, industrial, and military services of the country."[15] Urban, industrial society was decimating the strength of the nation by damaging the moral and physical health of the people.

During the nineteenth century, statistics became a powerful tool in constructing these public health dangers. Louis René Villermé in France and William Farr in England, for example, statistically linked increases in mortality to urban, industrial society.[16] Demographic investigations and a new faith in statistics showed, in the studies of Villermé and Farr, that the poor died at a much higher rate than the rich and that the poor in the cities, especially, had higher rates of mortality than those in the countryside. Villermé believed the solution to environmental improvement was to "civilize" the working classes, because those with the least "civilization" suffered the most from diseases and early death.[17] Farr, on the other hand, saw lack of sanitary provisions as the main problem and became part of the great sanitary movement in England, led by Edwin Chadwick. To Farr and Chadwick, cleaning up the working poor meant implementing large engineering projects, such as creating sewer lines, drainage systems, and clean water supplies.[18] By the 1860s, much of London had been transformed by these efforts under the Metropolitan Board of Works.[19]

In the second half of the nineteenth century, in England and on the continent, compulsory public health changes were mandated by states, which explicitly linked improved sanitation with solving problems of poverty and inequality. In New York City, city inspector Cornelius B. Archer noted that while it was commendable to have built underground drains for waste in wealthy areas of the city, "the districts where the poorer classes of our citizens 'most do congregate'" had an even greater need for sewers.[20] The German physician Rudolph Virchow, for example, believed that public health was essential to a democratic nation, and that "political medicine" would improve the lives of the poor.[21] Technologies of public health developed significantly over the second half of the century, including increasing numbers of indoor toilets. Yet slums and poverty still existed, with their outdoor privies and cesspools. While the reforms of the 1850s and even the 1860s tended to be driven by an optimism that sanitary improvements would lead to better lives for the working classes, the last part of the century was more pessimistic.[22]

Images of working-class neighborhoods as impenetrable and dangerous contributed to systematic slum clearances and the demolition of narrow alleyways and courts replaced by wide boulevards. As with earlier in the century, concerns about the physical environment were wedded to concerns about the moral environment. In order to bring order and cleanliness to the cities, reformers sought to reshape urban geographies. In Paris, Baron Haussmann's radical restructuring of the city pushed the working classes to the outskirts, where new factories were constructed to draw them out of the city center. "Haussmannization" meant new sewers, water supplies, and trees, but it also meant the displacement of the working poor. His creation of boulevards and parks forced 350,000 people from their homes.[23] Slum clearances often had the effect of creating more housing pressures, which meant more overcrowding for families who did not want to leave their neighborhoods or needed to stay close to their places of work. Andrew Mearns, whose 1883 *The Bitter Cry of Outcast London* helped expose the continuing dangers of London's slums, wrote:

> These wretched people must live somewhere. They must live near the centres where their work lies. They cannot afford to go out by train or tram into the suburbs; and how, with their poor emaciated, starved bodies, can they be expected—in addition to working twelve hours or more, for a shilling, or less,—to walk three or four miles each way to take and fetch? It is notorious that the Artisans' Dwellings Act has, in some respects, made matters worse for them. Large spaces have been cleared of fever-breeding rookeries to make way for the building of decent habitations, but the rents of these are far beyond the means of the abject poor. They are driven to crowd more closely together in the few stifling places still left to them.[24]

While writers like Mearns sympathetically represented the problems of slum living, they simultaneously constructed the urban poor as moral "others" who needed to be rescued. Alternatively, in the name of public health, reformers sought to link the health dangers of slums to national deterioration, pushing for stricter sanitary laws and the improvement of working-class housing.[25]

While the supposed moral contagion of the poor and concerns about the healthiness of the urban environment continued to be pressing matters to public health reformers, the late nineteenth century saw a new way to represent public health dangers: the science of bacteriology. Whereas the "sanitary idea" of reformers such as Farr and Chadwick looked to the environment and engineering projects to solve the sanitation problems they encountered in poor communities, the bacteriological approach targeted individuals as transmitters of disease.[26] Bacteriology promised a new approach to the urban poor that offered hope for healthier populations, but there were obvious class implications in the association of microbes with individuals. The working poor continued to be linked with filth and disease, but descriptions of their living conditions and bodies now drew on the new language of germs and infection. For example, the physician Hippolyte Marié-Davy explicitly used a microbiological rhetoric in describing the slums: "the lodgings of the poor are impregnated from top to bottom with putrid or putrescent matter of all kinds … We also find in some of these houses 50 to 60 times more microbes than in the air of the foulest sewer."[27] According to historian David S. Barnes, these descriptions represented the poor as "little better than microbes themselves."[28]

At the same time, theories of disease rooted in eugenic and degenerationist ideas enforced the view that urban workers had deteriorated physically and morally. While the intention of bacteriology and the sanitary idea was to improve the lives of the poor, eugenic and degenerationist thinkers who argued that disease was hereditary challenged these public health efforts by stressing the containment and even the sterilization of populations considered feeble or dangerous.[29] Cities and factories themselves came to be seen as public health dangers, since they produced sources of national weakness. Nations strove to demonstrate their strength to be able to compete economically at home and in the race for colonies, developing policies to limit the damage that could be caused by "unfit" members of their populations. Improved hygiene now meant stronger nations, with working-class men who had the bodies to contribute to imperial projects and working-class women who had the knowledge to raise healthy children.[30] As with bacteriology, these "nationalist" approaches to public health also focused on individual bodies. I will pick up this discussion below when I turn to poverty and welfare.

THE FAMILY AND GENDER RELATIONS

If "filth," physical and moral, was considered one of the main components of the new industrial society, another was the disruption to stable family relations and gender roles. According to historian Jeffrey Weeks, "the fundamental problem as conceived by middle-class moralists was the effect of industrialisation and urbanisation, and in particular factory work, on the working-class family and the role of the woman within it."[31] The picture many historians have drawn of preindustrial work, in agriculture and cottage industries, is one where men, women, and children worked together, and household and workplace were harmonious. According to the French historian Elinor Accampo:

> When production took place within the home, work and family fused in a number of ways. Labor shared time and space with eating, sleeping, lovemaking, childbearing and childrearing, and socializing with friends and kin. Family and household concerns frequently and spontaneously broke up the sixteen-hour workday. Equally important, the bond between work and family had cultural significance. Men, women, and children often labored as a team. Parents passed skills on to their children, trained and disciplined them, and initiated them into the secrets and associations of their trades. Marriages formed around work relationships and in turn reinforced those relationships. Even when the family members labored at unrelated tasks, the common effort to sustain a family income bound them together.[32]

Industrialization, so the traditional story goes, took work out of the home, devalued women's work, and separated families. Some historians have since critiqued this picture, with Amanda Vickery, a British historian, arguing, for example, that there was no "golden age" where families happily worked together and women shared status with men, which "gave way to an exploitative wage economy which elevated the male breadwinner and marginalized his dependants."[33] Women's work and status, as Katrina Honeyman and Jordan Goodman have shown clearly, have consistently been secondary in the labor market, a status most evident at times of change and conflict, and reflected in domestic relations.[34]

Yet there is no question that industrialization meant significant changes to the everyday patterns of life for working people. As the British historian E. P. Thompson famously argued, time became regulated by the clock and the factory whistle, rather than the seasons and the rising and setting sun.[35] Workers had to mold their lives outside the workplace to fit in with these new configurations. And just as new work patterns often took families out of their homes and overcrowded slums became the norm for so many in industrial cities, dominant ideologies stressed the centrality of the home to social stability and national strength. The moral ethos of the new bourgeoisie, for which cleanliness was so foundational, also emphasized fixed gender roles.

Middle-class moralists imagined families where wives stayed at home focused on the responsibilities of social reproduction, bearing and rearing children, while men focused on the tasks of production, working and providing for their families. Women, as mothers and wives, ideally created domestic spaces that were healthy, calming, and comfortable. Men, as workers and breadwinners, expected to return to homes in which they would be cared for. This male breadwinner ideal, where men earned enough money to support their families without contributions from wives and children, was also attractive to working-class men, for a variety of reasons I will discuss below.

To many middle-class observers, the specter of women working in factories and mines signalled a world turned upside down. Investigators worried that working-class girls had little domestic knowledge, because they had to spend their youth employed outside their homes rather than being trained in the tasks of social reproduction. A committee of physicians and surgeons from Birmingham, England, submitted a report to the British Parliament in the 1840s concluding that working-class girls who worked in factories "marry totally ignorant of all those habits of domestic economy which tend to render a husband's home comfortable and happy."[36] The same arguments came out of Germany in the late nineteenth century, with the expansion of women's factory work, as observers worried about the impact of women's work on "'the health and well-being of the whole nation'."[37] Historian Kathleen Canning has shown that in the 1880s and 1890s, the German labor code restricted women's factory work in the interests of providing women more time to learn domestic skills.[38] Similar "protective legislation" was enacted in other countries to limit the types and hours of women's work and to encourage them into domestic occupations.[39]

Many writers lamented the effects of industrialization and urbanization on working-class households. According to Friedrich Engels in his 1844 study of Manchester, industrialization worked against the bourgeois vision of a normative family life, but the middle classes blamed working-class men and women for circumstances that were out of their control:

> The social order makes family life almost impossible for the worker. In a comfortless, filthy house, hardly good enough for mere nightly shelter, ill-furnished, often neither rain-tight nor warm, a foul atmosphere filling rooms over-crowded with human beings, no domestic comfort is possible. The husband works the whole day through, perhaps the wife also and the elder children, all in different places; they meet night and morning only, all under perpetual temptation to drink; what family life is possible under such conditions? Yet the working-man cannot escape from the family, must live in the family, and the consequence is perhaps most demoralizing for parents and children alike. Neglect of all domestic duties, neglect of the children, especially, is only too common among the English working-people, and only too vigorously fostered by the existing institutions of society. And children growing up in this savage way, amidst these demoralizing influences, are expected to turn out goody-goody and moral in the end! Verily the requirements are naïve, which the self-satisfied bourgeois makes upon the working man![40]

Engels faulted the industrial capitalist system for creating this distorted family life, but he also supported a vision of family where men worked while women remained at home. Similarly, the French Republican politician, Jules Simon argued in *L'Ouvrière* (1860) that factory life was unnatural for women, who belonged at home with their families: "Any form of social organization that uproots wives from their husbands and children is a poorly regulated one that does not allow … women to be women."[41] Industrial society, in Simon's view, prevented the fulfilment of natural gender roles.

While Engels used visions of disrupted family and gender relations to critique industrial capitalism, working men also used these fears to their advantage to protect their own jobs. Mechanization posed significant challenges to men's claims to authority based on artisanal skills, and these challenges had wider implications for how working-class men and women interacted. Historian Anna Clark has shown that British men's arguments that their manhood was contingent on being able to maintain wives and children at home bolstered both their own claims for higher wages and their efforts to remove women from competition in the workplace.[42] Male workers tied their claims to political citizenship to being able to demonstrate their respectability by being breadwinners who provided for nonworking wives.[43] According to historian Laura L. Frader, French working men did not appeal to the male breadwinner ideal as strongly as did British men, but they did support a notion of the family where women were removed from the workforce, and thus supported a family wage.[44]

The language used by working men to critique women's industrial work was remarkably similar to that of middle-class observers. Both emphasized the dangers to the working-class family. A cotton worker from Manchester, England, testified to a Select Committee investigating factory conditions in 1831 that female factory workers "cannot do any of the work that it is necessary for a menial servant to do; they are ignorant of those things, and we say that if they are not fit for servants, they will make very poor wives for working men."[45] In 1850, a petition from laboring men to the British Parliament to improve factory conditions argued that long hours kept women from "acquiring that domestic knowledge which is so absolutely necessary for young females to possess, before they become wives, and mothers of families."[46] James Burn of New York commented in the 1860s that factory girls "are neither fitted for wives by a due regard for the feelings and wishes of their husband, nor a knowledge of the simple rudiments of housekeeping."[47] It went without saying that these young women were supposed to become wives and perform domestic work similar to that of servants.

The politics of working-class movements and labor unions also adopted the "rhetoric of domesticity" to try to bolster men's economic positions by emphasizing women's importance to the home. According to the men of the Chartist movement in Britain in the 1830s and 1840s, factory work for women was ruining working-class communities. The solution, for Chartists, was to raise men's wages and give them a stronger political voice.[48] L'Atelier, a French working-class publication, commented in the 1840s that "Woman was not made to manufacture our products or to occupy our factories, she must devote herself to the education of our children, to the cares of her household."[49] By asserting that women belonged at home rather than in factories, working-class men would benefit from both improved domestic care and less competition in the labor market. Working-class women, according to Clark, found the male breadwinner ideal attractive because it promised them responsible husbands.[50]

Yet the male breadwinner ideal ignored the pressures under which poor families lived. For most working-class families, the idea that women could stay at home without contributing an income was unrealistic, since households often needed earnings from wives and children. Historian Laura Oren has shown that one impact of the male breadwinner ideal was that English wives suffered from insufficient diets, which had negative impacts on their health.[51] In Hamburg, a construction union publication described women's sacrifices:

> The man, the one who after all has to work [sic], consumes the largest share of the available food. The children too have as much as possible. In most cases the mother is left out—she has to be satisfied with one or two mouthfuls if there is not enough to go around, and lives on bread, coffee, and potatoes.[52]

And the pressures on men to be the breadwinners meant that their failures to provide challenged dominant models of working-class masculinity.

The gaps between expectations and working-class couples' lives sometimes were expressed through domestic violence. Husbands frustrated with their own limited earnings abused their wives for failing to bring them meals on time or for complaining about the quality of their housing situations. One London wheelwright's wife claimed, for example, that her husband beat her "for no other reason than that I had no dinner provided for him at times when he came home."[53] Frederick Jones of the West Midlands in England defended himself in 1886 against his wife's charge of assault by claiming she failed to get his meals to him at work.[54] The discursive construction of gender roles thus had very physical impacts on women's bodies. Commentators like Engels worried that households where wives worked while husbands were unemployed were "turned upside down," and that "it is easy to imagine the wrath aroused among the working-men [sic] by this reversal of all relations within the family."[55] Situations like these materially affected relationships between spouses, where men were hostile to their wives for earning income when they were unable (See Figure 7.2).[56]

FIGURE 7.2 Théophile Alexandre Steinlen, *Misère*, 1896. Courtesy of Bibliothèque nationale de France.

Before the courts, wives also expressed their own frustrations with their husbands' failures as breadwinners. They used the gender expectations to their own benefit. In England, women summoned their husbands, asking for separation and maintenance orders, to force their husbands to uphold their roles as providers. In a 1921 West Midlands case, a wife "stated that [her husband] had never given her a wage since the marriage day. She had never had a wife's place."[57] Other women argued that they wanted a separation because their husbands never provided them with a proper home. Elizabeth Billingham of the small West Midlands town of Cradley Heath told the magistrates that she and her husband had been married for ten years "and never had [her husband] provided her with a home that could be called a home."[58] According to historian Joanna Bourke, "of all the dreams dreamt by working-class women, marriage followed by full-time housewifery was the most widely shared."[59] When employment conditions did not support a male breadwinner's family wage, men and women suffered both economically and culturally.

POVERTY AND WELFARE

In critiques of industrial society, images of filthy cities and disrupted families were accompanied by a third prominent and interrelated theme: dire poverty. Perhaps above all, the impoverishment of the working classes and fears about the creation of a criminal- or underclass dominated representations of work and society in the long nineteenth century. Particularly in the later part of the century, when social Darwinism began to permeate western thought, commentators wondered what would happen to societies filled with urban slums, unhealthy laboring populations, and growing admissions to mental hospitals.[60] Workers appeared to degenerate and to be degenerate, unable to control their children who roamed the streets as waifs, beggars, and criminals (See Figure 7.3).[61]

FIGURE 7.3 A slum in the East End of London. Credit: Chronicle / Alamy Stock Photo.

Slum life and poverty corrupted mind and body, and according to the hereditary theories prevalent in the later nineteenth century, this corruption once learned would be passed down to future generations, eroding the quality and strength of the nation. According to the French psychiatrist Bénédict Morel, writing as early as 1857:

> The working classes are equally, in many cases, the involuntary victims of hard necessities, that bring forth misery and the disorder in intellectual, moral and religious education. Their physical health, compromised as much by the nature of their work as by the excess to which they abandon themselves, is reflected in the constitution of their children and incessantly tends to perpetuate and transmit itself with a progressive physical and moral degradation.[62]

Morel here combines environmental understandings of the impact of poverty with blaming the victims, both of which for him resulted in hereditary degeneration. Nations focused on industrial competition, imperial greatness, and military strength could not afford to watch their working populations deteriorate.

In general, by the late nineteenth century commentators shifted from describing the working poor through a language of moral failure or economic anxiety to a language of hereditary degeneration, although blaming the individual never fully disappeared. For example, concerns about prostitution, which had been prevalent throughout the century, became voiced in the new language of degeneration and heredity. Rather than seeing prostitution as the result of the lack of viable economic options for poor women, which caused them to "fall," moralists and medical men put it down to a hereditary taint. Prostitutes became increasingly marginalized from their working-class communities as the century wore on, and prostitution came to be understood less as a desperate way to make money than as a pathologized identity.[63]

Fears associated with poverty became exacerbated with the "great depression," which lasted from the 1870s to the 1890s. Increasing numbers of people out of work became suggestive of mobs and mob violence, visions that were only fuelled by the Paris Commune of 1871 and the London unemployed demonstrations of the 1880s. Middle- and upper-class observers wrote of the horrors of "outcast London" and "the dangerous classes" of Paris. Through their writings, they stressed the differences and distances between themselves and the working poor, emphasizing the foreignness of the sights, smells, tastes, sounds, and material culture of the slums. Andrew Mearns, in his 1883 *Bitter Cry of Outcast London*, warned that, "seething in the very centre of our great cities, concealed by the thinnest crust of civilization and decency, is a vast mass of moral corruption, of heart-breaking misery and absolute godlessness, and that scarcely anything has been done to take into this awful slough the only influences that can purify or remove it." His description emphasizes the difficulty of the reader, presumably of the middle classes, entering into the world of the poor:

> To get into them you have to penetrate courts reeking with poisonous and malodorous gases arising from accumulations of sewage and refuse scattered in all directions and often flowing beneath your feet; courts, many of them which the sun never penetrates, which are never visited by a breath of fresh air, and which rarely know the virtues of a drop of cleansing water. You have to ascend rotten staircases, which threaten to give way beneath every step, and which, in some places, have already broken down, leaving gaps that imperil the limbs and lives of the unwary. You have to grope your way along dark and filthy passages swarming with vermin. Then, if you are not driven back by the

intolerable stench, you may gain admittance to the dens in which these thousands of beings who belong, as much as you, to the race for whom Christ died, herd together.[64]

Simultaneously distancing and uniting classes, Mearns speaks to the foreignness of the impoverished Londoners.

Charles Booth, also an "explorer" of London, tried to understand the city's poverty by categorizing different classes ranging from the vagrant and criminal to the comfortable middle and upper classes. He mapped these classes across London, to indicate the extent of poverty and where it existed (Figure 7.4). While Booth sought to look at social class "scientifically" and was sympathetic to the situation of the urban poor, degenerationist and moralist thinking still pervaded his work. For example, in describing what he called Class A, the lowest class, Booth comments that "their life is the life of savages ... They degrade whatever they touch, and as individuals are perhaps incapable of improvement ... There appears no doubt that [the class] is now hereditary to a very considerable extent."[65] Class B, the very poor, according to Booth, "is not one in which men are born and live and die, so much as a deposit of those who from mental, moral, and physical reasons are incapable of better work."[66] Booth and others contributed to the idea of the "unemployable," those men (especially) who formed an underclass whose idleness, proclivity towards criminal behavior, and mental or physical deficiency prevented them from belonging to the respectable working poor.

Views about what caused the working classes to suffer from poverty shaped the strategies used to try to fix the problem. For much of the nineteenth century, those with the power to alleviate poverty tended to blame the poor for their own condition or see

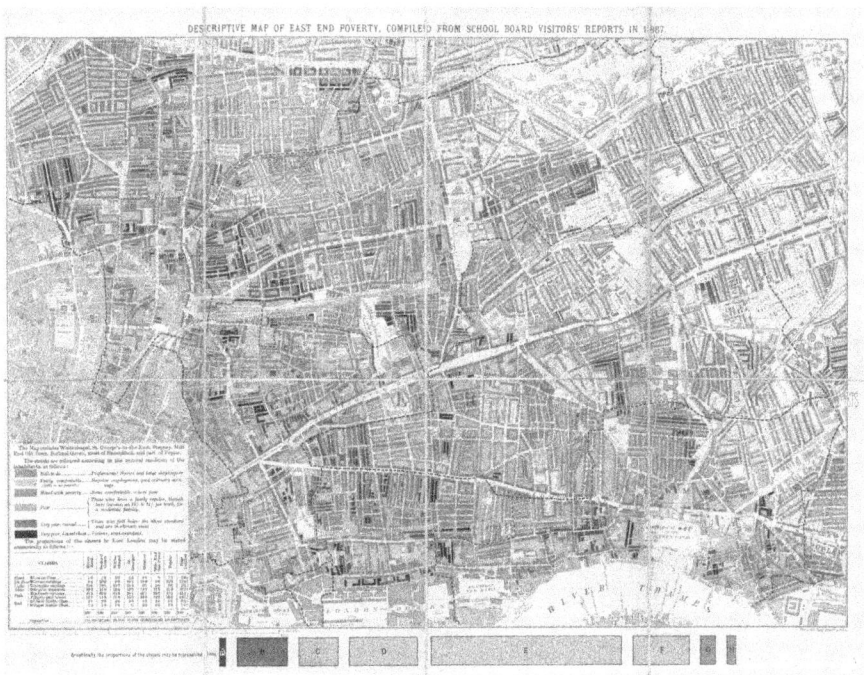

FIGURE 7.4 Charles Booth, map of East End poverty, 1889. Credit: Antiqua Print Gallery / Alamy Stock Photo.

economic inequality as part of the natural order. The distribution of relief was meant to reinforce certain norms of behavior, particularly with regard to gender and class roles. Poor men and women who were not considered "respectable" were often denied assistance or forced to perform tasks in return for aid. Religious and religiously inspired charities sponsored soup kitchens, alms houses, and relief subscriptions for those they considered the "deserving" poor, who usually included the elderly, orphans and neglected children, the ill and infirm, and sometimes women on their own, like widows. They also included families who faced sudden emergencies, such as an illness of the breadwinner or a difficult childbirth for a mother.[67] Representations of the deserving poor emphasized their respectability, their efforts to remain independent, and their commitment to hard work. The "undeserving" poor were irresponsible, drunk, promiscuous, and work shy, and these characteristics caused them to be unsuccessful as laborers and as members of families and society.

The willingness to work, especially for men, was a key sign of deservedness, and this was built into the largest system of European state welfare of the first three-quarters of the nineteenth century: the English Poor Law. The Poor Law originated in Elizabethan times, but the policies that dominated the period under study here came from the Poor Law Amendment Act of 1834, or the New Poor Law. Ideologically, the New Poor Law reinforced middle-class notions of family roles, which included the male breadwinner responsible for his wife and children. Able-bodied men without work were blamed for their joblessness, and the only way they were supposed to receive assistance from the New Poor Law was in a workhouse. In the workhouse, families were separated, and individuals were forced to wear uniforms, eat barely nutritious food, and perform unproductive labor such as breaking stone or picking oakum. The "workhouse test" was intended to separate the truly destitute from slackers, who would be unwilling to trade their freedom for relief. While the workhouse system was supposed to humiliate those unable to remain independent, the numbers of men and women forced to rely on the Poor Law meant that much relief continued to be awarded as "out-relief," outside the workhouse in people's own homes. In fact, the workhouses wound up housing mostly the elderly, the infirm, and orphans, categories of people considered deserving but who had nowhere else to go.[68]

Both public and private relief systems often required that visitors check up on the households of the working poor to make sure their assertions of need were reliable, revealing that authorities distrusted the word of the poor. In the later nineteenth century, these visits shifted to focus on maternal and child welfare, with middle-class women entering the homes of the poor to observe and instruct mothers about proper hygiene and childcare.[69] As nations worried about depopulation and the strength of their military and workforces, policymakers developed welfare programs to try to stem the tide of infant mortality and adult weakness. During the late nineteenth and early twentieth centuries, many countries introduced programs such as free school meals, public health clinics for mothers, milk dispensaries, and child protection services (See Figure 7.5).[70] Many of these programs came from a more "scientific" representation of poverty.

Fears about unemployment and what might happen to unemployed men also drove nations to build state welfare programs. Even though towns and regions had suffered from slumps associated with the new industrial order that threw entire workforces out of work, it was not until the end of the nineteenth century that "unemployment" as a category came to describe a structural problem of industrial capitalism. For the majority of the century, being out of work was considered the fault of the individual, who simply did not try hard enough to find a job. Being out of work was a moral failing that reflected

FIGURE 7.5 Mobile kitchen in Berlin, c. 1900. Credit: INTERFOTO / Alamy Stock Photo.

the laziness or immorality of a worker rather than a lack of employment. The depression of the late nineteenth century, which lasted from the 1870s through the 1890s, forced "respectable," independent men who had lost their jobs to look for relief. They often wound up tramping in search of work and participated in protests about the lack of state assistance. This led to a reassessment about the causes of poverty and unemployment and spurred states to develop welfare programs directed towards respectable men. Unemployment came to be understood as part of the industrial system rather than the fault of an individual.

In the late nineteenth and early twentieth centuries, France, Germany, and Britain as well as other nations instituted programs such as state-sponsored public works schemes, health insurance, unemployment insurance, and old-age pensions. These programs were proactive and defensive, an effort to smooth over the social disruption experienced by the working poor. By the end of the nineteenth century, Britain, France, Germany, and the United States all had electorates that included working-class men. This had an impact on the development of welfare programs and new languages of citizenship to emphasize commonalities of nation rather than differences of class. Governments worried that without state assistance, the respectable working classes would become indistinguishable from the "dangerous" or "criminal" classes, the "residuum," those unable to or uninterested in living respectable lives. The goal of these welfare programs was to make workers productive and keep the nation strong and competitive. Otto von Bismarck in Germany, for example, instituted a fairly comprehensive welfare scheme including health insurance, accident insurance, disability insurance, and old-age pensions, which he hoped would help keep the working classes from turning to socialism. Britain and France both looked to Germany as they laid the foundations for their own welfare states in the early twentieth century.

One of the central narratives concerning work and society in the long nineteenth century told of the disruption caused by industrialization and urbanization. Historians have often used the traces of the past to depict the story of the nineteenth century as a reactive one, with various public and private entities trying to solve the social problems of industrialization, particularly those associated with public health, family relations, and poverty. In many instances, this narrative has portrayed those with social power conflating the poor and working classes with the problems of industrialization. The poor came to stand for filth, family disorganization, gender disruption, criminality, and degeneration. They were a sign that industrialization and urbanization needed to be investigated and managed, not left to develop organically. This management ranged from the development of public health organizations to welfare schemes to the radical restructuring of cities. It also included the intimate contact of middle-class visitors descending on poor neighborhoods to teach poor women "proper" domestic tasks and hygiene.

The powerful cultural sources—the texts and images of social disruption and environmental degradation—have shaped the dominant stories we tell about work and society in the nineteenth century. We cannot deny these powerful documents. Yet the discourses shaped by these texts and images tend to victimize the working poor, rendering them helpless before the forces of industrialization and urbanization, which meld them into degenerate, almost subhuman beings. There are other stories to tell from these sources that resist this victimization and that demonstrate the ways the working poor fought back against efforts to see their lives as no more than the filth in which they lived. Other chapters in this collection flesh out these stories of working-class agency.

CHAPTER EIGHT

The Political Culture of Work

FIONA A. MONTGOMERY

At the beginning of the nineteenth century, work for most people continued largely as it had done for the previous two centuries. Agriculture was by the far the biggest employer even in the UK, where industrialization was well underway. Harvest time and haymaking saw men, women, and children working together. In the period 1800–1920, however, class and gender came to regulate access to work, and could also determine its economic value. The progress of industrialization throughout Europe, which by 1920 would bring about change in working patterns and occasion the concept of separate spheres (with the man assuming a public role and the woman a private one), was patchy both in geographical areas and in the ways in which it developed. Britain led the world in industrialization in the late eighteenth and nineteenth centuries and only it and Belgium were industrial societies by 1850. France was still overwhelmingly rural in the nineteenth century and Germany's industrialization did not take off until after unification in 1871. Nevertheless, increasing mechanization and industrialization led to a gendered division of labor that ensured the downgrading of women's skills and the introduction of restrictive practices while also altering the conditions and pace of work for all laborers. Working practices reflected the needs of industrialists.

Although working men (and of course women) were excluded from formal politics for a large part of the nineteenth century, they still played a part in many aspects of political activity. The initial reaction to the introduction of machinery was fear, especially among artisans, that their skills would be superseded, leading to underemployment at best and destitution at worse. Technology was considered a threat to their skill set and to their standing in the community, and to avoid deskilling they mounted a three-pronged attack: exclude or marginalize women; take control of new technology; and redefine working processes. Sometimes these were used singly, at others in concert. Both in the UK and in continental Europe workers employed a number of strategies to turn back the clock. These included machine breaking, strikes, political protest, and the marginalization of women workers.

POLITICAL MOVEMENTS IN THE FIRST HALF OF THE NINETEENTH CENTURY

Examples of machine breaking can be found in the Middle Ages, but as a modern form of protest it dates to the Industrial Revolution. As a tactic, however, it enjoyed limited success. By 1780, the British Parliament refused to ban cotton-spinning machinery, signalling that there would be no going back. The most well-known episode of machine breaking in the UK was that of the Luddites. Beginning in Nottinghamshire in 1811, Luddism spread throughout Lancashire, Yorkshire, and Derbyshire, encompassing not merely machine breaking, but also arson, theft, and murder. Parliament responded by making machine breaking a capital offense, seeing it not only as a protest against mechanization but also as part of a larger political critique of the government. Sporadic machine breaking continued in England until around 1842; a major outbreak occurred with the Captain Swing riots in 1830 when agricultural laborers rioted over the introduction of new threshing machines that threatened their livelihoods.[1] On the continent, machine breaking was never as common in the early years as it had been in Britain. There were outbreaks against power looms and the use of unskilled and female labor in Krefeld (1828), Aachen (1830), and Silesia (1844). The last big outburst came in the 1848 German revolution.[2]

As industrialization progressed in the UK, protest developed into a political debate over actual working conditions in factories, as in textiles where workers spent long hours amid dangerous machinery breathing a fog of dust that could lead to lung disease. In this debate, perceptions of work and the language used to describe it are very interesting. Work in cotton factories in the UK was described as slavery, not by the workers themselves, but by middle-class Tory reformers. Working from a philanthropic, one-nation Tory perspective that put particular emphasis on the paternalist obligation of the privileged towards the poor, men such as Richard Oastler, Lord Shaftesbury, and John Fielden pointed out the advantages that foreign slaves had, compared to white ones (i.e. factory workers). In a series of letters to the *Leeds Mercury* in September 1830 entitled "Yorkshire Slavery" Oastler contrasted the life of white "slaves" with those of blacks:

> Thousands of little children, both male and female, *but principally* female, from seven to fourteen years of age are daily *compelled to labour* from six o'clock in the morning to seven in the evening ... ye are indeed sacrificed at the shrine of avarice, *without even the solace of the negro slave;* ye are no more than he is, *free agents* ... Ye live in the boasted land of freedom, and *feel* and mourn that *ye are slaves*, and slaves without the only comfort which the negro has. He knows it is his sordid, mercenary master's interest that he should *live* be *strong* and healthy. Not so with you.[3]

He pointed out that there was no need to go the West Indies to find slavery as it was happening on their very doorsteps. Sentiments such as this gave rise to a movement to shorten the working day that consisted of evangelical Tories and factory workers organized in short-time committees. It met strong opposition from manufacturers and mill owners who argued that cutting the working day would lead to economic ruin for both workers and owners with a loss of markets and a cut in wages.

A select committee (1832) and a royal commission (1833) illustrated the various standpoints of the debate.[4] The ten hour movement concentrated on humanitarian aspects of the harmful effects of long hours on children, while the royal commission centered on wastage and inefficiency. The ten hour movement also included factory workers who wanted the working day to be reduced to ten hours for *all* workers. They were not averse to using women and children as propaganda. As an alternative to classical political economy's emphasis on laissez-faire, in which men were considered independent agents able to take care of themselves, working-class radicals and workers developed the idea of fair employment designed to empower the adult male worker. They argued that the legal protection of labor should be part of a social contract between government and adult men (women were firmly classed as dependents). The problem was that the labor market was unregulated. Employers and government leaders considered working men to be free agents with property in their own person and labor, and therefore free to negotiate their working conditions. Workers, however, felt that the market was rigged against them with capitalist employers having all the power.

As the Glasgow cotton spinner James McNish put it when giving evidence to the Sadler Committee:

> The Glasgow combinations for ten hours thought that while slaves were protected they were not ... that their labour which forms their principal property, was left completely open to be trampled upon by every avaricious employer as he chose; they were therefore determined ... to reduce those hours of labour, for the benefit both of themselves and their children.[5]

The "official" stance was that legislation should only cover those who were not free agents and therefore unable to make a legal contract: children. Accordingly, with the 1833 Factory Act children aged under nine could not work; those aged nine to thirteen were restricted to no more than forty-nine hours in one week or nine hours in one day; those thirteen to eighteen had a working week of no more than sixty-nine hours or twelve in one day.

This did not appease the ten hour movement. Its members continued to campaign and in 1847 they secured the Ten Hours Act which stated that women and adolescents aged between thirteen and eighteen should work no more than ten hours a day for five days a week and eight hours on Saturday. Both working men and employers, however, were aware that reducing hours was the thin end of the wedge. John Dennistoun (Member of Parliament for Glasgow) argued in 1847 that the bill was dishonest, as it was termed a "Bill for limiting the hours of labour of young persons and females in factories." He therefore wished to put this question to those who had charge of the bill: "Will the Bill not also affect adult male labour?"[6] Which of course was what the operatives wanted.

The usual arguments had been aired in Parliament. As Dennistoun argued not only would it cut adult hours, but it would also damage commerce: "This might appear a trivial affair; but in reality it would be a loss of two millions sterling per annum."[7] Even those in favor were somewhat patronizing. The people deserved this measure because they had behaved themselves:

> They had for many years besought Parliament to grant them a Ten Hours Bill; and ... the manner in which they had agitated the question entitled them to the most favourable consideration of the Legislature. They had sought to obtain it by the most peaceable means; they had never had recourse to violent agitations, to strikes, or combinations against their employers. They never had committed a breach of the peace at any of the great meetings held upon this question, but their conduct had always been characterised by regularity, and by manifestations of loyalty. It would, therefore, be only an act of justice to those loyal, peaceable, and industrious men to pass this Bill.[8]

By bringing factory conditions to public notice, a political alliance of workers (un enfranchised) and philanthropists (enfranchised) had brought the issue into political debate.

While those in the UK had been demanding the right to work less, continental workers were campaigning for the right to work. Lyon silk workers protested against conditions in 1831, 1834, and 1848. In 1831 the demand for silk dropped leading to a reduction in wages. In an effort to maintain their standard of living, workers tried to have a minimum price imposed on silk. The refusal of the manufacturers infuriated the workers, who went into open revolt. An army of twenty thousand crushed an armed uprising. This attempt ended with no minimum price and the workers no better off. A further revolt occurred in 1834 when employers tried to reduce wages. The government crushed the rebellion in a bloody battle, and deported or imprisoned ten thousand insurgents. This 1848 revolt then became part of the revolution of 1848.[9]

The year 1848 saw revolution break out throughout Europe with a cry for national self-determination and political participation. The emphasis varied from country to country, but economic factors, liberal and democratic ideas, and outmoded political institutions all played a part. Helge Berger and Mark Spoerer, however, demonstrate that "economic misery" as a result of the severe economic fluctuations of 1845 to 1847 provided the impetus for peasants and artisans to become revolutionaries.[10]

In France, economic hardship undoubtedly played a large role. Since 1830 the population of Paris had grown from 785,862 to over 1,053,000 in 1848.[11] However, neither employment nor agricultural output had kept pace. This resulted in a decline in living standards that was exacerbated by a European slump in the 1840s and significant unemployment in France generally and in Paris in particular. While the economy began to recover from 1847, it did not get a chance to blossom because the outbreak of revolution resulted in shops closing, leaving craftsmen without work at a time when charity was inadequate and there was no help forthcoming from the government.

In Paris, the unemployed campaigned for the "Right to Work," which gave rise to a short-lived system of national workshops. In practice, however, they did not provide work but only registered the unemployed and gave them a small dole. Furthermore, the division in the labor force was very evident. Peasants did not see their interests as in any way allied with urban workers. To pay for the national workshops, an extra tax was levied and this fell mainly on the peasantry who could see no reason why they should be squeezed further. The new conservative Constituent Assembly, in an attempt to deal with the financial crisis, shut down the workshops on June 21, which led to the June Days (June 24–26, 1848) in which more than ten thousand on both sides lost their lives. The "Right to Work" can be viewed not only as a protest for improved living conditions but also as a cry against social inequality. However, as an attempt to introduce socialism, it was a failure and demonstrated the vast gulf between industrial workers and the peasantry.

The German labor force at the time of the revolution of 1848 was still dominated by peasants who outnumbered both craftsmen and factory workers. In 1846 and 1847, prices outstripped wages and unemployment rose, leading to riots. The German middle classes revolted against what they saw as outmoded absolutism. In contrast to the focus on high politics among middle-class radicals, the 1848 Workers' Congress of Berlin and Frankfurt discussed practical concerns. They advocated protection of handicrafts, apprentices, and journeymen in what was essentially an embryonic liberal social policy. Artisan and handicraft workers whose status and position were threatened by mechanization led the Workers' Congress.

The revolutions of 1848, although widespread, were a failure; the forces of conservatism won the day and unrest was viciously suppressed throughout Europe. The UK did not experience revolution but it did have two coterminous protest movements: Chartism and the Anti-Corn Law League. Chartism grew out of disappointment at the lack of tangible improvements in working-class life. Propaganda from the 1832 Reform Act had led working-class radicals to expect great things from the Whig government. Instead there was still no ten-hour day for textile workers, trades unions had suffered defeat, the New Poor Law of 1834 brought in a harsh system of workhouses and an end to outdoor relief, and the economy was in a slump.

Chartism sought political reform to give working men a chance to improve their situations and protect their families. Their demands in the charter included universal *male* suffrage, annual parliaments, and pay for Members of Parliament (see Figure 8.1). Male Chartists viewed women as their husbands' helpmeets at best, useful for collecting signatures, participating in campaigns to buy from shopkeepers backing the cause, and supporting strike action. A demand for the franchise for women was quickly dropped and many Chartist men belittled women who wanted to hold their own meetings. Such arguments did not convince all women. In 1839, an address from the Newcastle upon Tyne Female Political Union stated unequivocally, "we have been told that the province of women is her home, and that the field of politics should be left to men; this we deny ... Is it not true that that the interests of our fathers, husbands, and brothers, ought to be ours?"[12] Shared experience, therefore, was justification for political action. Solidarity between men and women had been previously seen in Glasgow in the 1820s, when women and children struck against the replacement of male spinners by lower-paid workers, including women, in an attempt to uphold trade solidarity. In this context, women's sometimes violent protests were described as "harmless exhibitions of feeling or folly or weakness."[13] The Chartist movement, however, supported excluding all women from the workplace and from politics, and women's working interests were ignored. The Chartists thus appropriated bourgeois domestic ideology as a means of putting pressure on the government. Yet the appeal to domesticity did not save the movement from failure. The failure of Chartism led to working men campaigning for the franchise in cooperation with established political parties. Collaboration between the Reform League (a working-class political organization in the 1860s) and the Liberal Party led to the "Lib–Lab" Alliance.

Similarly, the movement for Corn Law Repeal was happy to use its female supporters as fundraisers. Women ran the Great Bazaar that lasted seventeen days and raised £25,000 at Covent Garden in 1845. Female supporters organized separate petitions calling for repeal, arguing that "they considered truly enough, they were as much interested in the question as the men." Women's petitions often emphasized the feminine aspects of a political issue. Those against the Corn Laws argued that it was not the role of the state to regulate the price of basic provisions and so obstruct domestic economy.[14]

Simon Morgan argued that women's "respectable" involvement with the League was vital in establishing it as a national movement.[15] He maintains that such fundraising gave a fillip to later women's political activities, in particular their campaign for the suffrage. While middle-class women were active in the movement, Paul Pickering and Alex Tyrrell found "little evidence" of working-class women's involvement.[16] Unlike Chartism, the anti-Corn Law movement was a success, and both laws were repealed in 1846. Despite different outcomes, both movements provided political education for the marginalized (women and the working classes).

FIGURE 8.1 Chartist meeting, 1848. Photo: Hulton Archive / Getty Images.

GENDER POLITICS AND INDUSTRIALIZATION

Both mechanization and the division of labor altered relationships between men and women in the workplace, in part by deskilling the work process. Women were hired at lower wages than men, for lower-skilled jobs, undercutting men's wages and threatening their control over the work process. One way in which male workers responded was to use the strike as a political weapon against both women and employers. Hatters, calico printers, tailors, and framework knitters were among the trades striking against women workers in the period 1806–11, with no success.[17] The London Tailors' Union was one of the strongest unions in Britain until the beginning of the nineteenth century when capitalist fabric merchants began to produce "ready-made" clothes that were manufactured by unskilled, often female workers as piece work done at home. The breakdown of male craft domination that resulted not only meant a loss of manly status, but also falling wages and underemployment. This was common in most trades where skilled men were replaced by cheaper, unorganized female labor.

When in May 1834 the union came out on strike demanding the end of piece work and home work, women were brought in to strike break. Robert Owen's Grand National Consolidated Trades Union's (GNCTU) magazine, *The Pioneer*, with its "A page for the ladies" (later renamed "Woman's Page") contained letters criticizing the men's actions and pointing out that the working man was often a greater enemy than the employer. The question of whether women had the right to work for lower wages than men was also posed:

> Certainly not, was woman considered equal to man, and did she enjoy the same rights and privileges; but since man has doomed her to inferiority, and stamped an inferior value upon all the productions of industry, the low wages of woman are not the

voluntary price she sets upon her labour, as the price which is fixed by the tyrannical influence of male supremacy.[18]

The answer was equal pay. However, the strike collapsed at the end of May, and the union then left the GNCTU, which itself folded. Nonetheless, we see with this example that women on occasion realized that men were working against their interests.

In general, artisans worked to exclude women while male spinners were prepared to countenance women and children working, as long as such work was subsidiary and under male supervision. In the early nineteenth century, the introduction of the self-acting mule was designed to break the power of the male spinners. Operating steam-powered mules in factories required less skill than working handlooms, and employers in the UK attempted to substitute much cheaper female and child labor. Male artisans, however, aimed to ensure that a lower value was put on women's work by stressing the element of skill needed for the occupation. Similarly, in areas of France, men worked power looms, which were said to require greater strength. Here, women found employment in handloom weaving and by 1850 dominated the trade.[19] Regardless of the gendered shifts in labor in a particular region, whenever women began to work at a particular job, that occupation lost status and brought in lower wages.

Whereas previously male strength might have been cited as a requirement for certain positions, once technology began to be applied to a process such as spinning or typesetting, there was no reason for a gendered division of labor. However, skill continued to be seen as a masculine preserve. Throughout the century, male workers persisted in promoting the value of their work as a means of safeguarding their position in working-class life. Women's work, therefore, was characterized as secondary and unskilled or at best, less skilled and part-time, and was paid accordingly. Men took over supervisory roles and were able to persuade employers that this was a necessary part of the use of the new technology. Such an emphasis chimed in with the newly emerging bourgeois values of the family with its stress on the stay-at-home wife supported by a wage-earning husband. Whether consciously or subconsciously, artisans in particular accepted the prevailing beliefs concerning suitable work for men and women. This was evident in attitudes to women working underground in the mining industry, which occasioned the beginnings of protective legislation.

Mining practices had changed little over the centuries with whole families working together. By the 1840s, however, middle-class commentators in the UK were increasingly exercised by what they saw as the immoral aspects of men and women working together half-dressed in damp conditions. Working conditions therefore were brought into the political arena, particularly when *The Times* publicized pictures of mine work. Reformers had no doubt that such employment could only detract from a woman's ability to be a good wife and mother. Their concern was with morality not exploitation. As the surgeon Michael Thomas Sadler commented:

> I strongly disapprove of females being in pits; the female character is totally destroyed by it; their habits and feelings are altogether different; they can neither discharge the duties of wives nor mothers. I see the greatest differences in the homes of those colliers whose wives do not go into the pits in cleanliness and good management. It is a brutalizing practice for women to be in collieries; the effect on their morals is very bad; it would be advisable to prevent females from going into pits.[20]

As a result of such concern, the 1842 Mines Act, the first piece of gender legislation, banned women and children under the age of ten from working underground (see Figure 8.2). This legislation resulted entirely from middle-class concerns; there was no groundswell of favorable opinion from the miners themselves.[21] However, it did not provide alternative employment for women, which meant that they had no option but to ignore its provisions and continue to work illegally without protection. In the UK, the Mines Act affected around five thousand women and girls who were faced with the problem of finding jobs elsewhere. As the *Wigan Times* was later to put it, young women were "scattered in all directions for a livelihood, families were broken up never to be united again; sent to procure employment in towns where they were exposed to temptations in forms that had never assailed them before."[22]

The situation in Belgium differed from that of the rest of Europe. There it was generally accepted that women would work in heavy industry such as mining, textiles, and chemical industries. Although reformers attempted to use the same domestic ideology to remove women from underground work in mines, they were unsuccessful, not simply because it would lead to hardship for women, but because of general labor shortages. Indeed, the number of women miners increased in the 1850s. Belgium also continued to employ a large number of married women in mining. By contrast, Germany (between 1878 and 1881), Austria (1884), France (1874), and Sweden (1891) restricted women's work to

Women Coal Bearers.

From: Taylor (I.), *The Mine*, 1829.

The usual method of carrying the coal from the place where it was dug to the entrance of the mine was by means of sledges drawn by horses up a gentle slope. Where the mine was not large enough for horses to work, men pushed the coal on a low carriage: where the ascent is too steep for this method, women bearers were employed carrying buckets on their backs.

FIGURE 8.2 Women coal bearers, 1829. Courtesy of Wellcome Collection via Wikimedia.

the surface of the mines. Belgium did not formally exclude women from underground work until 1911.

Although laissez-faire attitudes remained strong throughout the nineteenth century, protective legislation became more common over this period, applied first to children and then to women. In Prussia in 1839, the employment of children under the age of nine in factories or mines was forbidden, while under-sixteens were restricted to ten hours a day with no night or Sunday work. Other parts of Germany such as Baden, Bavaria, and Saxony also promoted factory legislation and from the 1850s factory inspectors were appointed. Germany was well ahead of France, which still lacked a means of enforcement as late as 1880. The French government had enacted legislation in 1841 banning work for children under eight and night work for those aged under thirteen but it was never effectively implemented.

The move towards protective legislation increased after the abortive Paris Commune of 1871. In March of that year insurrection broke out in the French capital after months of the city being besieged by the Prussian Army, leaving the population starving and in dire straits. Revolutionaries ruled Paris for two months under a socialist commune before regular troops violently suppressed it. The failure of the commune was disastrous for the French labor movement: its leaders were dead, jailed, or exiled. The International Working Men's Association (the First International), established in 1864 to foster cooperation across borders among various working-class organizations and parties, was outlawed in France. The only organization surviving was a much-weakened cooperative movement that was nonrevolutionary, seeking peaceful reform.[23] The failure of the commune led some working-class leaders to adopt gradualist approaches, as we see with France's first socialist party, the French Section of the Workers' International (SFIO), founded in 1879. Advocating gradual reform, it never achieved the success of the German Social Democratic Party (SPD).

To combat the threat of socialism, countries acted in different ways. In Germany, Chancellor Otto von Bismarck put in place antisocialist laws before deciding a better policy would be to beat the Socialists at their own game. He enacted a series of legislation from 1883 establishing health and accident insurance and retirement pensions in order to make socialism less attractive to workers. The term "state socialism" was coined to describe this. Similarly, legislation such as the French Labor Law of 1892 that limited night work for women, girls, and children in dangerous occupations such as those involving chemicals could be seen as an attempt to obviate the need for socialism by protecting workers. In practice, however, the law only drove women into unregulated jobs in sweatshops and domestic production. In 1900, Sweden forbade the employment of women in the four weeks after birth but provided no support, so again women had to work in unregulated areas. Governments usually lacked suitable means of enforcing such legislation. Thus in 1842, in the UK there was only one inspector for two thousand collieries and he never went underground! French factory legislation was not effective till 1900. Exceptions also existed for much of this legislation. The ten-hour day was not introduced in France until 1904 but workers in silk mills often worked eleven hours. Similarly, the German Labor Code of 1891 excluded homeworkers engaged in garment making and needlework in a domestic setting from the welfare benefits system.

Such protective legislation may have been designed with the best of intentions but it took no account of the realities of the fact that women had to work to support themselves and their families. On the whole protective legislation disadvantaged women workers because it made them less useful than men. For example, women were unable to clean machinery at the end of their shifts after the 1844 Factory Reform Act, which led to a drop in badly needed wages. As Mary Lynn Stewart demonstrated, the French 1892 Legislation tied women into low-paid jobs.[24] Protective legislation also infantilized women by classing them differently from men and, in the UK, including them with children as in need of protection. Many feminists such as Emma Paterson, founder of the Women's Protective and Provident League (the first women's trade union) disapproved of this legislation since it denied women the status of rational adults. This led to a realization that since male-dominated trade unions ignored women's interests, women needed their own organizations.

By contrast, in France, authorities were more interested in protecting children rather than women *and* children.[25] In France, it was accepted that both single and married women worked for wages. France had a higher proportion of married working women than any other European power during the period 1870–1914.[26] Reformers argued that limiting women's work hours might improve infant mortality. Infant mortality was a concern not simply because industry needed a healthy labor force but also because of worries over a declining birth-rate. This was particularly disquieting because France had been decisively beaten in the Franco-Prussian War of 1870–1 and should there be another war they would be at a severe disadvantage. This was an issue around which all—Solidarists, the left, and bourgeois feminists—could unite. Social Catholics, radical republicans, and employers argued that a shorter working day would mean increased efficiency and productivity.[27]

While workers wanted to exclude women, employers at times helped their cause by stressing the need for women to remain in the home; thus employers and men were in an unofficial alliance. They also organized work on paternalist lines. Not only were men seen as natural supervisors, but women's subordinate position was reinforced by the prevailing system of punishment and rewards. Women were punished for a greater range of misdemeanours, often of a trivial nature, such as unbecoming behavior (gossiping, laughing, making fun of the managers), while men were fined for rowdy behavior. Thus factory owners wanted to enforce a moral code, which would strengthen factory discipline.[28]

TOWARDS AN ACCEPTANCE OF WOMEN'S WORK

Women have always played an important role in agriculture. As agriculture became mechanized, however, men took over the skilled work and domestic ideology (where men's roles were in the public sphere and women's in the home) came into play: "The period from about 1780 was crucial, marking a transition from *Hausmutter*, working in partnership with her husband presiding over agricultural estates, to *Hausfrau* or housewife, the guardian of the private sphere."[29] This meant that men intruded into what had been traditional areas of women's work.

In small agricultural enterprises women did practically everything, but generally those tasks associated with strength, skill, or control were seen as men's. As harvesting technology shifted from the use of the sickle to the heavier scythe, women's role in harvesting was reduced. Throughout Europe, the scythe with its perceived need for strength and skill was considered the preserve of men.[30] As in manufacturing, agriculture was transformed by mechanization, and machine breaking took place. The most notable example is probably the Swing riots, which occurred in Kent, East Anglia, and southern

England in 1830 and 1831. As well as widespread destruction of threshing machines (seen as a threat to laborers' livelihoods), rick burning, and cattle maiming, rioters also made wage demands and destroyed workhouses and tithe barns. Small farmers were often in sympathy with this cause (even if they did not support the actual tactics) since they too suffered from high rents, the need to pay tithes, and the poor law rates.[31] Similarly in France in 1851, agrarian agitation encompassed workers and small-scale producers protesting against crop prices and low wages, and demanding the suffrage. Such alliances did not survive long into the century, however, and protests against low wages in the 1870s were unsuccessful. By this time in England attention was being directed to fighting for the franchise.

In a perceptive article, Denise Fink demonstrates how women's position in Danish dairying changed as agriculture became mechanized.[32] Dairying was labor-intensive (see Figure 8.3). In 1836 Danish women were given training and as a result secured good jobs with high wages and status. As the century progressed, dairying became more economically successful which meant that it was considered no longer feasible to leave it in the hands of women, however well-qualified; male management with male strength, knowledge of technology, and more suitable clothing was what was required. Women therefore became marginalized in Denmark. By the 1880s men had taken over as dairy advisers. While men took over leadership, middle-class women who had played a full role in dairying turned away from hard work, so that it changed from "a female craft to a male science."[33]

With the general loss of field workers, farmers in the UK, France, and Belgium used agricultural gangs to provide the necessary labor, a practice that was denounced by bourgeois reformers because the character of the work made women unsuitable for their

FIGURE 8.3 Benjamin Waterhouse Hawkins, *Milk*, c. 1845. Photo: Oxford Science Archive / Print Collector / Getty Images.

true vocation as wives and mothers. Evidence given to the 1867 *Commission on the Employment of Children, Young Persons and Women in Agriculture* stated:

> Not only does [such employment] almost unsex a woman, in dress, gait, manners, character, making her rough, coarse, clumsy, masculine; but it generates a further very pregnant social mischief, by unfitting or indisposing her for a woman's proper duties at home … The farmers, almost to a man … express the opinion that the proper place for a young single girl is in a household, and not upon the land.[34]

Women's position in agriculture therefore became part of political debate. As late as 1892, however, Belgium still had fifty-seven thousand women working in such gangs. The importance of agriculture as an employer should not be underestimated: the 1896 French Census revealed that it outstripped both the service sector and manufacturing (agriculture, 2,760,000; service, 1,729,000; manufacturing, 1,716,000).[35]

The late 1880s and 1890s saw a labor shortage, especially in the factories of the Rhineland and Westphalia. This led to an increasing number of both married and single women working outside the home. Some mill owners, in an attempt to reconcile the need for workers with a belief that women's rightful place was in the home, introduced cooking and sewing lessons. In this the multiple positions that women held within society—workers, mothers, wives—are evident. Employers were also concerned with male and female workers fraternizing. The 1891 German Labor Laws recommended segregating male and female workers, but in the Rhineland only a few Catholic textile employers did so. Factory inspectors tried to enforce separation of the sexes, sometimes by ensuring separate entrances for men and women.[36]

As women became increasingly involved in work outside the home, they began to participate to a greater extent in strikes. Women took part in sporadic protests in small-scale craft industries and in the textile trades. In Britain women were involved in Luddism and other disputes and were often described as worse than the men. Women sometimes instigated strikes, as during the July Monarchy when twenty women fur cutters (one of the early mechanized trades) in Paris walked out to protest a cut in wages and tried to get the support of the other women. The National Guard arrested five women, of whom four were convicted of illegal coalition. Women shawl cutters also struck against the introduction of machines in a week-long action in September 1831. In 1834 women joined male wood gilders to demonstrate against the use of prison labor.[37] Women also took part in isolated strikes between 1839 and 1847 in the woollen towns of Lodève and Mazamet. At Elbeuf forty homeworkers struck after losing their jobs when new machines were introduced. Troops had to be called out to put down the disturbance. On such occasions, the authorities did not see such activity as the work of the women themselves but either as the acts of men dressed as women, or as women simply doing what their husbands told them.

Women saw industrial action as one way in which they could better their conditions to enable them to fulfil their domestic responsibilities. Thus silk weavers in Krefeld campaigned for an extra half-hour lunch break (which would enable them to prepare food for their families), clean canteens, a changing room for women workers, and a room for breaks. The strike was resolved before a lockout.[38] Women began to join workers' committees such as in the textile factories of Crimmitschau in Saxony. Crimmitschau was the center of a large textile industry and women had become used to fighting for their own interests. From August 22, 1903 to January 18, 1904 one of the longest-lived strikes in Germany occurred, in which women struck and played a full role (see Figure 8.4).

Indeed, mill owners and civic authorities considered that the women's behavior was "notably worse than men." The police arrested a woman for "loitering" in the street from 8:45 a.m. to after 10:00 p.m. claiming that this was not the action of a respectable woman who "does not belong out on the street, rather in the house" and therefore she must be part of the strike.[39] Notice the emphasis on respectability and the supposition that a woman's place was in the home. She was jailed for a day but this did not discourage others from protesting. Nor did fining them or keeping them in custody for hours at a time.

Women also formed associations such as the Glasgow Female Power Loom Association representing 12,498 power looms and developed "for their mutual protection against the encroachment of tyrannical men, and the reduction of masters."[40] Women, aware that they were being used as cheap labor, joined the GNCTU.[41] From its inception the GNCTU supposedly offered support to women trade unionists, but men immediately showed unease at best or outright hostility at worst. This attitude was evident in what became known as the "Couriau Affair." In April 1913, Emma Couriau, a printer, applied to join her local printers' union in Lyon. Printing represented a well-paid, highly skilled trade at which women could perform as well as men but were not equally paid. Women printers therefore represented a threat to male printers' livelihoods, especially since the number of women printers increased threefold in the decades from 1866 to 1906.[42] Women were used as a means of introducing new machines. They had also been used as strike breakers in the printing industry since 1862, and in 1901 Marguerite Durand (founder of the feminist newspaper paper *La Fronde*) agreed to strike break at Nancy with the female printers. Thus when printers formed a National Federation in 1881, they vowed "to oppose, by all legal means, the employment of women typesetters."[43]

FIGURE 8.4 Women textile workers who struck for the ten-hour day, Crimmitschau, 1904. Photo: ADN-Bildarchiv / ullstein bild via Getty Images.

Given this context, it is not surprising that Couriau's application to join her local printing union was denied. Hostility towards her was so great that despite it being official policy to accept women, not only did the union refuse Couriau's application, it also drove out her husband, Louis, on the grounds that he had "let" her work. This seemed to convince feminists that working-class men were against women working, especially when the central committee dismissed the Couriaus' appeal. Emma set up her own female typographers' union in September 1913 seeking admission to the federation. This was vetoed in January 1914. However, an additional resolution to be debated at the 1915 congress asked that sanctions should be taken against those refusing to admit women. The affair received national attention, and as Charles Sowerwine points out, it forced workers to accept, "the reality of women's work ... If the Couriau affair is 'an index of attitudes towards women', it indicates not the persistence of misogyny but a step and an evolution towards egalitarianism."[44] Interestingly, the anarchist Georges Yvetot's analysis echoed that of the London tailoresses in 1834: "If man is the slave of his wages, woman is as well ... Working like man ... bound to the same fatigues, the same dangers, the same risks, a woman is paid less ... Under the influence, the authority, the stupidity and the cruelty of the male, woman is condemned to be, despite herself: several times mother, domestic, Courtesan."[45] At the beginning of the twentieth century, the French Confederation Générale du Travail, an organization that affiliated several trade unions, worked to organize women. The Couriau Affair demonstrated that at on the eve of the First World War, unions and their political allies no longer promoted policies assuming women's work to be unnatural.[46]

SUFFRAGE AND WAR

By the end of the nineteenth century, the extension of the male franchise throughout Europe gave rise to the possibility of political parties devoted to the interests of the working classes. While socialist parties attracted the support of working-class men in France and Germany, in the UK, for most of the late nineteenth century, working men voted liberal. The 1885 election saw eleven working men returned to Parliament as liberal MPs. The British Socialist movement tended to be more middle-class, lacking mass appeal to the working class. Instead, trade-based organizations represented workers. The Labour Representation Committee (LRC) formed in 1900 by the Trades Unions Congress resulted from the trade unions movements' conviction that their interests would be best served with their own political representation in Parliament, especially as employers seemed to be working increasingly against the well-established, old craft unions, for example in coal and cotton. The LRC, however, lacked mass membership (trade unions were not affiliating to it) and therefore the finances necessary to make a difference.

As employers became more organized and successful in curtailing union power, support for the LRC grew. In 1899, the *Lyons v. Wilkins* case limited picketing rights. In 1901, as a result of the House of Lords' decision that a trade union was financially liable for the actions of its agents, the Taff Vale Railway Company sued the Amalgamated Society of Railway Servants for picketing damages and was awarded £23,000. This made strike action impossible and the only way forward was to persuade Parliament to change legislation. To do so, true Labour MPs, not Lib–Lab were needed. Taff Vale led to an influx of unions to the LRC, including the first of the miners' unions, the Lancashire and Cheshire Miners' Federation. In 1906, the LRC changed its name to the Labour

Party.[47] Working conditions therefore had had a massive impact on the working class, and therefore national politics.

Women too realized that they needed their own political representation. Many Socialists argued that men's suffrage should come first. Women's suffrage associations were in existence from the mid-1850s throughout Europe and were mostly led by educated bourgeois women who prioritized education and employment. This limited outlook led to the development of the suffragist movement, yet there was also a strong feminist movement within socialism that fought against "the sexism of male socialists and the social conservatism of middle-class women's movements."[48] The biggest socialist women's movements were in Germany, Austria, and the United States. Many socialist parties were ambivalent towards female suffrage. The First International was hostile to women's work and unenthusiastic towards women in politics. The Second International prohibited cooperation with bourgeois groups. Socialist women were expected to focus on the socialist movement not on women's rights. Nonetheless, international socialists took the view that "the increasingly public character of women's labour had to be matched with an equally public political role."[49]

With the outbreak of the First World War, suffrage was no longer a priority for women. Most advocated war work, but some were pacifists and this split the suffrage movement. In wartime the family household was torn apart. Women were pushed into work and therefore were no longer in the private sphere. For working-class women the First World War brought an expansion in employment but not a change in the way their work was viewed. Thus women continued to nurse, although in much more horrific surroundings, but they also took over the jobs vacated by men fighting at the front. They were involved in shipbuilding on the Clyde and in Germany where they worked as riveters; they ran the Paris Metro, worked in munitions, the chemical industries, and transport. However, wages were still paid at a fraction of men's.

Protective legislation was abandoned in both France, "tacitly ... under the stress of circumstances in the new industries opened to women,"[50] and Germany, until it was feared that overwork would lead to a breakdown in women's health. France introduced a day of three eight-hour shifts to reduce the working day and Germany an eight-hour day in munitions factories. By splitting shifts, however, it was possible to obviate the need for breaks and actually increase hours.

As in the UK, it was realized that women had a double burden of working for the war effort and running a home. Nurseries, crèches, rest rooms, and women supervisors became normal. In Germany, despite such incentives, married women were still not eager to work in factories; for example, in Bavaria in 1917 only 29 percent of the labor force was married compared to around one-third in 1907. By 1917 the number of women working in engineering, the metallurgical, chemical, and mining industries as well as iron and steel had increased by around six times compared to 1913. Such figures were only an extension of the prewar situation but one that was very visible. This increased fears that women were taking over men's jobs thus blurring the distinctions between what should be men's work and what women's.

In an attempt to mollify the unions and the men, processes were split into many different stages so that employers could argue that one man was not being replaced by one woman and of course cut costs. Nevertheless, men still were against women doing the same or similar jobs even when women joined unions and worked for equal pay. Furthermore, women were under no illusion that their work was to be temporary and should be relinquished once the war was over.

An interesting political attitude to women's work is evident in the way major nations reacted to the idea of women becoming part of the armed forces. Here the question of what constituted citizenship was vital. Men were considered citizen-soldiers. They defended the state because they had a stake in it. This point of view meant that women could be excluded. If men expressed their contribution to the common good through military duties, women were thought to do so through motherhood. This changed somewhat during the First World War, when Britain, Russia, the United States, and Germany embraced the idea of women's military auxiliary corps. France did not. As far as France was concerned, women were not citizens and did not have a duty to the nation. They were needed in war work because of the manpower shortage but were not being called to national service. As Margaret and Patrice Higonnet pointed out, taking on men's jobs did not improve their status relative to men, for the simple reason, men were now in an even more masculine role: that of a combatant.[51] By 1918, one hundred thousand British women were serving in the auxiliary corps while French women were doing exactly the same jobs as civilians.

After the war, although not necessarily as a consequence, women were enfranchised to some extent in countries such as Germany, Austria, and the UK. Some neutral countries like the Netherlands and Scandinavia gave women the vote while in some combatant countries like France, Italy, and Belgium they had to wait until after the Second World War. Defeat in Germany and Austria and consequent revolution brought in socialist governments that enfranchised women.

By the end of the period, all working men and many working-class women had a stake in political society. Action had moved from machine breaking to exercising the franchise. Attitudes towards women's work, however, remained much the same and the body politic and therefore the political culture remained overwhelmingly male. By 1921 fewer women were working in industry than there had been before the war. Furthermore, any chance of fairer, let alone, equal pay proved to be nothing but a dream, even though the Treaty of Versailles had promised "equal remuneration for work of equal value."[52] Women continued to be seen as wives and mothers, and only incidentally as workers. Even in the nascent Soviet Union, where work was considered equally important for men and women, most women "remained economically dependent housewives" in the postwar period, even though they did have a higher rate of workforce participation than did women in the West.[53]

CHAPTER NINE

Work and Leisure

W. SCOTT HAINE

The relationship between work and leisure underwent dramatic transformations between 1820 and 1920. The technological, entrepreneurial, and social changes across the century between the Battle of Waterloo and the end of the First World War reconfigured leisure and its relation to work, family, and nation. The consolidation of the Industrial Revolution in Britain, along with rapid urbanization that would make the island nation the first predominantly urban society in history, spread throughout Europe over the course of the century, bringing with it factories, railroads, growing cities, and mass-circulation newspapers and journals covering all facets of an expanding realm of leisure activities. We see the golden age of mass literacy and the apogee of the printed word, as well as not only the dawn of modern media—film and radio—but also the growing complexity of reading publics and urban spectators who enjoyed a sort of "virtual reality," even before the rise of the computer.

Modern leisure emerged not just as a diversion from or complement to work but also as time distinct unto itself and increasingly at the discretion of and focused on the individual rather than the group, whether at work, at home, or in the neighborhood. Indeed, a labor–leisure dialectic emerged during this period in which entrepreneurs realized that free time could be commodified in an almost limitless fashion, and that leisure allowed human creativity to blossom. The result was new forms of music, dance, and literature, along with the emergence of new technologies such as film, the phonograph, and at the very end of the era covered in this chapter, the radio. Although not fully developed during this time, the modern amusement park that could integrate all these new bodily and mental expressions can be discerned from the international expositions, world's fairs, and urban landscapes devoted to strolling, seeing, and experiencing. To these "virtual" journeys to other places was added actual travel, at the seaside and in the mountains and deserts, increasingly accessible by train, bicycle, and eventually automobiles. The calendar of leisure activities changed during this period as well. Traditional Christian holy days (with their often semi-pagan elements) such as carnival and saints' feasts declined, as did regional fairs and market days. In their place, a more rational, regulated, and spatially and temporally delimited set of leisure activities emerged. Nevertheless, some of the magic and wonder of long-standing aspects of leisure activities, such as the intoxication of dancing, singing, and the comedic crowds, carried over into modern leisure.

Drinking, eating, and socializing remained at the heart of working-class life across this entire era. Domestic spaces remained small and crowded, and as urban outdoor spaces became more regulated, pubs, taverns, cafés, and restaurants gained in importance. Only at the end of our era do we see workers starting to be able to create a more stable and developed home life that kept men out of the taverns and women tied more to their own homes rather than neighborhood networks. Public institutions began to recede from the center of working-class leisure life when laborers were able to buy and enjoy new consumer durables in their homes; nonetheless, pianos, phonographs, and radios—the first great mechanical devices of the new age of mechanized leisure—were debuted in public.

URBAN LEISURE

At the dawn of the nineteenth century, the time of the peasant, artisan, and urban worker was porous and riddled with unforeseen moments of spontaneity and unexpected interruptions. In the cities, most workshops were on busy streets with the result that the distinction between work and sociability was often blurred. Traditionally among artisans, and even among early factory workers, time spent at work was not rigidly regulated and workers often talked, sang, gambled, drank, and even played sports while on the job. Outside of the workplace, collective dancing, singing, a spontaneous public theater, and community sporting events such as early football matches that moved through the streets of the city and towns were hallmarks of working-class leisure. In addition, general merry-making associated with carnival and the market place contributed to the creation of deep community bonds through recreation. (see Figure 9.1). These activities also often inverted and mocked the power structure and those in authority. These "carnivalesque" moments, when the ordinary hierarchies and routines of daily life were turned upside-down, were regular occurrences, especially in Catholic countries, with their many saints' days and religious festivals.[1] Religion provided a moment for the community of the faithful, or a community of workers united under the protection of their trade's patron saint, to strengthen bonds that had a dimension other than shared work experience. Community-based leisure in streets, open fields, and village squares generated a sense of neighborliness and a feeling of "collective effervescence," and group solidarity.[2]

FIGURE 9.1 Walter Gelkie, *Fair Gamblers*, early nineteenth century. Photo: The Print Collector / Print Collector / Getty Images.

But steadily from the time of such early disciplinarian manufacturers as Josiah Wedgwood, work time was closely monitored. In early factories, a clear demarcation between the space and time of work and that of leisure was established by means of regulated entry into and exit from the workplace, the use of timekeeping devices and bells to signal the beginning and end of the work day, as well as closely supervised breaks in the work routine. As a result, leisure activities that once might have happened on the shop floor moved to the street and cafés, music hall, or athletic field. In addition, popular animal sports and athletics were driven from open spaces in rural areas with the enclosure movement, and in cities and towns with the passage of ordinances meant to ensure public order and cleanliness. This was especially true of animal sports centered around baiting various animals such as badgers, bears, and bulls. In Great Britain, bear-baiting died out in the eighteenth century, partially due to the expense of importing long-extinct bears; it was formally outlawed in 1835. Bull-baiting, in which dogs attacked bulls in order to bring them down, was outlawed in the same year. With the end of bear- and bull-baiting went the end of the "civic pageantry" that surrounded it, when the animals were paraded through the city and the marketplace became a stage.[3] Cock- and dog-fighting were also banned in 1835, as part of the same bill introduced by South Durham Member of Parliament Joseph Pease, a member of the Royal Society for the Prevention of Cruelty to Animals, founded in 1824. Yet these sports were difficult to eradicate, and later legislation (the 1911 Protection of Animals Act) made it illegal to keep a place for the purposes of "fighting or baiting any animal."[4] These sports endured in part because they were occasions for gambling, and as they were increasingly criticized as being too bloody they moved from outdoor spaces to pubs and taverns.

In general, public spaces for both organized and spontaneous leisure activities diminished in the first half of the nineteenth century. As cities grew, state and municipal authorities worried about the threats that crowds posed to political stability, especially given the history of urban unrest and violence in capitals such as London and Paris. During carnival celebrations in Paris in 1831, crowds sacked the Abbey of Saint-Denis.[5] In Manchester in the 1830s, museums, parks, and gardens not normally accessible to the poor were opened to all, in an attempt to draw off attendance at Chartist demonstrations. Popular crowds were also considered dangers to public health in the wake of repeated cholera epidemics. The working classes were increasingly seen as "dangerous classes," inherently predisposed to criminality and other forms of disorder.[6] At the same time, the expansion of commerce and manufacturing, and the growth of urban middle-class populations, shifted priorities of city planning towards production, circulation, and consumption. In this context, spontaneous football matches in the city's streets or popular festivities such as the festival of laundresses, in which laundry-women paraded through the streets of Paris, became seen as outmoded uses of shared urban spaces.

As leisure moved inside, coffee houses, cafés, and pubs became more important in working-class life. In Paris, the number of cafés grew from around three thousand in 1789 to twenty-two thousand in 1870; by the late 1880s, that number had grown to thirty-three thousand. In 1909, Paris could boast 11.25 drinking establishments per resident, compared to New York's 3.15 and London's paltry one-to-one ratio.[7] Yet even one pub per Londoner meant that there were plenty of spaces where working-class men and women could gather when they were not working. In England, pubs provided playing cards, billiard tables, and shove ha'penny boards, along with bowling and skittles alleys. All of these activities were accompanied by gambling, another favorite activity of working-class men. Pubs and cafés became more attractive as the organization of work changed.

Mechanization meant that workers had to be more attentive, and could not talk, joke, or drink for fear of being seriously injured in the machine. A quickening of the pace of production as well as increased policing of the workplace also encouraged a separation of work and leisure. As work became more routinized and tiring, leisure activities outside of work hours provided a source of much-needed relaxation and socializing. It is therefore not surprising that, as Hugh Cunningham has shown, among skilled workers in England a desire for increased leisure time outpaced demands for higher wages during the period 1840–70.[8]

Pubs were often the incubators of friendly societies and cooperatives. These working-class associations proliferated across the early nineteenth century in Britain and were a means by which workers built financial and intellectual capital. By pooling their resources, workers created a safety net that protected them from illness, work-related accidents, and old age. These associations also served as a way for workers to educate themselves. Even at the end of the century, when Parisian workers pooled their resources to buy plots of suburban land to build their own houses, café owners often served as the "banker." The pub could also serve as a center for politicization, and politics and leisure were often intertwined in the nineteenth century. The Parisian entrepreneur Denis Poulot worried about workers' propensity to critique the class bias of bourgeois newspapers that they read while in the café (Figure 9.2).[9]

If the pub was often the center of working-class life, it also connected workers to a larger world. One of the first great achievements of working-class associational networks happened in Britain, where mechanics' institutes and friendly societies collected sufficient

FIGURE 9.2 Reading the newspaper in the tavern, 1876. Photo: Prisma / UIG / Getty Images.

funds to send, via railroad, tens of thousands of workers to the Crystal Palace world exhibition in London in 1851. Many employers contributed, with some even giving workers time off with pay to attend the exhibition.[10] This was the dawn of working-class tourism. Yet while such societies played a big role in getting workers to beaches across Britain, not many could afford excursions to the European continent.

One of the most spectacular leisure activities that expanded the reach of the pub was the development of the music hall and a popular music culture, stimulated by the mass printing and distribution of song via sheet music (see Figure 9.3). In Paris, café-concerts had a more satirical edge and in Vienna concerts fused music with dance. Working-class publics came together in dance halls on the outskirts of Vienna and in rented halls in New York City. Sales of sheet music encouraged singing on streets and in cafés and then helped to develop an emerging star system. There was often much audience participation, as at carnival. In working-class café-concerts, known derisively as *beuglants* (*beugler* means "to bellow") the audience sang along with performers; attempts to restrain audiences were never fully successful.[11]

Paris best epitomized a culture of urban leisure in the late 1860s. By the end of this decade Haussmannization had created broad boulevards lined with grand cafés and luxurious department stores, as well as spacious new parks at either end of the city. The 1867 World Fair drew Parisians and tourists. In the French capital, not only was luxury commodified and on display on the boulevards and in shop windows, but also other aspects of the urban landscape, such as the catacombs and the sewers, were major tourist draws. At the end of the century the Eiffel Tower, built for the 1889 *Exposition universelle*, became a symbol of Parisian modernity as well as an icon of the French capital's nickname of the "city of light." The Paris Metro (1900) provided ease of transportation throughout the city. By the turn of the century, Paris had all the elements of a modern amusement

FIGURE 9.3 Music hall patrons, c. 1830. Photo: Hulton Archive / Getty Images.

park. While this centerpiece of modern leisure would not emerge until the twentieth century, Walt Disney did look to nineteenth-century pleasure gardens, such as the Tivoli Garden in Denmark, for inspiration.

YOUTH CULTURE AND MODERN INVENTIONS

By the late nineteenth century, the sheer spectacle of the city inspired the youth to dream. With urban renovation in Paris, traditional street life and trade were increasingly limited to working-class districts where they became objects of the tourist gaze. Working-class youth were often at the center of new youth cultures of consumption and display, as with the Apaches—one of several urban gangs—and their "siren" *Casque d'Or* (golden helmet), a nickname given to the prostitute Amélie Hélie, made famous during a 1901 trial of Joseph Pleigneur for murdering his rival for Amélie's affections and business. Although Pleigneur was not a member of the Apaches his trial led to a vogue in music-hall numbers parodying them, while also encouraging working-class youth to reject the discipline of the factory for the Apache lifestyle.[12] As "slumming" in the café-concerts of working-class Paris gained in popularity, singers and dancers of working-class origins could build successful careers.

Working-class youth culture became a tourist attraction, but it also elicited concerns. By the late nineteenth century, legislation across Europe had raised the age at which youth could enter the labor force, while the decline of artisanal production and the rise of factories had eliminated the odd jobs that youth had often performed and that straddled the work/leisure divide. But as youth went to school and lived in large cities filled with the "temptations" of modern consumer society moralists across the political spectrum started the first moral panic about juvenile delinquency. Even Friedrich Nietzsche called on the youth to disdain the "pseudo-wants of city life." The American psychologist G. Stanley Hall inspired European thinkers to consider adolescence as a stage of "storm and stress."[13] Hall invited both Freud and Jung to lecture to his students at Worchester University before the First World War. In the United States, Jane Addams responded to concerns over idleness among the young at her settlement house in Chicago. Addams had been influenced by the British housing reformer Octavia Hill and her development of the settlement movement, which sought to ensure that bourgeois and working-class families would live in closer proximity in order to achieve the moral elevation of the working class. Addams focused on the need to provide proper spaces and activities for youth and inspired the construction of playgrounds. In the decades leading up to 1914 European cities ranging from Cologne to Manchester followed the example of the United States in building swimming pools, athletic stadiums, and recreational parks. Youth centers and settlement houses staged Punch and Judy shows, gave readings of classic children's literature, or showed morally uplifting films.

But by 1914 the public house, or pub, had been joined by other menacing means of corrupting youth, from the candy store to the cinema to the news kiosk. Juvenile protective agencies across Europe warned that sweets and gambling tempted children to steal and sell their textbooks for extra cash. Newspapers, along with allegedly corrupting youth, also fanned middle-class fears in sensationalist prose and photographs of adolescent gangs cruising and carousing in the streets of European cities from the Hooligans of London, to the Apaches in Paris, to the Platen in Vienna, and the Malaria in Turin.

Cinema also became a cause of concern. Cinema was a breathtaking development. Only little more than a decade passed between the first public showing of a moving picture in Paris 1895 to the construction of the first great cinema palaces. By 1910 cinema was at the center of leisure in all European societies and by 1914 some of the first great sociological studies of leisure concerning movie audiences had been carried out. These studies confirmed the strong presence of women at the movies, raising age-old concerns that first emerged in the eighteenth century about the moral impact of novel-reading on women.

The technology of modern cinema emerged first in the United States with the work of Thomas Alva Edison. In France, the Lumière brothers, Louis and Auguste (often called "the founding fathers of modern film"), worked in a Lyon factory that manufactured photographic equipment and supplies. They developed a combination movie camera and projector that, handheld, could be cranked by hand and could project movie images to several spectators. It was dubbed the *Cinematographe* and patented in February 1895. After showing films in their Lyon basement on December 28, 1895, the Lumières presented the first commercial and public exhibition of a projected motion picture to a paying public in the world's first "movie theater" in the *Salon Indien*, at the Grand Café on Paris' Boulevard des Capucines. The twenty-minute program included ten short films, including the famous fifty-second short *Arrivée d'un train en gare à La Ciotat* (*Arrival of a Train at La Ciotat*), which some sources reported was shocking to its first unsophisticated viewing audience who jumped out of the way.

The cinema was not a shock for long. Merely three years later, in 1898, the Lumières' catalog had over one thousand titles. Rivals in London and Berlin could not keep pace with them or another set of French brothers, the Pathé frères. From 1896 Charles and Emile Pathé would become the largest producers of films in the world. Around 1906 and 1907, their movies comprised over a third of the films shown on screens in the United States. Another French innovator, Georges Meliès, developed his own camera (a version of the Kinetograph), and set up Europe's first film studio (1897) pioneering artificial illumination within a greenhouse-like structure that featured both a glazed roof and a series of retractable blinds. In this imaginative environment he created the illusions that would become a staple of horrors films such as *Le Manoir du Diable (The Devil's Castle*, 1896) and his pioneering science-fiction film *Le Voyage dans la Lune* (*A Trip to the Moon*, 1902).

Until about 1906, cafés, along with carnivals, kinetoscope parlours, amusement arcades, and sideshows, were the main venue for movies. Only by 1906 did purpose-built cinemas become prominent in downtowns and increasingly in most outlying neighborhoods (see Figure 9.4). The growth in the following years up to the First World War was exponential: by 1914, Britain had 3,800 cinemas. London alone had almost five hundred and could seat four hundred thousand people, more than five times the capacity of music halls, which began to fall into the shadow of "the dream factory." By 1913, a quarter million Londoners went to the cinema every day and children often received two pennies pocket money: one for the ticket and the other for sweets. That working-class children had the money to go to the movies and buy candy indicated an improvement of living standards that contributed more generally to the expansion of commercialized leisure.[14] Some movie palaces were vast venues that hosted multiple forms of music, image, and festivity. The Hippodrome in Paris, "the biggest cinema in the world," opened on December 14, 1907, with a full orchestra; the opening-night audience watched eighteen short films, listened to choral singing, and witnessed a boxing match. By 1916, Russians had become dazzled

FIGURE 9.4 The Hippodrome Cinema in Paris, 1914. Courtesy of Wikimedia.

by the silver screen. The sprawling but soon-to-be swept-away empire had four thousand cinemas that screened five hundred new movies to more than 180 million customers that year. About 10 percent of the urban population (or 20 percent of the entire population) watched a movie every day.[15]

Audiences were far from entranced passive spectators. The succession of different types of entertainments and genres of film (from adventure to melodrama to commodity to horror) required a steadily shifting sensibility; the continual coming and going in the audience, and the live music accompaniment and sometimes narration also broke any fixed concentration. Only by the 1930s had a uniform sequence to film viewing become established. One Parisian journalist noted in October 1911:

> The public enter and leave in the middle of the show ... Our spectators tend to be people who go the cinema for an hour to experience diverse emotions and have their curiosity satisfied quickly. They love short dramas and pretty comedies. They appreciate the news of the week and films about distant lands, exotic tribes, and natural history.[16]

Working-class women found the cinema a liberator. Instead of spending Saturday alone at home while their husbands were at the café or pub, they now had an outside venue to frequent. Girls also went to the movies, although less often than boys, as they did not exercise as much control over their time and money. Migrant communities had their own theaters. The most nuanced picture of audiences in pre-First World War Europe comes from the pioneering dissertation written in 1913 by Emilie Altenloh. She studied the provincial city of Mannheim and found that spectators at its cinemas were indeed stratified, with the working class paying 10 *pfennings* and the local elite paying ten times that much for a box seat (they also showed up in evening dress as if going to the opera). In between sat the middle class of officers, engineers, and tradespeople. Altenloh also found that while working-class women and children attended the cinema regularly, working-class men who were members of the Social Democratic Party (SPD) or of trade unions typically "agreed with the conservative cinema reform movement, rejecting the cinema as an 'epidemic' and a 'scourge.'"[17] They looked instead to leisure and education clubs developed by the SPD to provide alternative cultural venues for their members.

In film and in literature a "fictionalist" turn occurred in the second half of the nineteenth century in which there was a greater acceptance of—and enthusiasm for—"the communal and persistent habitation of imaginary worlds."[18] We see this with the rise of science fiction and the detective genre. The development of mass-marketed fiction in the late nineteenth century along with the spread of movie theaters thrust into the center of popular culture stories connected to the emerging genres of modern fantasy whether about detectives, science fiction, or still undiscovered cultures and worlds in exotic places in the world's jungles and deserts. In literature, Sir Arthur Conan Doyle's detective-hero Sherlock Holmes and Marcel Allain and Pierre Souvestre's mesmerizing criminal Fantômas captivated the reading public in narratives that integrated science and logic with mystery and the supernatural. In 1913, Louis Feuillade created a series of silent films based on the character Fantômas that combined realism and fantasy. In novel and film, the arch-villain took readers and spectators into working-class neighborhoods, romanticizing these areas for bourgeois and worker alike.[19] These imaginative leaps of detection, adventure, and science fiction helped acclimatize their adherents to virtual reality long before the late twentieth century. At the end of the nineteenth century we see emerging the modern phenomena of fan-based communities following every step of their heroes, the most extreme example of which were Sherlock Holmes' "Baker Street Irregulars," although the letters to the editor of fantasy and detective magazines from the late nineteenth century are filled with other examples. The emergence of working-class hobbying, from gardening to photography to electronics, also overlapped with these literary and cinematic passions.

SPORT, LEISURE, AND NATIONALISM

Modern sport emerged in the first capitalist nation, Britain, and drew upon the same economic and moral imperatives. Sport was rule- and contest-based, with clear means of determining winners and losers. The foundations of both modern industry and modern sport were in place in England by the 1770s. There, the modern rules of horse racing were established in 1750, of boxing in 1743, and of cricket in 1744. Tony Collins argues that the creation of "commonly agreed, national, written laws governing the playing of sport" emerged at this time as a corollary to the commercialization of sport.[20] For the first time, we see attempts to attract a paying public to sporting events as a means to generate profit out of what had often before been informal, community-based pastimes. Extravagant sporting events designed to attract paying spectators were all the more seductive due to the presence of gambling, which riveted attention more than the theater or the fair. By 1815, most newspapers followed sporting events. Weekly and monthly sporting journals also emerged and competed with each other, such as *Bells Life* (1822), whose great rival, *The Field*, was founded in 1853. As sport gained a growing public audience, aristocratic patrons who had pioneered the commercialization of sport withdrew, and sporting entrepreneurs, often publicans, rose to prominence.

While the commercialization of sport offered many opportunities for working-class men and women to be spectators, playing sports became less common, in part due to the rise of amateurism in elite English schools. Amateurism became an important cultural value, taught through sport, in which the key was not to win but to uphold a high moral code of disinterested accomplishment and friendly competition. Sport was considered a means of socialization, teaching future leaders how to rule enterprises and the empire after graduation. The value placed on amateurism provided a justification for the exclusion of the working-class from sporting competitions. Along with the Football Association (FA, est. 1863) the associations governing the sports of rowing (1861), track and field (The Amateur Athletic Club, 1866), and cricket (administered since the late eighteenth century by Marylebone Cricket Club) excluded tradesmen, artisans, laborers, and working mechanics. However, professionalization opened up opportunities for working-class men to compete. In the first decade of the FA finals (1872–85), only public-school alumni played, but after the legalization of professionals in 1885 no club composed of middle-class members ever again appeared in an FA Cup (see Figure 9.5).[21] Thus, in little over a decade, the sport went from being a playful pastime of middle-class boys and young men to a working-class sport. With professionalization, the style of play changed, as the sport became an avenue of fame and upward social mobility. Professionalization also contributed to making football a mass spectator sport; whereas 3,500 spectators viewed the 1876 FA Cup between the Wanderers and the Old Etonians, the 1901 FA Championship between Tottenham Hotspur and Sheffield United drew a crowd of 114,815 to the Crystal Palace stadium.[22] As with the pub, the music hall, and the cinema, the sporting field was free of the restrictions of the factory and provided a sense of place and community in the heart of working-class neighborhoods, even if stadiums were increasingly enclosed and segmented in terms of space and time. Nonetheless, audiences bonded and displayed some of the collective effervescence once associated with village life at carnival. By 1900, daily newspapers of almost every large town primed the fans for the big game that was often celebrated or mourned in a pub late Saturday night.

France became the center of the sport of bicycling and a pioneer in athletic centralization. France's much larger territory and much slower rate of agricultural modernization and industrialization resulted in a much more dispersed population which found cycling an ideal way to expand their horizons. The precocious bureaucratization of France after 1600 was turned to good use as French newspapers and sporting personalities helped create the modern media and organizational structure of world sport. Although first developed in Britain, as early as the 1860s France had become the world leader in the recently invented bicycle. The first cycling road race was Paris to Rouen in 1869 subsidized by the periodical *Le Vélocipède Illustré*. The Franco-Prussian War (1870–1) and Paris Commune (1871) stalled growth of the sport, but by the 1890s, with more efficient two-wheelers, the Paris–Brest–Paris race became a major annual event. During this same decade the French staged a high-profile running event, the Paris–Belfort run, then the first ever motorcar race from Paris to Rouen, and finally the Paris marathon. Two newspapers played a key role in organizing and marketing these events: *Le Vélo* and *L'Auto-vélo* (later shorted to *L'Auto*). It was under this format that the latter paper, under the editorship of Henri Desgrange, initiated the Tour de France in 1903.[23] Even in its initial year, one hundred thousand people watched in person and millions more followed in the newspapers. By the end of the decade, the Italians had created their equivalent with the Gia d'Italia.

The founder of the Tour de France, Desgrange, promoted cycling as a means of producing model workers due to the self-discipline needed to train during the week for

FIGURE 9.5 Newcastle United v. Sunderland, c. 1904. Photo: Bob Thomas / Popperfoto / Getty Images.

the weekend's race. In a fictive letter to a cyclist-in-training, Desgranges wrote: "No preoccupations, no enemies, no passing love affairs, the week spent quietly waiting for Sunday, and Sunday's victory filing the following week. Your boss, whom I saw, is most pleased with you."[24] However, while he saw cycling as a means of moral improvement, he worried that it could also create a sense of independence, not to mention financial success, which would cause working-class athletes to move beyond their station in society. As Christopher Thompson has shown, half of the racers who competed in the Tour de France between 1909 and 1939 had backgrounds as manual laborers, while the other half were clerks or worked in low-level service jobs.[25] Racing paid much better than these positions, and prize money could be used to supplement ordinary wages or to start a small business.

Pierre de Coubertin and Jules Rimet were the founders, respectively, of the modern Olympics Games (1896) and the International Governing Body of Football (FIFA, 1904). An aristocrat, de Coubertin resolutely followed the code of the amateur and believed the revival of the sporting contests that had helped create western civilization would regenerate the modern European elite, in particular the French elite that he thought particularly prone to degeneration. Ironically, even at the Olympics prior to the 1920s, working-class Irish Americans and Native Americans were standouts. At the 1908 London Games, the tension between an elite culture of amateurism and a reality of successful working-class athletes came to a head at the start of the games, when the Irish American athlete who carried the American flag refused to drop Old Glory in honor of the British king, and at the end of the marathon when British officials helped a disoriented and dehydrated Italian runner over the finish line and the Americans protested (successfully) that the unaided John Joseph "Johnny" Hayes, one of ten members of the Irish American Athletic Club at the games, was the rightful winner.[26]

Sport had been intimately connected to politics in central and eastern Europe from the French Revolution and Napoleonic eras, as new or aspiring nations wished to erase the stigma of defeat at the hands of the French. The turner movement started in Germany by Friedrich Ludwig ("Father") Jahn after the Napoleonic conquest of the German states. Drawing on the work of earlier German gymnastic instructors and adding his own ideas, Jahn outline twenty-nine separate exercises, including some drawn from the Greek pentathlon and a wide range of others that he invented, ranging from climbing, dancing, and jumping to balancing, bathing, fasting, lifting, pulling, and writing. The goal was to mold a strong character centered on self-control. After opening the first *Turnplatz*, or open-air gymnasium, in Berlin in 1811, Jahn supervised their rapid spread. Young gymnasts were taught to regard themselves as members of a kind of guild for the emancipation of their fatherland. After the revolution of 1848 the Turner movement split between a conservative wing following Jahnian nationalism and a working-class offshoot never fully tied to the German SDP (founded 1863). By 1900 working-class Turners numbered 37,000 and by 1910, 153,000. Both wings of this immensely popular sporting movement agreed that English sports were too work-oriented and focused unduly on competition and records. The German Turners would later reject Courbertin's call to join the Olympic Games. Even at the end of the nineteenth century, Turner remained the primary organized athletic movement in Germany (with over one million members), as opposed to the emergent game of soccer (eighty-two thousand) that held its first German championships only in 1903.

In Scandinavia, Sweden's Per Henrik Ling created a northern variant on the Turner movement following the wars with Russia in the early nineteenth century (the Finnish

War, 1808–9). In Ling's case, more attention was paid to the health benefits of exercise than national unification. The Turner movement spread across eastern Europe in part because its potent synthesis of recreation, sport, and nationalism appealed to various ethnicities and national groups that, in turn, wanted their own nations, and often in opposition to the domination of the German-speaking Austrian Empire. When the Swedish Martina Bergman Osterberg founded the first college for female physical educators in England in 1892, she explained the need for such education as being "to accelerate the progress of the race."[27] Those seeking to improve the health of the working classes championed Swedish gymnastics. In the early twentieth century, the Rowntree factory sponsored lessons in gymnastics and swimming for its female employees. Unlike earlier forms of leisure that occurred spontaneously at the workplace, swimming and gymnastics lessons were held after work hours, and were "orderly and disciplined and directed to consciously utilitarian ends," that is, the future health of the English working classes.[28]

Germany and Russia's emergence as industrial powers late in the century was not accompanied by any vital new innovations in leisure and recreation. Instead, they largely borrowed from the western pace setters. However, Germany elaborated and developed the association between leisure and the nation-state, already pioneered in France and Great Britain. In Germany, universal male conscription often facilitated learning to play musical instruments, which helped diffuse music and choral societies across the new nation. After unification Germans often promoted the construction of national monuments through subscription. These monuments became sites for festivals and celebrations and were highly successful in instilling national consciousness. The SPD and trade unions organized festivals for the working classes, including May Day, the commemoration of the revolution of 1848, and the death of Ferdinand Lassalle, founder of German Social Democracy. These festivals were carnivalesque, in which working-class men and women dressed up in costumes and masks, danced, drank, and ate to excess, "notwithstanding the panoply of measures introduced to prevent them doing so."[29]

Between 1900 and 1914 reflections upon the status of industrial society and the consequences of the emergence of leisure became common. Ernest Engel, a statistician in the government of Saxony, hoped for a smooth and gradual augmentation in incomes, fearing that if income rose too rapidly then workers would be prone to spend it on drink. This had been the case in Belgium in the 1850s.[30] Indeed, many agreed that higher wages were worth little if drink and tobacco consumption went up. On the eve of the First World War, Karl Oldenberg worried that affluence had brought in its train the civilizational diseases of drink and tobacco and that such new desires had eroded customs. But a more optimistic intellectual trend argued that consumption played a big role in raising the level of civilization. Innovative studies of consumption now provided a benchmark for the evolving nature of leisure and recreation and showed that while previously most spending had been on food, by 1900 this was not the case, and showed that drink did not cause poverty. In his *Principles of Economics* (1890), Alfred Marshall argued that leisure was "used less and less as an opportunity for mere stagnation … there is a growing desire for those amusements, such as athletic games and travelling, which develop activities, rather than indulge any sensuous craving."[31] Marshall was optimistic that leisure and consumerism were a means of improving the human condition.

With the outbreak of the First World War, all nations strove to maximize efficiency of both human and industrial capital, and recognized that leisure and rest were vital to keep workforces at peak capacity. The academic study of fatigue and exhaustion, as well as the philanthropic and moralistic impulse for recreation, leisure, and consumption, was now viewed as a means to keep the home workers and battlefront soldiers in peak condition. As a result, investment in public recreation grew during the First World War for women, who faced long working hours. As Tony Collins noted concerning Great Britain and France, "football became a feature of working life for thousands of women."[32]

The war altered leisure patterns for women, who entered the industrial workforce in unprecedented, huge numbers. With higher wages and less parental or spousal supervision, women could patronize pubs and cafés, music halls, and cabarets, where they were just as likely as men to drink. For example, in Paris the number of women arrested for public drunkenness jumped from 10 percent of the total brought before the police courts just before the outbreak of war in the summer of 1914, to 20 percent within the first months of the conflict. As a Prefecture of Police report noted, as women went into better paying industrial jobs related to the war effort, they ceased to engage in prostitution and engaged in behavior previously deemed to be "masculine."[33]

During the war, shoppers' leagues proliferated across Europe, but were especially prominent in central Europe due to the British blockade. Within four months of the war's start the German government created a national committee for consumer interests representing seven million households and over a quarter of the population. Similar organizations emerged in Vienna, Budapest, and Prague in the Austro-Hungarian Empire. The passion for organization within the Reich also saw the inclusion of cooperatives and housewives' organizations with roots in both the churches and political parties. Ultimately Germany and the Central Powers lost the war not only due the failure of its spring 1918 offensive and growing presence of American forces but also by losing the battle of the home front. Rather than unifying the nation, the regime's rationing system exacerbated class and status tensions: impoverished consumers attacked soldier's wives and those with few if any children resented mothers with many children for "unfair" special allowances.[34]

As revolution became both more palpable and possible as the war dragged on, governments promised their workers a better life after all the sacrifices: the eight-hour day was established across most of Europe. In some cases, as in the electrical plant in Dortmund, Germany, establishing an eight-hour day allowed for the hiring of demobilized soldiers without firing workers already in place.[35] The decision to shorten the working day without reducing wages was a response to widespread concerns that the "radical working-class movement" might take over control of factories, following the example of the Russian revolutionaries in 1917.[36] Government observers of the eight-hour day often expressed ambivalence, but leisure spending essentially doubled by 1935, becoming a source of economic growth.

The creation of the League of Nations brought in its train a number of international organizations, especially the International Labour Organization (ILO), dedicated to the betterment of the working classes of the world. The ILO saw the enactment of eight-hour days and vacations as a way to improve the leisure of the working class. Across the interwar era, it helped create documentation for the study of the history of leisure with such projects as a 1934 survey on popular music and song and popular arts carried out jointly with the Institute for Intellectual Cooperation. Moreover, by 1919 investigators were no longer concerned exclusively with the share of workers' expenditure on food, lodging, and recreation but with establishing a basic consumption norm—a standard of living index.[37] In essence, by 1919 government bureaucrats and scholars across Europe realized that the working class was moving from an age of subsistence into an age of consumerism.

Finally, a new media emerged at the end of the war, radio. Coming out of the tinkering of hobbyists, the radio became a communication technology that was one of the necessities of war. On September 6, 1920, the first radio broadcast was a prize fight in the United States, and on July 2, 1921, all of France filled public squares and cafés to hear the first "simulcast" of a boxing match between French champion Georges Carpentier and the American Jack Dempsey. Three hundred thousand people around the world heard the fight as it unfolded.[38] This world championship prizefight, a transatlantic broadcast, united the French and American public almost as intimately as a match in a public square in the early nineteenth century, as each punch and each parry was immediately communicated (commercialized) and bodies writhed in grotesque pain and heroic triumph.

During the age of industry, unprecedented attempts were made to isolate leisure into specific venues and times of day, and to define it as the opposite to work. Leisure thus emerged as the opposite of work in both mental and physical space. As employers strove to focus the attention of their workers fully on the job, pent-up urges and desires had to be repressed. But once off the job the worker felt a sense of liberation and a conviction that his time was his own, which was equally unprecedented. Leisure then became more than ever a world apart where a person could do and think as they pleased, and increasingly workers believed they deserved this time and space. Daydreams, desires, and fantasies that built up during the workday were unleashed after work, whether at a bar, a sporting event, or while reading or watching a film. Leisure became the time to be and make one's self.

A new labor–leisure dialectic developed, especially in sport, where discipline and competition became sources of pleasure. As work time decreased and pay rose, workers had a growing number of ways to fulfil their fantasies. At the same time, entrepreneurs used their imaginations to create new industries such as the modern publishing of music or the cinema, each based upon fulfilling the pent-up desires and imaginations of worker after the end of their labors. Thus leisure was not only "time off," but it also provided inspiration to create new industries that would monetize the imagination. The commodification of leisure and many of its contemporary aspects have their roots in the nineteenth-century imagination. We see this with the fans of Sherlock Holmes or other detective and fantasy figures, who created clubs where they could play at being their heroes—an early form of "virtual" reality. In essence, the modern industrial world modernized and industrialized the long-standing tension and productive interplay between laborious toil and carnivalesque release.

NOTES

Introduction

1 Chapter One.
2 Robert C. Allen, *The British Industrial Revolution in Global Perspective* (Cambridge: Cambridge University Press, 2009), 212–13.
3 John Hinshaw and Peter N. Stearns, *Industrialization in the Modern World: From the Industrial Revolution to the Internet*, vol. 2: R–Z (Santa Barbara, CA: ABC-CLIO, 2014), 227.
4 Lucien Febvre, "History and Psychology," in *A New Kind of History from the Writings of Lucien Febvre*, ed. Peter Burke, trans. K. Folca (New York, NY: Harper & Row, 1973), 9.
5 Clifford Geertz, *The Interpretation of Cultures: Selected Essays* (New York, NY: Basic Books, 1973), 5.
6 Jay Winter, "Preface: Labour History at War," *Labour History* 106 (May 2014): iii. See also Ann Curthoys, "Labour History and Cultural Studies," *Labour History* 67 (November 1994): 12–22.
7 William H. Sewell, Jr., *Work and Revolution in France: The Language of Labor from the Old Regime to 1848* (Cambridge: Cambridge University Press, 1980); Joan Wallach Scott, *Gender and the Politics of History* (New York, NY: Columbia University Press, 1988).
8 Dick Geary, "Labour History, the 'Linguistic Turn' and Postmodernism," *Contemporary European History* 9, no. 3 (2000): 454.
9 C. Knick Harley, "British and European Industrialization," in *The Cambridge History of Capitalism*, vol. 1: *The Rise of Capitalism from Ancient Origins to 1848*, eds. Larry Neal and Jeffrey G. Williamson (Cambridge: Cambridge University Press, 2014), 497.
10 David S. Landes, *The Unbound Prometheus: Technological Change and Industrial Development in Western Europe from 1750 to the Present* (Cambridge: Cambridge University Press, 1972), 84.
11 Harley, "British and European Industrialization," 506.
12 Joseph Kirwan, *A Descriptive and Historical Account of the Liverpool and Manchester Railway, from its First Projection to the Present Time: Containing All the Facts and Information that have Yet Appeared on the Subject, with Numerous Interesting and Curious Original Details, Estimates of Expenses, &c. &c.* (Glasgow: W. R. M'Phun, 1831), 1.
13 Theodore S. Hamerow, *The Birth of a New Europe: State and Society in the Nineteenth Century* (Chapel Hill: University of North Carolina Press, 1983), 19.
14 Laura S. Strumingher, *Women and the Making of the Working Class: Lyon 1830–1870* (Montreal: Eden Press, 1979), 60.
15 Christopher Johnson, "Economic Change and Artisan Discontent: The Tailors' History, 1800–1848," in *Revolution and Reaction: 1848 and the Second French Republic*, ed. Roger Price (London: Croom Helm, 1975), 87–114.
16 Christopher Johnson, "Patterns of Proletarianization: Parisian Tailors and Lodève Woolen Workers," in *Consciousness and Class Experience in Nineteenth-Century Europe*, ed. John Merriman (New York, NY: Holmes & Meier, 1979), 69.

17 Nancy L. Green, "The Sweatshop as Workplace and Metaphor," in *Ready-to-Wear and Ready-to-Work: A Century of Industry and Immigrants in Paris and New York* (Durham, NC: Duke University Press, 1997), 138.
18 Deborah Simonton, *A History of Women's Work: 1700 to the Present* (London: Routledge, 1998), 135.
19 Kathleen Canning, *Languages of Labor and Gender: Female Factory Work in Germany, 1850–1914* (Ann Arbor: University of Michigan Press, 1996), 42–3.
20 Marilyn J. Boxer, "Women in Industrial Homework: The Flowermakers of Paris in the Belle Epoque," *French Historical Studies* 12, no. 3 (March 1982): 407, 409.
21 Robert C. Allen, *The Industrial Revolution: A Very Short Introduction* (Oxford: Oxford University Press, 2017), 5–7.
22 Jeff Horn, Leonard N. Rosenband, and Merritt Roe Smith, "Introduction," in Jeff Horn, Leonard N. Rosenband, and Merritt Roe Smith, eds., *Reconceptualizing the Industrial Revolution* (Cambridge, MA: MIT Press, 2010), 23–4.
23 "By the Frameworck Knitters. A Declaration," in *Writings of the Luddites*, ed. Kevin Binfield (Baltimore, MD: Johns Hopkins University Press, 2004), 89.
24 Maxine Berg, *The Machinery Question and the Making of Political Economy, 1815–1848* (Cambridge: Cambridge University Press, 1982), 2.
25 Jonathan Sperber, *The European Revolutions, 1848–1851* (Cambridge: Cambridge University Press), 5.
26 Harley, "British and European Industrialization," 493.
27 Ibid., 503.
28 Landes, *The Unbound Prometheus*, 188.
29 Friedrich Engels, *The Condition of the Working-Class in England in 1844*, trans. Florence Kelley Wischnewetzky (London: Swan Sonnenschein & Co., 1892), 27.
30 *Réflexions d'un ouvrier tailleur, sur la Misère des Ouvriers en général, la durée des journées de travail, le taux des salaires, les rapports actuellement établis entre les Ouvriers et les Maîtres d'ateliers, la nécessité des associations d'ouvriers comme moyen d'améliorer leur condition* (Lyon: Imprimerie J. Perret, n.d.), 2.
31 Friedrich Engels, "Draft of a Communist Confession of Faith" [1847] in Karl Marx and Friedrich Engels, *The Communist Manifesto*, ed. Jeffrey C. Isaac (New Haven, CT: Yale University Press, 2012), 49.
32 Jonathan Earle, "Wage Slavery," in *Slavery in the United States: A Social, Political, and Historical Encyclopedia*, ed. Junius P. Rodriguez, 2 vols. (Santa Barbara, CA: ABC-CLIO, 2007), 1, 500.
33 Emma Rothschild, "Political Economy," in *The Cambridge History of Nineteenth-Century Political Thought*, eds. Gareth Stedman Jones and Gregory Claeys (Cambridge: Cambridge University Press, 2011), 750.
34 Chapter One.
35 Chapter Two.
36 Harley, "Industrialization in Britain and Europe," 507.
37 Eric Dorn Brose, "The Political Economy of Early Industrialization in German Europe, 1800–1840," in *Reconceptualizing the Industrial Revolution*, eds. Horn, Rosenband, and Smith, 108.
38 Eric J. Hobsbawm, *Industry and Empire from 1750 to the Present Day: The Birth of the Industrial Revolution*, rev. ed. by Chris Wrigley (New York, NY: The New Press, 1999), 102.
39 Jean-Antoine Chaptal, *De l'industrie française* (1819), 2:29 quoted in Anna Bezanson, "The Early Use of the Term Industrial Revolution," *Quarterly Journal of Economics* 36, no. 2 (1922): 346.

40 Bezanson, "The Early Use of the Term Industrial Revolution," 347.
41 Arnold Toynbee, *Lectures on the Industrial Revolution of the 18th Century in England. Popular Addresses, Notes and Other Fragments* (New York, NY: The Humboldt Publishing Co., n.d. [1884]), 28.
42 Daniel C. S. Wilson, "Arnold Toynbee and the Industrial Revolution: The Science of History, Political Economy and the Machine Past," *History & Memory* 26, no. 2 (2014): 144–5.

Chapter One

1 Louis De Jaucourt, "Oisiveté," in *Encyclopédie, ou dictionnaire raisonné des sciences, des arts et des métiers, etc.*, eds. Denis Diderot and Jean le Rond d'Alembert, vol. 11 (1765), 445–6. University of Chicago: ARTFL Encyclopédie Project (Spring 2016 Edition), Robert Morrissey and Glenn Roe (eds), http://encyclopedie.uchicago.edu (accessed July 18, 2017).
2 Louis Chevalier, *Laboring Classes and Dangerous Classes in Paris During the First Half of the Nineteenth Century*, trans. Frank Jellinek (New York, NY: Howard Fertig, 1973).
3 Jean-Baptiste Say, *Traité d'économie politique, ou simple exposition de la manière dont se forment, se distribuent, et se consomment les richesses*, 2 vols. (Paris: De l'Imprimerie de Crapelet, 1803), 1: xliii.
4 Clarisse Vigoureux, *Parole de providence* (Paris: Bossange père, 1834), 57–8.
5 Kenneth Pomeranz, *The Great Divergence: China, Europe, and the Making of the Modern World Economy* (Princeton, NJ: Princeton University Press, 2000); Robert C. Allen, *The British Industrial Revolution in Global Perspective* (Cambridge: Cambridge University Press, 2009).
6 Prasannan Parthasarathi, *Why Europe Grew Rich and Asia Did Not: Global Economic Divergence 1600–1850* (New York, NY: Cambridge University Press, 2011).
7 Jeff Horn, Leonard N. Rosenband, and Merritt Roe Smith, eds., *Reconceptualizing the Industrial Revolution* (Cambridge, MA: MIT Press, 2010).
8 Karl Polanyi, *The Great Transformation* (New York, NY: Farrar & Rinehart, 1944); Pomeranz, *The Great Divergence*.
9 Dipesh Chakrabarty, *Provincializing Europe: Postcolonial Thought and Historical Difference* (Princeton, NJ: Princeton University Press, 2000): Allen, *The British Industrial Revolution*.
10 Andrew Ure, *Philosophy of Manufactures; or, An Exposition of the Scientific, Moral, and Commercial Economy of the Factory System in Great Britain* (London: Charles Knight, 1835), x.
11 Edward Baines, *History of the Cotton Manufacture in Great Britain* (London: H. Fisher, R. Fisher and P. Jackson, 1835).
12 Charles Babbage, *Memoir of the Life and Labours of the Late Charles Babbage* (1880; Cambridge, MA: MIT Press, 1988), 194, quoted in Simon Schaffer, "Babbage's Intelligence: Calculating Engines and the Factory System," *Critical Inquiry* 21, no. 1 (1994): 209; Adolphe Blanqui, *Histoire de l'économie politique en Europe depuis les anciens jusqu'à nos jours*, 2 vols. (Paris: Guillaumin, 1837), 2:399.
13 Jules Michelet, *Le Peuple* (Geneva: G Fallot, 1846), 33, 29, 32, 31, 33.
14 Denis Poulot, *Le sublime, ou Le travailleur comme il est en 1870, et ce qu'il peut être: Question sociale* (Paris: Librairie internationale, 1870).
15 Sheila Ogilvie and Markus German, eds., *European Proto-industrialization* (Cambridge: Cambridge University Press, 1996); David Howell, "Proto-industrial Origins of Japanese Capitalism," *The Journal of Asian Studies* 51, no. 2 (1992): 269–86.

16 J. C. L. Simonde de Sismondi, *Études sur l'économie politique*, 2 vols. (Paris: Treuttel et Würtz, 1837), 1:41.

17 Etienne Cabet, *Propagande communiste, Ou questions à discuter et à soutenir ou à écarter* (Paris: Prévôt, 1842), 2. Emphasis in original.

18 Charles F. Sabel and Jonathan Zeitlin, "Historical Alternatives to Mass Production: Politics, Markets, and Technology in Nineteenth-Century Industrialization," *Past & Present* 108 (August 1985): 163.

19 Charles F. Sabel and Jonathan Zeitlin, eds., *World of Possibilities: Flexibility and Mass Production in Western Industrialization* (Cambridge: Cambridge University Press, 1997).

20 Alain Cottereau, "La désincorporation des métiers et leur transformation en publics intermédiaires: Lyon et Elbeuf 1790–1814," in *La France, malade du corporatisme? XVIIIe–XXe siècles*, eds. Steven L. Kaplan and Philippe Minard (Paris: Belin, 2004).

21 Jean-François Géraud, "Des habitations-sucreries aux usines sucrières: La 'mise en sucre' de l'île Bourbon (1783–1848)" (unpublished PhD thesis, Université de La Réunion, 2002), p. 283.

22 See, for example, "Les noirs, M., Dupin et sa statistique: Moyenne de la vie du nègre et de l'ouvrier anglais," *L'Atelier* (Paris), May 1845, 127.

23 François Jarrige, *Au temps des "tueuses de bras": Les bris de machines à l'aube de l'ère industrielle* (Rennes: Presses Universitaires de Rennes, 2009).

24 Claude Henri de Rouvroy, comte de Saint-Simon, *Opinions littéraires, philosophiques et industrielles* (Paris: Bossange père, 1825), epigram on title page.

25 Claude Henri de Rouvroy, comte de Saint-Simon, *Nouveau Christianisme, dialogues entre un conservateur et un novateur: Premier dialogue* (Paris: Bossange père, 1825), 66.

26 Friedrich List, *The National System of Political Economy*, trans. Sampson S. Lloyd (1841; Kitchener, ON: Batoche, 2001).

27 Pierre-Édouard Lemontey, "Influence morale de la division du travail," *Raison, folie, chacun son mot, petit cours de morale mis à la portée des vieux enfans* dans *Œuvres de P.E. Lemontey*, 7 vols. (1801; Paris: A. Sautelet et Co., 1829), 1:201.

28 "L'Echo de la fabrique," *Journal industriel de Lyon et du département du Rhone* 17 (19 February 1832): 5.

29 Karl Marx and Friedrich Engels, *Manifesto of the Communist Party* (1848), in Marx and Engels, *Selected Works*, trans. Samuel Moore with Friedrich Engels, 3 vols. (Moscow: Progress Publishers, 1969), 1:18.

30 Alessandro Stanziani, *Bondage: Labor and Rights in Eurasia from the Sixteenth to the Early Twentieth Centuries* (New York, NY: Berghan, 2014), 72.

31 Caroline Oudin-Bastide and Philippe Steiner, *Calcul et morale: Coûts de l'esclavage et valeur de l'émancipation (XVIIIe–XIXe siècle)* (Paris: Albin Michel, 2015).

32 David Northrup, *Indentured Labor in the Age of Imperialism, 1834–1922* (Cambridge: Cambridge University Press, 1995).

33 Paul Leroy-Beaulieu, *Traité théorique et pratique d'économique politique*, 6th ed., 2 vols. (1890; Paris: Libraire Félix Alcan, 1914), 1:108, 738.

34 Charles Fourier, *Théorie des quatre mouvemens et des destinées générales: Prospectus et annonce de la découverte* in *Œuvres complètes de Ch. Fourier*, 2nd ed., 6 vols. (Paris: Société pour la propagation et pour la réalisation de la théorie de Fourier, 1841–5), 1:289.

35 Charles Fourier, *Théorie de l'unité universelle,* in Fourier, *Œuvres complètes de Ch. Fourier*, vol. 2, 180–1.

36 Victor Considerant, *Contre M.Arago: Réclamation adressée à la Chambre des députés* (Paris: Au Bureau de la Phalange, 1840), 12. Emphasis in original.

37 Charles Fourier, *L'Association et le travail attrayant* (Paris: Librairie de la bibliothèque démocratique, 1873).
38 Jules Lechevalier, *Études sur la science sociale* (Paris: Eugène Renduel, 1832), 65.
39 Richard Sennett, *The Craftsman* (New Haven, CT: Yale University Press, 2008).
40 Pierre Charnier (1828), quoted in Ludovic Frobert and George Sheridan, *Le solitaire du ravin: Pierre Charnier (1795–1857), prud'homme tisseur et canut* (Lyon: ENS-Éditions, 2014), 84.
41 Michelet, *Le Peuple*, 20. Emphasis in original.
42 Karl Marx, *The Eighteenth Brumaire of Louis Bonaparte*, trans. Daniel de Leon, 3rd ed. (Chicago, IL: Charles H. Kerr & Company, 1913), 145.
43 François Vatin, *Le travail: Economie et physique (1780–1830)* (Paris: Presses universitaires de France, 1993).
44 Philippe Lefebvre, *L'invention de la grande entreprise: Travail, hiérarchie, marché (France, fin XVIIIe–début XXe siècle)* (Paris: Presses universitaires de France, 2003).
45 Alain Cottereau, "Sens du juste et usages du droit du travail: Une évolution contrastée entre la France et la Grande-Bretagne au XIXe siècle," *Revue d'histoire du XIXe siècle*, 33 (Dec. 2006), 105.
46 Anson Rabinbach, *The Human Motor: Energy, Fatigue, and the Origins of Modernity* (New York, NY: Basic Books, 1990); Peter-Paul Bänziger and Mischa Suter, eds., *Histories of Productivity: Genealogical Perspectives on the Body and Modern Economy* (London: Routledge, 2016).

Chapter Two

1 Gustave Flaubert, *Madame Bovary: Provincial Ways*, trans. Eleanor Marx-Aveling. February 25, 2006. Project Gutenberg. http://www.gutenberg.org/2/4/1/2413/ (accessed January 23, 2018).
2 Jean-Pierre Chaline, "The Cotton Manufacturer in Normandy and England during the Nineteenth Century," *Textile History* 17, no. 1 (1986): 19–26.
3 John H. Clapham, *The Economic Development of France and Germany, 1815–1914*, 4th ed. (Cambridge: Cambridge University Press, 1968).
4 Chaline, "The Cotton Manufacturer," 19.
5 Michelle Facos, *An Introduction to Nineteenth-Century Art* (New York, NY: Routledge, 2011), 228–9.
6 Linda Nochlin, "The Image of the Working Woman," in *Representing Women* (New York, NY: Thames and Hudson, 1999), 83.
7 Ibid, 85.
8 Judith G. Coffin, *The Politics of Women's Work: The Paris Garment Trades, 1750–1915* (Princeton, NJ: Princeton University Press, 1996).
9 Nochlin, "The Image of the Working Woman," 81.
10 Facos, *An Introduction*, 219.
11 According to the 1896 census 87 percent of workers in cloth and clothing and half of textile workers were women. Françoise Battagliola, *Histoire du travail des femmes* (Paris: Éditions de la Découverte, 2000), 25. On the "problem" of the woman worker in the nineteenth century, see Joan Wallach Scott, "The Woman Worker," in *A History of Women in the West: Emerging Feminism from Revolution to World War*, eds. Geneviève Fraisse and Michelle Perrot (Cambridge, MA: Harvard University Press, 1993): 399–426 and Joan Wallach Scott, *Gender and the Politics of History* (New York, NY: Columbia University Press, 1988).

12 Tim Barringer, *Men at Work: Art and Labour in Victorian Britain* (New Haven, CT: Yale University Press, 2005), 129.
13 Nochlin, "The Image of the Working Woman," 94.
14 Martin A. Danahay, *Gender at Work in Victorian Culture: Literature, Art and Masculinity* (Burlington, VT: Ashgate, 2005), 1.
15 Madeleine Reberioux, *Images du travail: Peintures et dessins des collections françaises* (Paris: Éditions de la Réunion des musées nationaux, 1985), 17.
16 Danahay, *Gender at Work*, 2.
17 Ibid., 62.
18 Barringer, *Men at Work*, 26.
19 The Gentle Author, "Wheatley's Cries of London," *Spitalfields Life*, January 26, 2011. http://spitalfieldslife.com/2011/01/26/wheatleys-cries-of-london/ (accessed July 20, 2017).
20 The Gentle Author, "The Lost Cries of London: Reclaiming the Street Trader's Devalued Tradition," *The Guardian*, November 24, 2015. https://www.theguardian.com/cities/2015/nov/24/lost-cries-of-london-liberty-vagabonds-street-theatre (accessed July 20, 2017); The Gentle Author, "The Cries of London," *Discovering Literature: Romantics and Victorians*, May 15, 2014. https://www.bl.uk/romantics-and-victorians/articles/the-cries-of-london (accessed July 20, 2017).
21 Vincent Milliot, *"Les Cris de Paris," ou le peuple travesti: Les représentations des petits métiers parisiens (XVIe–XVIIIe siècles)* (Paris: Publications de la Sorbonne, 1995), 133.
22 Anne Higonnet, "Real Fashion: Clothes Unmake the Working Woman," in *Spectacles of Realism: Body, Gender, Genre*, eds. Margaret Cohen and Christopher Prendergast (Minneapolis: University of Minnesota Press, 1995), 137–62; Milliot, *"Les Cris de Paris."*
23 See Luc Sante, *The Other Paris* (New York, NY: Farrar, Straus and Giroux, 2015) for a fascinating and generously illustrated exploration of working-class Paris.
24 Aimée Boutin, *City of Noise: Sound and Nineteenth-Century Paris* (Urbana: University of Illinois Press, 2016).
25 Charlotte Denoël, "Les cris de Paris," *Histoire par l'image*, January 2007. http://www.histoire-image.org/etudes/cris-paris (accessed July 25, 2016).
26 Milliot, *"Les Cris de Paris,"* 19.
27 Robert Massin, *Les Cris de la ville: Commerces ambulants et petits métiers de la rue* (Paris: Gallimard, 1978), 126.
28 Ibid., 161.
29 Boutin, *City of Noise*, 35–60.
30 *Elle coud, elle court, la grisette!* Maison de Balzac, October 14, 2011–January 15, 2012 (Paris: Paris Musées, 2011). Exhibition catalogue. See also Victoria E. Thompson, *The Virtuous Marketplace: Women and Men, Money and Politics in Paris 1840–1870* (Baltimore, MD: Johns Hopkins University Press, 2000), 19–27, and Jennifer Jones, *Sexing la Mode: Gender, Fashion and Commercial Culture in Old Regime France* (Oxford: Berg, 2004).
31 Beatrice Farwell, *The Charged Image: French Lithographic Caricature, 1816–1848* (Santa Barbara, CA: Santa Barbara Museum of Art, 1989), 111.
32 A reviewer of the English translation of Balzac's *Scenes of Parisian Life* comments on the usefulness of Balzac's characterization of the *grisette*, perceived internationally as a fixture of the Parisian landscape: *The London and Paris Observer or Weekly Chronicle of Literature, Science, and the Fine Arts*, vol. 10 (Paris: A and W. Galignani, 1834), 728.
33 There may have been more in the original series, but, "the most complete editions still in existence contain no more than 47 plates," according to Loÿs Delteil, *Manuel de l'amateur d'estampes du XIXe et du XXe siècle (1801–1924)*, 4 vols. (Paris: Dorbon-Aîné, 1925), 1:30.

34 Claire Haru Crowston, *Fabricating Women: The Seamstresses of Old Regime France (1675–1791)* (Durham, NC: Duke University Press, 2001); Jones, *Sexing la Mode*.
35 Crowston, *Fabricating Women*, 23–73.
36 Higonnet, "Real Fashion," 144–5.
37 Nina Kushner, *Erotic Exchanges: The World of Elite Prostitution in Eighteenth-Century Paris* (Ithaca, NY: Cornell University Press, 2013), 67.
38 Valerie Steele, *The Corset: A Cultural History* (New Haven, CT: Yale University Press, 2001), 41.
39 Charles Philipon (1800–61) was a celebrated caricaturist and publisher of the satirical journals *La Caricature* and *Le Charivari*. See Farwell, *The Charged Image*.
40 Steele, *The Corset*, 45.
41 Coffin, *The Politics of Women's Work*, 90.
42 Ibid., 94.
43 Valerie Steele, *Paris Fashion: A Cultural History* (New York, NY: Oxford University Press, 1988), 71.
44 Eunice Lipton, *Looking into Degas: Uneasy Images of Women and Modern Life* (Berkeley: University of California Press, 1986), 131, 128.
45 Ibid., 132.
46 Lynn Mae Alexander, *Women, Work, and Representation: Needlewomen in Victorian Art and Literature* (Athens: Ohio University Press, 2003), 57.
47 Linda Nochlin, *Realism* (1971; repr., London: Penguin Books, 1990), 113.
48 André Guillerme, *La naissance de l'industrie à Paris: Entre sueurs et vapeurs, 1780–1830* (Seyssel: Champ Vallon, 2007), 357–8.
49 Nochlin, *Representing Women*.
50 Linda Nochlin, "Morisot's *Wet Nurse*," in *Women, Art, and Power and other Essays (1988)* reprinted in *Women Artists: The Linda Nochlin Reader*, ed. Maura Reilly (New York, NY: Thames and Hudson, 2015), 161–73.
51 Charles Baudelaire, "Le peintre de la vie moderne," in *Ecrits esthétiques* (Paris: Union Générale d'éditions, 1986), 360–404. See also Jerrold Siegel, "Bourgeois Life and the Avant-Garde," in *Modernity and Bourgeois Life: Society, Politics, and Culture in England, France, and Germany since 1750* (New York, NY: Cambridge University Press, 2012), 483–525.
52 Nochlin, "Morisot's *Wet Nurse*," 164.
53 Ibid., 164.
54 David Baguley, *Emile Zola: L'Assommoir* (Cambridge: Cambridge University Press, 1992), 26.
55 Marni Kessler, *Sheer Presence: The Veil in Manet's Paris* (Minneapolis: University of Minnesota Press, 2006), 21.
56 Ibid., 22; Lipton, *Looking into Degas*, 143.
57 Lipton, *Looking into Degas*, 144.
58 Nancy L. Green, *Ready-to-wear and Ready-to-work: A Century of Industry and Immigrants in Paris and New York* (Durham, NC: Duke University Press, 1997); Battagliola, *Histoire du travail des femmes*.
59 Anne Montjaret, *La Sainte-Catherine: Culture festive dans l'entreprise* (Paris: Éditions du C. T. H. S, 1997).
60 Kristina Huneault, *Difficult Subjects: Working Women and Visual Culture, Britain 1880–1914* (Burlington, VT: Ashgate, 2002), 1.
61 Deborah Thom, *Nice Girls and Rude Girls: Women Workers in World War I* (New York, NY: I.B. Tauris, 2000).

62 Scott, "The Woman Worker"; Michelle Perrot, *Les Femmes ou les silences de l'histoire* (Paris: Flammarion, 1988); Mary Lynn Stewart, *Women, Work, and the French State: Labour Protection and Social Patriarchy, 1879–1919* (Kingston: McGill-Queen's University Press, 1989); Helen Harden Chenut, *The Fabric of Gender: Working-Class Culture in Third Republic France* (University Park: Pennsylvania State University Press, 2005).

Chapter Three

1   On modern "ages," the series by Eric J. Hobsbawm, written decades ago, remains a good overview: *The Age of Revolution, 1789–1848* (New York, NY: Vintage, 1996); *The Age of Capital, 1848–1875* (New York, NY: Vintage, 1996); *The Age of Empire, 1875–1914* (New York, NY: Vintage, 1989); and *The Age of Extremes, 1914–1991* (New York, NY: Vintage, 1996).
2   Robert Marks, *The Origins of the Modern World: A Global and Environmental Narrative from the Fifteen to the Twenty-First Century*, 3rd ed. (Lanham, MD: Rowman and Littlefield, 2015).
3   Leonard R. Berlanstein, *The Working People of Paris, 1871–1914* (Baltimore, MD: Johns Hopkins University Press, 1984), 90.
4   Kenneth Pomeranz, *The Great Divergence: China, Europe, and the Making of the Modern World* (Princeton, NJ: Princeton University Press, 2001).
5   Tessie P. Liu, *The Weaver's Knot: The Contradictions of Class Struggle and Family Solidarity in Western France, 1750–1914* (Ithaca, NY: Cornell University Press, 1994).
6   Alice Conklin, *France and Its Empire since 1870* (Oxford: Oxford University Press, 2014). There is abundant recent literature on Haiti. See, for instance, Laurent Dubois, *Avengers of the New World: The Story of the Haitian Revolution* (Cambridge, MA: Harvard University Press, 2005).
7   Bruce Laurie, *Working People of Philadelphia, 1800–1850* (Philadelphia, PA: Temple University Press, 1980), 27.
8   Mark Traugott, ed. and trans., *The French Worker: Autobiographies from the Early Industrial Era* (Berkeley: University of California Press, 1993), 274.
9   Donald Reid, *Paris Sewers and Sewermen: Realities and Representations* (Cambridge, MA: Harvard University Press, 1991).
10 Balzac, *Eugénie Grandet*, trans. Marion Ayton Crawford (New York, NY: Penguin, 1955), 34.
11 Traugott, *French Worker*, 252, 275.
12 Alfred E. Kelly, ed. and trans., *The German Worker: Working-Class Autobiographies from the Age of Industrialization* (Berkeley: University of California Press, 1987), 14.
13 Eric Arnesen, *Waterfront Workers of New Orleans: Race, Class, and Politics, 1863–1923* (Urbana: University of Illinois Press, 1994), 40.
14 Émile Zola, *L'Assommoir*, trans. Leonard Tancock (New York, NY: Penguin, 1970), 169.
15 Traugott, *French Worker*, 69.
16 Ibid., 206.
17 Émile Guillaumin, *The Life of a Simple Man*, trans. Margaret Crosland (Hanover: New Hampshire University Press, 1983), 114.
18 Nelson Lichtenstein et al., *Who Built America? Working People and the Nation's Economy, Politics, Culture, and Society*, vol. 2 (New York, NY: Worth Publishers, 2000), 207.
19 Judith F. Stone, *The Search for Social Peace: Reform Legislation in France, 1890–1914* (Albany: State University of New York Press, 1985).

20 Kelly, *German Worker*, 27.
21 Ibid., 292.
22 Doris Beik and Paul Beik, eds. and trans., *Flora Tristan, Utopian Feminist: The Travel Diaries and Personal Crusade* (Bloomington: Indiana University Press, 1993), 129.
23 Kelly, *German Worker*, 27.
24 Ibid., 201.
25 Reginald E. Zelnick, ed. and trans., *A Radical Worker in Tsarist Russia: The Autobiography of Sëmen Ivanovich Kanatchikov* (Palo Alto, CA: Stanford University Press, 1986), 15.
26 Michelle Perrot, "On the Formation of the French Working Class," in *Working-Class Formation: Nineteenth-Century Patterns in Western Europe and the United States*, eds. Ira Katznelson and Aristide Zolberg (Princeton, NJ: Princeton University Press, 1986), 91.
27 Beik, *Flora Tristan*, 82, 84, ff.
28 Traugott, *French Worker*, 130.
29 Ibid., 223; Guillaumin, *Simple Man*, 114.
30 Zelnick, *Radical Worker*, 86
31 Ibid., 51.
32 Guillaumin, *Simple Man*, 104.
33 Reid, *Paris Sewers*.
34 Kelly, *German Worker*, 84, 153.
35 Leslie Page Moch, *The Pariahs of Yesterday: Breton Migrants in Paris* (Durham, NC: Duke University Press, 2012), 33.
36 Traugott, *French Worker*, 349.
37 Jacques Rancière, *The Nights of Labor: The Workers' Dream in Nineteenth-Century France*, trans. John Drury (Philadelphia, PA: Temple University Press, 1989), 54, 66, 60, 57.
38 Emilie Carles, *A Life of Her Own: The Transformation of a Countrywoman in Twentieth-Century France*, trans. Avriel H. Goldberger (New York, NY: Penguin, 1992).
39 Kelly, *German Worker*, 21–3.
40 Ibid., 21.
41 Mary Jo Maynes, *Taking the Hard Road: Life Course in French and German Workers' Autobiographies in the Era of Industrialization* (Chapel Hill: University of North Carolina Press, 1995), 121, quote 123.
42 Kelly, *German Worker*, 123, 130, 133.
43 Ibid., 141, 150, 153.
44 Ibid., 361.
45 Traugott, *French Worker*, 349.
46 Zola, *L'Assommoir*, 33.
47 Kelly, *German Worker*, 64.
48 Judith G. Coffin, *The Politics of Women's Work: The Paris Garment Trades, 1750–1915* (Princeton, NJ: Princeton University Press, 1996), 121, 125.
49 Coffin, *Politics of Women's Work*, 129, 162; see also Nancy Green, *Ready-to-Wear and Ready-to-Work: A Century of Immigrants in Paris and New York* (Durham, NC: Duke University Press, 1997), 163.
50 Ibid., 141, 151.
51 Moch, *Pariahs of Yesterday*, 32
52 Ibid., 94.
53 Kelly, *German Worker*, 252.
54 Alain Corbin, *Women for Hire: Prostitution and Sexuality in France after 1850*, trans. Alan Sheridan (Cambridge, MA: Harvard University Press, 1990), 6.

55 Ibid., 58.
56 Beik, *Flora Tristan*, 68 ff.
57 Ibid., 165 ff.
58 David L. Ransel, ed. and trans., *Olga Semyonova Tian-Shanskaia, Village Life in Late Tsarist Russia* (Bloomington: Indiana University Press, 1993), 130–1.
59 Gay L. Gullickson, *Unruly Women of Paris: Images of the Commune* (Ithaca, NY: Cornell University Press, 1996), 89 ff; Beik, *Flora Tristan*, 15–16.
60 Jürgen Kocka, "Problems of Working-Class Formation in Germany: The Early Years, 1800–1875," in *Working-Class Formation*, eds. Katznelson and Zolberg, 320.
61 Ian Donnachie, *Robert Owen: Social Visionary* (Edinburgh: John Donald, 2000).
62 Robert Owen, *A New View of Society* (New York, NY: Prism Key Press, 2013), 36.
63 Ibid., 51.
64 Traugott, *French Worker*, 252,
65 Ibid., 252, 254, 257, 270–1, 275.
66 Ransel, *Olga Semgonova*, 46.
67 Ibid., 108.
68 Guillaumin, *Life of A Simple Man*, 35.
69 Kelly, *German Worker*, 318.
70 Traugott, *French Worker*, 120 ff.
71 Kelly, *German Worker*, 15; David L. Hoffman, *Peasant Metropolis: Social Identities in Moscow, 1929–1941* (Ithaca, NY: Cornell University Press, 1994), 62–3.
72 Sean Wilentz, *Chants Democratic: New York City and the Rise of the American Working Class* (Oxford: Oxford University Press, 1984), 33.
73 Kelly, *German Worker*, 400–5.

Chapter Four

1 James R. Farr, *Artisans in Europe, 1350–1914* (Cambridge: Cambridge University Press, 2000), 31.
2 William H. Sewell, Jr., *Work and Revolution in France: The Language of Labor from the Old Regime to 1848* (Cambridge: Cambridge University Press, 1980), 88.
3 Farr, *Artisans in Europe*, 289.
4 Ibid., 282.
5 Roger Magraw, *A History of the French Working Class. Volume 1: The Age of Artisan Revolution* (Oxford: Blackwell, 1992), 58.
6 E. P. Thompson, "The Tramping Artisan," *The Economic History Review* New Series 3, no. 3 (1951): 301.
7 Rainer Liedtke, *Jewish Welfare in Hamburg and Manchester, c. 1850–1914* (Oxford: Clarendon Press, 1998), 195.
8 Fabrice Laroulandie, *Les ouvriers de Paris* (Paris: Éditions Christian, 1997), 194.
9 Sewell, *Work and Revolution in France*, 175.
10 Quoted in Laroulandie, *Les ouvriers de Paris*, 40.
11 Christiane Eisenberg, "'Artisans' Socialization at Work: Workshop Life in Early Nineteenth-century England and Germany," *Journal of Social History* 24, no. 3 (1991): 509.
12 Laroulandie, *Les ouvriers de Paris*, 31.
13 Victoria E. Thompson, *The Virtuous Marketplace: Women and Men, Money and Politics in Paris, 1830–1870* (Baltimore, MD: Johns Hopkins University Press, 2000), 113; Helen Harden Chenut, *The Fabric of Gender: Working-Class Culture in Third Republic France* (University Park: Pennsylvania State University Press, 2005), 180.

14 Farr, *Artisans in Europe*, 5.
15 Quoted in E. P. Thompson, *Making of the English Working Class* (New York, NY: Vintage, 1963), 236.
16 Eisenberg, "Artisan's Socialization at Work," 510–11.
17 Laroulandie, *Les ouvriers de Paris*, 21.
18 Sewell, *Work and Revolution in France*, 173.
19 William Lovett, *The Life and Struggles of William Lovett, In His Pursuit of Bread, Knowledge, and Freedom* (London: Trübner & Co., 1876), 21.
20 Lovett, *Life and Struggles of William Lovett*, 25.
21 Ibid., 30–1.
22 Thompson, *Making of the English Working Class*, 203.
23 Christopher Johnson, "Economic Change and Artisan Discontent: The Tailors' History, 1800–1848," in *Revolution and Reaction: 1848 and the Second French Republic*, ed. Roger Price (London: Croom Helm, 1975), 87–114.
24 Laura Strumingher, *Women and the Making of the Working Class: Lyon, 1830–1870* (St. Alban's, VT: Eden Press, 1979), 8.
25 Magraw, *History of the French Working Class*, 1:100.
26 Barbara Alpern Engel, *Between the Fields and the City: Women, Work, and Family in Russia 1861–1914* (Cambridge: Cambridge University Press, 1996), 102.
27 Deborah M. Valenze, *The First Industrial Woman* (Oxford: Oxford University Press, 1995), 105.
28 Valenze, *First Industrial Woman*, 91.
29 Rose L. Glickman, *Russian Factory Women: Workplace and Society, 1880–1914* (Berkeley: University of California Press, 1984), 143–4.
30 Karl Ittman, *Work, Gender and Family in Victorian England* (Houndmills: Macmillan, 1995), 49.
31 Ittman, *Work, Gender and Family*, 64.
32 Ibid., 62.
33 Thompson, "Tramping," 306.
34 Sewell, *Work and Revolution in France*, 176.
35 Quoted in Thompson, *Making of the English Working Class*, 286.
36 Magraw, *History of the French Working Class*, 1:95.
37 Ibid., 103.
38 Geoffrey Crossick, "The Petite Bourgeoisie in Nineteenth-Century Britain: The Urban and Liberal Case," in *Shopkeepers and Master Artisans in Nineteenth-century Europe*, eds. Geoffrey Crossick and Heinz-Gerhard Haupt (London: Methuen, 1984), 85.
39 Thompson, *Virtuous Marketplace*, 113.
40 Laroulandie, *Les ouvriers de Paris*, 110.
41 Farr, *Artisans in Europe*, 290–1.
42 Robert Weinberg, *The Revolution of 1905 in Odessa: Blood on the Steps* (Bloomington: Indiana University Press, 1993), 55.
43 William E. Mitchell, *Kinship, Ethnicity and Voluntary Associations: Jewish Family Life in New York City* (London: Routledge, 2009), 176.
44 Mary Merryweather, *Experience of Factory Life: Being a Record of Fourteen Years' Work at Mr. Courtauld's Silk Mill at Halstead, in Essex*, 3rd ed. (London: Emily Faithfull and Co., 1862), 35.
45 Thompson, *Virtuous Marketplace*, 60.
46 Louis René Villermé, *Tableau de l'état physique et moral des ouvriers employés dans les manufactures de coton, de laine et de soie* (Paris: Jules Renouard et Cie, 1840), 2:50.

47 Maurice Le Prévost, "Du choix d'un état," *L'Ouvrier: Journal hebdomadaire illustré paraissant tous les samedis* 8 (June 22, 1861): 4.
48 Quoted in Thompson, *Making of the English Working Class*, 191.
49 D. S. (Prince), *Aperçu sur la condition des classes ouvrières en France et en Angleterre* (Paris: Chez Bureau, 1844), 14.
50 Archives nationales de France, F/12/2357–2358: Procès-verbaux de la commission d'enquête sur le commerce et la fabrication des broderies.
51 Villermé, *Tableau*, 2:51. Emphasis in original.
52 Ibid., 52.
53 Kathleen Canning, "Gender and the Culture of Work: Ideology and Identity in the World Behind the Mill Gate, 1890–1914," in *Elections, Mass Politics, & Social Change in Modern Germany: New Perspectives*, eds. Larry Eugene Jones and James Retallack (Cambridge: Cambridge University Press, 1992), 190–1.
54 Quoted in Canning, "Gender and the Culture of Work," 189.
55 Glickman, *Russian Factory Women*, 142.
56 Quoted in Thompson, *Making of the English Working Class*, 291.
57 Thompson, *Virtuous Marketplace*, 116.
58 Michael P. Fitzsimmons, *From Artisan to Worker: Guilds, the French State, and the Organization of Labor, 1776–1821* (Cambridge: Cambridge University Press, 2010), 123.
59 Sewell, *Work and Revolution in France*, 166.
60 Théodore Fix, *Observations sur l'état des classes ouvrières* (Paris: Guillaumin, 1846), 12.
61 Patrick Joyce, *Work, Society and Politics: The Culture of the Factory in Later Victorian England* (New Brunswick, NJ: Rutgers University Press, 1980), 140.
62 P. E. Razzell and R. W. Wainwright, eds., *The Victorian Working Class: Selections from Letters to the* Morning Chronicle (London: Frank Cass, 1973), 183–4.
63 Peter N. Stearns, *Paths to Authority: The Middle Class and the Industrial Labor Force in France, 1820–48* (Chicago: University of Illinois Press, 1978), 43.
64 Dietrich Mühlberg, ed., *Proletariat: Culture and Lifestyle in the 19th Century*, trans. Katherine Vanovitch (Leipzig: Édition Leipzig, 1988), 18.
65 Richard Biernacki, *The Fabrication of Labour: Germany and Britain, 1640–1914* (Berkeley: University of California Press, 1995), 94.
66 Stearns, *Paths to Authority*, 44.
67 Laroulandie, *Les ouvriers de Paris*, 32.
68 Tessie Liu, *The Weaver's Knot: The Contradictions of Class Struggle and Family Solidarity in Western France, 1750–1914* (Ithaca, NY: Cornell University Press, 1994), 224.
69 Biernacki, *Fabrication of Labour*, 115.
70 Mühlberg, *Proletariat*, 30.
71 Stearns, *Paths to Authority*, 92.
72 Joyce, *Work, Society, and Politics*, 180.
73 Stearns, *Paths to Authority*, 99.
74 Ittman, *Work, Gender, and Family*, 48.
75 Quoted in Joyce, *Work, Society, and Politics*, 149.
76 Biernacki, *Fabrication of Labour*, 112.
77 Yves Lequin, *Les ouvriers de la région Lyonnaise (1848–1914)* (Lyon: Presses universitaires de Lyon, 1977), 1:271.
78 Edward Shorter and Charles Tilly, *Strikes in France, 1830–1968* (Cambridge: Cambridge University Press, 1974), 106.
79 Andrew August, *The British Working Class, 1832–1940* (Harlow: Pearson Longman, 2007), 119.

80 Magraw, *History of the French Working Class*, 1:42.
81 Chenut, *The Fabric of Gender*, 37.
82 Biernacki, *Fabrication of Labour*, 438.
83 Ibid., 441.
84 Liu, *The Weaver's Knot*, 143.
85 Magraw, *History of the French Working Class. Volume 2: Workers and the Bourgeois Republic*, 44.
86 Joan Wallach Scott, *The Glassworkers of Carmaux* (Cambridge, MA: Harvard University Press, 1980), 120–4.
87 Jean-Claude Caron, "Représentations d'une culture de la protestation (Le Creusot, 1899–1900)," in *La voix & le geste: Une approche culturelle de la violence socio-politique*, eds. Philippe Bourdin, Jean-Claude Caron, and Mathias Bernard (Clermont-Ferrand: Presses universitaires Blaise Pascal, 2005), 185.
88 Quoted in Joyce, *Work, Society, and Politics*, 218–19.
89 Ibid., 213–14.
90 Angela Woollacott, *On Her Their Lives Depend: Munitions Workers in the Great War* (Berkeley: University of California Press, 1994), 66.

Chapter Five

1 John Rule, "The Property of Skill in the Period of Manufacture," in *The Historical Meanings of Work*, ed. Patrick Joyce (Cambridge: Cambridge University Press, 1987), 99–118.
2 Liliane Hilaire-Pérez, *La pièce et le geste: Artisans, marchands et savoir technique à Londres au XVIIIe siècle* (Paris: Albin Michel, 2013); Robert Halleux, *Le savoir de la main: Savants et artisans dans l'Europe pré-industrielle* (Paris: Armand Colin, 2009).
3 Patrick Verley, *L'échelle du monde: Essai sur l'industrialisation de l'Occident* (Paris: Gallimard, 1997), 107.
4 Thomas Le Roux, "Les puissances vives soumises aux forces mortes: Hygiénistes, corps ouvriers et machines au XIXe siècle en France (1800–1870)," in *Corps et machines à l'âge industriel, XIXe–XXe siècles*, eds. Laurence Guignard, Pascal Raggi, and Étienne Thévenin (Rennes: Presses universitaires de Rennes, 2011), 259–72; François Jarrige, "Le travail discipliné: Genèse d'un projet technologique au XIXe siècle," *Cahiers d'histoire: Revue d'histoire critique* 110 (October–December 2009): 99–116.
5 Liliane Hilaire-Pérez, *L'Invention technique au siècle des Lumières* (Paris: Albin Michel, 2000), 303.
6 Maxine Berg, *The Machinery Question and the Making of Political Economy 1815–1848* (Cambridge: Cambridge University Press, 1982); Christine MacLeod, *Heroes of Invention: Technology, Liberalism and British Identity (1750–1914)* (Cambridge: Cambridge University Press, 2007).
7 Alain Leménorel, Gabriel Désert, Philippe Dupré, Yannick Lecherbonnier, and Emmanuelle Réal, "Hydraulique, vapeur et industrialisation au XIXe siècle: La 'voie normande'," *Cahier des Annales de Normandie* 25 (1993): 7–22.
8 Anne Van Neck, *Les débuts de la machine à vapeur dans l'industrie Belge, 1800–1850* (Brussels: Palais des Académies, 1979), 598 ff.; Nick Von Tunzelmann, *Steam Power and British Industrialization to 1860* (Oxford: Clarendon Press, 1978).
9 Raphael Samuel, "Workshop of the World: Steam Power and Hand Technology in Mid Victorian Britain," *History Workshop Journal* 3, no. 1 (Spring 1977): 6–72.
10 David E. Nye, *American Technological Sublime* (Cambridge, MA: MIT Press, 1994), 46.

11 Edward Everett, *An Address Delivered Before the Massachusetts Charitable Mechanic Association* (Boston, MA: Dutton and Wentworth, 1837), 15.
12 Leo Marx, *The Machine in the Garden: Technology and the Pastoral Ideal in America* (1964; Oxford: Oxford University Press, 2000).
13 John A. Etzler, *The Paradise within the Reach of all Men without Labor, by Powers of Nature and Machinery: An Address to all Intelligent Men, in Two Parts* (Pittsburgh, PA: Etzler and Reinhold, 1833).
14 Gregory Claeys, "John Adolphus Etzler, Technological Utopianism, and British Socialism: The Tropical Emigration Society's Venezuelan Mission and Its Social Context, 1833–1848," *The English Historical Review* 101, no. 399 (April 1986): 351–75.
15 Maurice Daumas, ed., *Histoire générale des techniques, 3/ L'expansion du machinisme, 1725–1860* (1968; Paris: Presses universitaires de France, 1996), 92–3.
16 Quoted in Daumas, ed., *Histoire générale des techniques*, 92.
17 Bruno Belhoste and Konstantinos Chatzis, "From Technical Corps to Technocratic Power: French State Engineers and their Professional and Cultural Universe in the First Half of the 19th Century," *History and Technology* 23, no. 3 (2007): 209–25.
18 Jacques Guillerme and Jan Sebestik, "Les commencements de la technologie," in *Thalès* (Paris: Presses Universitaires de France, 1968), 1–72, reprinted in *Documents pour l'histoire des techniques*, ed. Maurice Daumas, no. 14 (2007): 50–121.
19 Edward P. Thompson, *The Making of the English Working Class* (1963; Toronto: Penguin Books, 1991); Adrian Randall, *Before the Luddites: Custom, Community and Machinery in the English Woollen Industry, 1776–1809* (Cambridge: Cambridge University Press, 1991); Kevin Binfield, ed., *Writings of the Luddites* (Baltimore, MD: Johns Hopkins University Press, 2004).
20 François Jarrige, *Au temps des tueuses de bras: Les bris de machines à l'aube de l'ère industrielle* (Rennes: Presses universitaires de Rennes, 2009).
21 Carl J. Griffin, *The Rural War: Captain Swing and the Politics of Protest* (Manchester: Manchester University Press, 2012).
22 Jules Michelet, *The People*, trans. G. H. Smith (New York, NY: Appleton and Company, 1846), 48; see also Paul Viallaneix, "Michelet, machines, machinisme," *Romantisme* no. 23 (1979): 3–15.
23 Michelet, *The People*, 50.
24 Karl Marx and Friedrich Engels, *Manifesto of the Communist Party*, trans. Samuel Moore (Chicago, IL: Charles H. Kerr & Company, 1906), 23, 24.
25 Ibid., 22–3.
26 Alf Hornborg, *The Power of the Machine: Global Inequalities of Economy, Technology, and Environment* (Walnut Creek, CA: AltaMir, 2001); Andreas Malm, *Fossil Capital: The Rise of Steam-Power and the Roots of Global Warming* (London: Verso, 2016).
27 Andrew Ure, *The Philosophy of Manufactures: Or, An Exposition of the Scientific, Moral, and Commercial Economy of the Factory System* (London: Charles Knight, 1835), 367; Jules Michelet, Preface to "Histoire du XIXe siècle," in *Œuvres completes de Jules Michelet*, 40 vols. (Paris: Flammarion, 1893–8), 24, 10.
28 Michel Chevalier, ed., *Exposition universelle de Londres de 1862*, quoted in Michèle Riot-Sarcey, *Le procès de la liberté: Une histoire souterraine du XIXe siècle en France* (Paris: La Découverte, 2016), 207.
29 John Tresch, *The Romantic Machine: Utopian Science and Technology after Napoleon* (Chicago, IL: University of Chicago Press, 2012); François Jarrige, ed., *Dompter Prométhée: Technologies et socialismes à l'âge romantique (1820–1870)* (Besançon: Presses universitaires de Franche-Comté, 2016).

30 Jonathan Beecher, *Fourier: The Visionary and his World* (Berkeley: University of California Press, 1990).
31 Mathieu Briancourt, *Visite au Phalanstère* (Paris: Librairie phalanstérienne, 1848), 127–8.
32 Pierre-Joseph Proudhon, "Machinery," in *System of Economical Contradictions, or, The Philosophy of Misery* trans. Benjamin R. Tucker (Boston, MA: Benjamin R. Tucker, 1888), 174.
33 Claude A. Costaz, *Essai sur l'administration de l'agriculture, du commerce, des manufactures et des subsistances, suivi de l'historique des moyens qui ont amené le grand essor pris par les arts depuis 1793 jusqu'en 1815* (Paris: Huzard, 1818), 149.
34 Irwin Feller, "The Draper Loom in New England Textiles, 1894–1914: A Study of Diffusion of an Innovation," *The Journal of Economic History* 26, no. 3 (1966): 320–47; Serge Benoit, "L'introduction des métiers Northrop," in *Tisser l'histoire: L'industrie et ses patrons, XVIe–XXe siècles*, eds. René Favier, Gérard Gayot, Jean-François Klein, Didier Terrier, and Denis Woronoff (Valenciennes: Presses universitaires de Valenciennes, 2009), 85–96.
35 Michelle Perrot, "Femmes et machines au XIXe siècle," in *Les femmes ou les silences de l'histoire* (Paris: Flammarion, 1998), 182.
36 Michelle Perrot, "Machines à coudre et travail à domicile," *Mouvement Social* no. 105 (October–December 1978): 161–4.
37 Monique Peyrière, *Recherches sur la machine à coudre, 1830–1889* (Paris, EHESS, 1990).
38 A. Godley, "Selling The Sewing Machine Around the World: Singer's International Marketing Strategies, 1850–1920," *Enterprise and Society* 7, no. 2 (June 2006): 266–314; David Arnold, *Everyday Technology: Machines and the Making of India's Modernity* (Chicago, IL: University of Chicago Press, 2013).
39 Yves Cohen, *Organiser à l'aube du taylorisme: La pratique d'Ernest Mattern chez Peugeot (1906–1919)* (Besançon: Presses universitaires du Franche-Comté, 2001), 106.
40 Henry Adams, "The Dynamo and the Virgin," in *The Education of Henry Adams* (Oxford: Oxford University Press, 1999), 320.
41 Julia Moses, "Accidents at Work, Security and Compensation in Industrialising Europe: The Cases of Britain, Germany and Italy, 1870–1925," *Annual Review of Law and Ethics* 17 (2009): 237–58.
42 Robert Salais, Nicolas Baverez, and Bénédicte Reynaud, *L'Invention du chômage* (Paris: Presses universitaires de France, 1986).
43 *Rapport sur la question du chômage, présenté au nom de la commission permanente du Conseil supérieur du travail* (Paris: Imprimerie nationale, 1896), viii, 323.
44 Christian Topalov, *Naissance du chômeur (1880–1910)* (Paris: Albin Michel, 1994), 266.
45 Peter H. Argersinger and Jo Ann E. Argersinger, "The Machine Breakers: Farmworkers and Social Change in the Rural Midwest of the 1870s," *Agricultural History* 58, no. 3 (July 1984): 393–410.
46 William Godwin Moody, *Our Labor Difficulties: The Cause, and the Way Out; Including the Paper on the Displacement of Labor by Improvements in Machinery* (Boston, MA: A. Williams & Co., 1878); John A. Hobson, "The Influence of Machinery Upon Employment," *Political Science Quarterly* 8, no. 1 (March 1893): 97–123.
47 Charles Gide, "De la coopération et des transformations qu'elle est appelée à réaliser dans l'ordre économique: Discours d'ouverture du Congrès international des Sociétés coopératives de consommation tenu à Paris, au Palais du Trocadéro, le 8 septembre 1889," in *Coopération et économie sociale (1886–1914)* (Paris: L'Harmattan, 2001), 133.

48 Dick van Lente, "The critique of industrial Technology in the Netherlands and other Western Countries in the Nineteenth Century," in *European Historiography of Technology*, ed. D. C. Christensen (Odense: Odense University Press, 1993), 55–67.
49 Alain Dewerpe, *Le Monde du travail en France (1800–1950)* (Paris: Armand Colin, 1989), 106.
50 Eric Hobsbawm, "Machine Breakers," *Past & Present* 1 (February 1952): 63; See also Beatrice and Sydney Webb, *Industrial Democracy* (London: Longman, 1897), 411.
51 Bernard H. Moss, *The Origins of the French Labor Movement: The Socialism of Skilled Workers, 1830–1914* (Berkeley: University of California Press, 1976).
52 Gérard Noiriel, *Workers in French Society in the 19th and 20th Centuries* (New York, NY: Berg, 1990), 84.
53 Philippe Lefebvre, *L'invention de la grande entreprise: Travail, hiérarchie, marché, France, fin XVIIIe–début XXe siècle* (Paris: Presses universitaires de France, 2003).
54 Patrick Fridenson, "Un tournant taylorien de la société française (1904–1918)," *Annales ESC* 42, no. 5 (September–October 1987): 1031–60; David Montgomery, *Workers' Control in America: Studies in the History of Work, Technology, and Labor Struggles* (Cambridge: Cambridge University Press, 1979), see especially 101–10.
55 Laura Lee Downs, *Manufacturing Inequality: Gender Division in the French and British Metalworking Industries, 1914–1939* (Ithaca, NY: Cornell University Press, 1995).

Chapter Six

1 Karl Fischer, *Denkwürdigkeiten eines Arbeiters*, ed. Paul Göhre (Jena: Eugen Diederichs Verlag, 1903), 123. Translated excerpts from Fischer's autobiography can be found in Alfred Kelly, ed., *The German Worker: Working-Class Autobiographies from the Age of Industrialization* (Berkeley: University of California Press, 1987), 51–63.
2 Leo Lucassen, *The Immigrant Threat: The Integration of Old and New Migrants in Western Europe Since 1850* (Urbana: University of Illinois Press, 2005), 29; David Kertzer, "Household Organization and Migration in Nineteenth-Century Italy," *Social Science History* 14, no. 4 (1990): 489–90.
3 Rachel G. Fuchs and Victoria Thompson, *Women in Nineteenth-Century Europe* (Houndmill: Palgrave Macmillan, 2005), 128.
4 Kertzer, "Household," 489–90.
5 Steve Hochstadt, *Mobility and Modernity: Migration in Germany, 1820–1989* (Ann Arbor: University of Michigan Press, 1999).
6 Colin G. Pooley and Shani D'Cruze, "Migration and Urbanization in North-West England circa 1760–1830," *Social History* 19, no. 3 (1994): 351.
7 Klaus J. Bade, *Migration in European History*, trans. Allison Brown (Malden, MA: Blackwell, 2003), 37.
8 Leslie Page Moch, *Moving Europeans: Migration in Western Europe Since 1650* (Bloomington: Indiana University Press, 2003), 111.
9 Bade, *Migration*, 69.
10 David Blackbourn, *The Long Nineteenth Century: A History of Germany, 1788–1918* (Oxford: Oxford University Press, 1998), 198.
11 Gay Gullickson, "The Sexual division of Labor in Cottage Industry and Agriculture in the Pays de Caux: Auffay, 1750–1850," *French Historical Studies* 12, no. 2 (1981): 190–2.

12 Moch, *Moving Europeans*, 114–15.
13 Lucassen, *Immigrant Threat*, 29–30.
14 Cormac Ó Gráda, *The Great Irish Famine* (Cambridge: Cambridge University Press, 2000), 48–50.
15 Cormac Ó Gráda and Kevin O'Rourke, "Migration as Disaster Relief: Lessons from the Great Irish Famine," *European Review of Economic History* 1, no. 1 (1997): 3–26.
16 Martin Dribe, "Dealing with Economic Stress through Migration: Lessons from Nineteenth Century Rural Sweden," *European Review of Economic History* 7, no. 3 (2003): 286 and 294–5.
17 Pooley and D'Cruze, "Migration," 349.
18 Javier Silvestre, "Temporary Internal Migrations in Spain, 1860–1930," *Social Science History* 31, no. 4 (2007): 540.
19 Deborah Simonton, "Women Workers; Working Women," in *The Routledge History of Women in Europe since 1700*, ed. Deborah Simonton (New York, NY: Routledge, 2006), 150.
20 Louise A. Tilly and Joan W. Scott, *Women, Work, and Family* (New York, NY: Rinehart and Winston, 1978); also Fuchs and Thompson, *Women*, 65–6.
21 Fuchs and Thompson, *Women*, 126.
22 J. Trent Alexander and Annemarie Steidl, "Gender and the 'Laws of Migration': A Reconsideration of Nineteenth-Century Patterns," *Social Science History* 36, no. 2 (2012), 224.
23 Rachel G. Fuchs, *Poor and Pregnant in Paris: Strategies for Survival in the Nineteenth Century* (New Brunswick, NJ: Routledge University Press, 1992), 14–15.
24 Barbara Alpern Engel, *Between the Fields and the City: Women, Work, and Family in Russia, 1861–1914* (Cambridge: Cambridge University Press, 1994), 3–16.
25 Ana Stolić, "Vocation or Hobby: Social Identity of Female Teachers in the Nineteenth Century Serbia," in *Gender Relations in South Eastern Europe: Historical Perspectives on Womanhood and Manhood in 19th and 20th Century*, eds. Slobodan Naumović and Miroslav Jovanović (Münster: LIT Verlag, 2004), 55–90.
26 Fuchs and Thompson, *Women*, 129; Lora Wildenthal, *German Women for Empire, 1884–1945* (Durham, NC: Duke University Press, 2001), 135, 144, 162–8.
27 Blackbourn, *Nineteenth Century Germany*, 192–3.
28 Bade, *Migration*, 103–4, 112–13, and 163.
29 Ibid., 102–4; Simone Wegge, "Occupational Self-selection of European Emigrants: Evidence from Nineteenth-century Hesse-Cassel," *European Review of Economic History* 6, no. 3 (2002): 372.
30 Bade, *Migration*, 107 and 112–13.
31 Mark Wyman, "Return Migration—Old Story, New Story," *Immigrants & Minorities* 20, no. 1 (2001): 3–4.
32 Silvestre, "Temporary Internal Migrations," 547–8.
33 Wegge, "Occupational Self-selection," 367.
34 Ran Abramitzky, Leah Platt Boustan, and Katherine Eriksson, "Europe's Tired, Poor, Huddled Masses: Self-Selection and Economic Outcomes in the Age of Mass Migration," *American Economic Review* 102, no. 5 (2012), 1836–7.
35 Tobias Brinkmann, "Why Paul Nathan Attacked Albert Ballin: The Transatlantic Mass Migration and the Privatization of Prussia's Eastern Border Inspection, 1886–1914," *Central European History* 43, no. 1 (2010): 47–83.
36 Mary Antin, *The Promised Land* (Boston, MA: Houghton Mifflin Company, 1912).

37 Robert Gildea, *Barricades and Borders: Europe 1800–1914* (Oxford: Oxford University Press, 1996), 273.
38 Adam McKeown, "Global Migration, 1846–1970," *Journal of World History* 15, no. 2 (2004): 155; Lucassen, *Immigrant Threat*, 51.
39 Bade, *Migration*, 158–60.
40 Staatsarchiv Münster (StAM), Oberpräsidium Münster (OPM) 5428, [01] Berlin, March 26, 1904.
41 StAM, OPM 5428, [09] Münster, May 28, 1904.
42 StAM, OPM 5428, [20] Lemberg, December 15, 1904.
43 Bade, *Migration*, 54–5 and 71.
44 StAM, OPM 6228, [163] Münster, July 1, 1909.
45 Lucassen, *Immigrant Threat*, 51–2.
46 StAM, OPM 6228, [296] Bochum, April 9, 1920.
47 Briant Lindsay Lowell, *Scandinavian Exodus: Demography and Social Development of 19th-century Rural Communities* (Boulder, CO: Westview Press, 1987), 64–5.
48 Wyman, "Return Migration," 1–2 and 8–9.
49 Bade, *Migration*, 79–81.
50 Angiolina Arru, "Networks and Logics of Migration: the Circulation of Credit among Immigrants in Nineteenth Century Italy," in *European Mobility: Internal, International, and Transatlantic Moves in the 19th and the Early 20th Centuries*, eds. Annemarie Steidl et al. (Vienna: V & R Unipress, 2009), 19–37.
51 Moch, *Moving Europeans*, 103, 105–7, 121; Bade, *Migration*, 61–3.
52 Ibid., 106–7.
53 David I. Jeremy, "Damming the Flood: British Government Efforts to Check the Outflow of Technicians and Machinery, 1780–1843," *Business History Review* 51, no. 1 (1977): 1–34.
54 Lucassen, *Immigrant Threat*, 32.
55 Rachel G. Fuchs, *Gender and Poverty in Nineteenth-Century Europe* (Cambridge: Cambridge University Press, 2005), 200–2.
56 Christoph Schmidt, *Ständerecht und Standeswechsel in Rußland 1851–1897* (Wiesbaden: Harrassowitz, 1994), 106–24.
57 Peter Kolchin, "Foreword," in Alexandr Nikitenko, *Up from Serfdom: My Childhood and Youth in Russia, 1804–1824* (New Haven, CT: Yale University Press, 2001), xii–xvi.
58 Christiane Harzig and Dirk Hoerder, *What is Migration History?* (Malden, MA: Polity Press, 2009), 39; Michael Hamm, ed., *The City in Late Imperial Russia* (Bloomington: Indiana University Press, 1986), 13–14 and 52–3.
59 Schmidt, *Ständerecht*, 122.
60 Stephen Nicholas, ed., *Convict Workers: Reinterpreting Australia's Past* (Cambridge: Cambridge University Press, 1988).
61 Stephen Nicholas and Peter Shergold, "Transportation as Global Migration," in ibid., 36–7.
62 Ann Taylor Allen, *Women in Twentieth-Century Europe* (Houndmills: Palgrave Macmillan, 2008), 12–14.
63 Ute Daniel, *The War from Within: German Working-Class Women in the First World War* (Oxford: Berg, 1997), 62.
64 Bade, *Migration*, 168–71.
65 Kai Rawe, Kriegsgefangene, "Freiwillige und Deportierte: Ausländerbeschäftigung im Ruhrbergbau während des Ersten Weltkrieges," in *Zwangsarbeit im Bergwerk: Der Arbeitseinsatz im Kohlenbergbau des Deutschen Reiches und der besetzten Gebiete im Ersten und Zweiten Weltkrieg*, vol. 1 *Forschungen* (Essen: Klartext, 2005), 35–62.

66 Bade, *Migration*, 173.
67 Dirk Hoerder, Jan Lucassen, and Leo Lucassen, "Terminologies and Concepts of Migration Research," in *The Encyclopedia of Migration and Minorities in Europe from the 17th Century to the Present*, eds. Klaus J. Bade, Pieter C. Emmer, Leo Lucassen, and Jochen Oltmer (Cambridge: Cambridge University Press, 2011), xxv–xxxii.
68 Dirk Hoerder, "Individuals and Systems: Agency in Nineteenth and Twentieth Century Labor Migrations," in Steidl et al., eds., *European Mobility*, 66.
69 Monika Glettler, "Czech Labor Migrants in Austria in the 19th and Early 20th Centuries," in Bade et al., eds., *Encyclopedia of Migration*, 302–3.

Chapter Seven

1 Charles Dickens, *Hard Times* (New York, NY: Penguin, 2003), 27.
2 Jeffrey Weeks, *Sex, Politics, and Society: The Regulation of Sexuality since 1800* (London: Longman, 1981), 28; Michel Foucault, *History of Sexuality, Volume I: An Introduction* (New York, NY: Vintage, 1990), 122–7.
3 Clive Emsley, Tim Hitchcock, and Robert Shoemaker, "London History—London, 1800–1913," *Old Bailey Proceedings Online*. www.oldbaileyonline.org, version 7.0 (accessed July 26, 2017); Rachel G. Fuchs, *Gender and Poverty in Nineteenth-Century Europe* (Cambridge: Cambridge University Press, 2005), 152; Emma Griffin, "Manchester in the Nineteenth Century," *Discovering Literature: Romantics and Victorians*, May 15, 2014. http://www.bl.uk/romantics-and-victorians/articles/manchester-in-the-19th-century (accessed July 25, 2017); Edward L. Glaeser, "Urban Colossus: Why is New York America's Largest City?" *FRBNY Economic Policy Review*, December 10, 2005. https://www.newyorkfed.org/medialibrary/media/research/epr/05v11n2/0512glae.pdf (accessed July 25, 2017).
4 Catherine J. Kudlick, *Cholera in Post-Revolutionary Paris: A Cultural History* (Berkeley: University of California Press, 1996), 63.
5 Marjorie Levine-Clark, *Beyond the Reproductive Body: The Politics of Women's Health and Work in Early Victorian England* (Columbus: Ohio University Press, 2004), 22.
6 George Rosen, *A History of Public Health* (Baltimore, MD: Johns Hopkins University Press, 1993), 264.
7 Ibid., 227.
8 Henry Mayhew, *London Labour and the London Poor: A Cyclopaedia of the Condition and Earnings of Those that Work, Those that Cannot Work, and Those that Will Not Work. Volume II: London Street-folk, Comprising Street Sellers, Street Buyers, Street Finders, Street Performers, Street Artizans, Street Labourers* (London: Griffin, Bohn, and Company, 1861), 446–50.
9 James Philips Kay, *The Moral and Physical Condition of the Working Classes Employed in the Cotton Manufacture in Manchester* (London: James Ridgway, 1832), 15–16.
10 Quoted in Levine-Clark, *Beyond the Reproductive Body*, 121–2.
11 Quoted in ibid., 123.
12 Jules Michelet, *The People*, trans. C. Cocks (London: Longman, Brown, Green & Longmans, 1846), 64.
13 *Royal Commission for Inquiring into the State of Large Towns and Populous Districts*, Second Report, Minutes of Evidence, Appendix, parts I and II, 1845 [602] [610], XVIII, 306.

14 Jack London, *The People of the Abyss* (New York, NY: Macmillan Company, 1903), 45–6.
15 General Board of Health, *Report of the General Board of Health on the Administration of the Public Health Act and the Nuisances Removal and Diseases Prevention Acts, from 1848 to 1854* (London: G. E. Eyre and W. Spottiswoode, 1854), 34.
16 Dorothy Porter, "Public Health," in *Companion Encyclopedia of the History of Medicine*, eds. W. F. Bynum and Roy Porter, 2 vols. (London: Routledge, 1993), 2:1231; Ann Elizabeth Fowler La Berge, *Mission and Method: The Early Nineteenth-Century French Public Health Movement* (Cambridge: Cambridge University Press, 1992), 59–67.
17 Ibid., 73.
18 Christopher Hamlin, *Public Health and Social Justice in the Age of Chadwick: Britain 1800–1854* (Cambridge: Cambridge University Press, 1998).
19 Lynda Nead, *Victorian Babylon: People, Streets and Images in Nineteenth-Century London* (New Haven, CT: Yale University Press, 2000), 14–26.
20 John Duffy, *A History of Public Health in New York City, 1625–1866* (New York, NY: Russell Sage Foundation, 1968), 412.
21 Porter, "Public Health," 1240–9.
22 Michelle Allen, *Cleansing the City: Sanitary Geographies in Victorian London* (Athens: Ohio University Press, 2008), 115–16.
23 T. J. Clark, *The Painting of Modern Life: Paris in the Art of Manet and His Followers* (Princeton, NJ: Princeton University Press, 1984), 37.
24 Andrew Mearns, *The Bitter Cry of Outcast London: An Inquiry into the Condition of the Abject Poor* (London: James Clarke and Co., 1883), 24.
25 Ann-Louise Shapiro, "Paris," *Housing the Workers, 1850–1914: A Comparative Perspective* ed. Martin J. Daunton (London: Bloomsbury, 2015), 58–9.
26 Porter, "Public Health," 1256.
27 Quoted in David S. Barnes, *The Great Stink of Paris and the Nineteenth-Century Struggle Against Filth and Germs* (Baltimore, MD: Johns Hopkins University Press, 2006), 136.
28 Ibid.
29 Anne Hardy, *Health and Medicine in Britain since 1860* (Basingstoke: Macmillan, 2001), 39–41.
30 Porter, "Public Health," 1255–6.
31 Weeks, *Sex, Politics, and Society*, 57.
32 Elinor Accampo, *Industrialization, Family Life, and Class Relations: Saint Chamond, 1815–1914* (Berkeley: University of California Press, 1989), 3.
33 Amanda Vickery, "Golden Age to Separate Spheres? A Review of the Categories and Chronology of English Women's History," *Historical Journal* 36, no. 2 (1993): 402.
34 Katrina Honeyman and Jordan Goodman, "Women's Work, Gender Conflict, and Labour Markets in Europe, 1500–1900," *Economic History Review* 44, no. 4 (1991): 608–28.
35 E. P. Thompson, "Time, Work-Discipline, and Industrial Capitalism," *Past & Present* 38 (December 1967): 56–97.
36 Quoted in Levine-Clark, *Beyond the Reproductive Body*, 39–40.
37 Kathleen Canning, "Social Policy, Body Politics: Recasting the Social Question in Germany, 1875–1900," in *Gender and Class in Modern Europe*, eds. Laura L. Frader and Sonya O. Rose (Ithaca, NY: Cornell University Press, 1996), 225.
38 Ibid., 224–5
39 Sonya O. Rose, "Protective Labor Legislation in Nineteenth-Century Britain: Gender, Class, and the Liberal State," in Frader and Rose, eds., *Gender and Class in Modern Europe*, 193–210.

40 Friedrich Engels, *The Condition of the Working Class in England* (1844. Chicago, IL: Academy Chicago Publishers, 1984), 159.
41 Quoted in Janet R. Horne, *A Social Laboratory for Modern France: The Musée Social and the Rise of the Welfare State* (Durham, NC: Duke University Press, 2002), 22.
42 Anna Clark, *The Struggle for the Breeches: Gender and the Making of the British Working Class* (Berkeley: University of California Press, 1995).
43 Keith McClelland, "England's Greatness, the Working Man," in *Defining the Victorian Nation: Class, Race, Gender and the Reform Act of 1867*, eds. Catherine Hall, Keith McClelland, and Jane Rendall (Cambridge: Cambridge University Press, 2000), 71–118.
44 Laura L. Frader, "Engendering Work and Wages: The French Labor Movement and the Family Wage," in Frader and Rose, eds., *Gender and Class in Modern Europe*, 146.
45 Quoted in Levine-Clark, *Beyond the Reproductive Body*, 50.
46 Ibid., 53.
47 Quoted in Christine Stansell, *City of Women: Sex and Class in New York, 1789–1860* (New York, NY: Knopf, 1987), 126.
48 Clark, *Struggle for the Breeches*, 197–247.
49 Quoted in Judith DeGroat, "The Public Nature of Women's Work: Definitions and Debates during the Revolution of 1848," *French Historical Studies* 20, no. 1 (1997): 34.
50 Clark, *Struggle for the Breeches*, 231–2.
51 Laura Oren, "The Welfare of Women in Laboring Families: England, 1860–1950," *Feminist Studies* 1, no. 3/4 (1973): 107–25.
52 Fuchs, *Gender and Poverty*, 117.
53 Nancy Tomes, "'A Torrent of Abuse': Crimes of Violence between Working-Class Men and Women in London, 1840–1875," *Journal of Social History* 11, no. 3 (1978): 331.
54 Marjorie Levine-Clark, *Unemployment, Welfare, and Masculine Citizenship: "So Much Honest Poverty" in Britain, 1870–1930* (Basingstoke: Palgrave Macmillan, 2015), 215.
55 Engels, *Condition of the Working Class*, 173.
56 Tomes, "Torrent of Abuse," 332.
57 Levine-Clark, *Unemployment, Welfare*, 215.
58 "Old Hill Police," *County Express*, June 15, 1901, 2.
59 Joanna Bourke, *Working-Class Cultures in Britain, 1890–1960: Gender, Class, and Ethnicity* (London: Routledge, 1994), 52.
60 Louise Hide, *Gender and Class in English Asylums, 1890–1914* (Houndmills: Palgrave Macmillan, 2014).
61 Lydia Murdoch, *Imagined Orphans: Poor Families, Child Welfare, and Contested Citizenship in London* (New Brunswick, NJ: Rutgers University Press, 2006).
62 Quoted in Sean M. Quinlan, *The Great Nation in Decline: Sex, Modernity, and Health Crises in Revolutionary France, c.1750–1850* (Aldershot: Ashgate, 2007), 204.
63 Julia Laite, *Common Prostitutes and Ordinary Citizens: Commercial Sex in London, 1885–1960* (Basingstoke: Palgrave Macmillan, 2012).
64 Mearns, *The Bitter Cry of Outcast London*, 1–2, 4.
65 Charles Booth, "Concerning the Whole District Under Review," in *Labour and Life of the People*, ed. Booth, *Volume 1: East London* (London: Williams and Norgate, 1889), 38.
66 Ibid., 44.
67 Fuchs, *Gender and Poverty*, 198–9.
68 Levine-Clark, *Unemployment, Welfare*, x.
69 Fuchs, *Gender and Poverty*, 211.
70 Ibid., 212–14.

Chapter Eight

1. Eric J. Hobsbawm and George Rudé, *Captain Swing* (Harmondsworth: Penguin Books, 1973).
2. John E. Archer, *Social Unrest and Popular Protest in England, 1780–1840* (Cambridge: Cambridge University Press, 2000), 48–55; Alessandro Nuvolari, "The 'Machine Breakers' and the Industrial Revolution," *Journal of European Economic History* 31, no. 2 (2002): 393–428; Jeff Horn, "Understanding Crowd Action: Machine-breaking in England and France, 1789–1817," *Proceedings of the Western Society for French History* 31 (2003): 138–52.
3. *The Leeds Mercury*, October 16, 1830.
4. *Parliamentary Papers* (PP) 1832 (706) XV Labour of Children in Factories; PP 1833 (450) XX Employment of Children in Factories. Royal Commission First Report. PP 1832 (706) XV Labour of Children in Factories, June 15, 1832.
5. Ibid.
6. *Hansard* House of Commons Debates, March 17, 1847, vol. 91 (cc 106–46).
7. Ibid.
8. Lord Feversham, *Hansard* House of Lords Debates, May 17, 1847, vol. 92 (cc 891–946).
9. Martyn Lyons, *Post-Revolutionary Europe, 1815–1856* (Basingstoke: Palgrave Macmillan, 2006).
10. Helge Berger and Mark Spoerer, "Economic Crises and the European Revolutions of 1848," *Journal of Economic History* 61, no. 2 (June 2001): 293–326.
11. René Heron De Villefosse, *Histoire de Paris* (Paris: Bernard Grasset, 1959), 323.
12. "Address of the Female Political Union of Newcastle upon Tyne to Their Fellow Countrywomen," *The Northern Star*, February 2, 1839 in *The Early Chartists*, ed. Dorothy Thompson (London: Macmillan, 1971), 128.
13. Anna Clark, *The Struggle for the Breeches: Gender and the Making of the British Working Class* (Berkeley: University of California Press, 1995), 36–140.
14. Sarah Richardson, *The Political Worlds of Women: Gender and Politics in Nineteenth-Century Britain* (New York, NY: Routledge, 2013), 117; see also Paul A. Pickering and Alex Tyrrell, *The People's Bread: A History of the Anti-Corn Law League* (London: Leicester University Press, 2000).
15. Simon Morgan, "Domestic Economy and Political Agitation: Women and the Anti-Corn Law League 1839–46," in *Women in British Politics 1760–1860: The Power of the Petticoat*, eds. Kathryn Gleadle and Sarah Richardson (London: Palgrave Macmillan, 2000), 116.
16. Pickering and Tyrell, *The People's Bread*, 131.
17. Clark, *The Struggle for the Breeches*, 120.
18. *The Pioneer*, April 5, 1834.
19. Gay L. Gullickson, *Spinners and Weavers of Auffay: Rural Industry and the Sexual Division of Labor in a French Village 1750–1850* (Cambridge: Cambridge University Press, 1986).
20. PP, *First Report of the Commissioners on the employment of children* (1842) vol. xv, 31.
21. Karen Hunt, *Equivocal Feminists: The Social Democratic Federation and the Woman Question, 1884–1911* (Cambridge: Cambridge University Press, 1996).
22. *Wigan Times*, April 7, 1860.
23. David A. Shafer, *The Paris Commune: French Politics, Culture, and Society at the Crossroads of the Revolutionary Tradition and Revolutionary Socialism* (Houndsmills: Palgrave Macmillan, 2005).

24 Mary Lynn Stewart, *Women, Work and the French State: Labour Protection and Social Patriarchy, 1879–1919* (Kingston: McGill-Queen's University Press, 1989).

25 Judith G. Coffin, *The Politics of Women's Work: The Paris Garment Trades, 1750–1915* (Princeton, NJ: Princeton University Press, 2014).

26 Philip Nord, "The Welfare State in France, 1870–1914," *French Historical Studies* 18, no. 3 (Spring 1994): 831.

27 Rachel G. Fuchs and Leslie Page Moch, "Pregnant, Single, and Far From Home: Migrant Women in Nineteenth-Century Paris," *American Historical Review* 93, no. 4 (October 1990): 1007–31.

28 Kathleen Canning, *Languages of Labour and Gender: Female Factory Work in Germany 1850–1914* (Ann Arbor: University of Michigan Press, 2002).

29 Deborah Simonton, "Women Workers, Working Women," in *The Routledge History of Women in Europe Since 1700*, ed. Deborah Simonton (London: Routledge, 2006), 149.

30 Nicola Verdon, *Rural Women Workers in Nineteenth-Century England: Gender, Work and Wages* (Rochester, NY: Boydell Press, 2002), 24.

31 Carl J. Griffin, "The Violent Captain Swing?," *Past & Present* 209 (November 2010): 149–80; and Carl J. Griffin *The Rural War: Captain Swing and the Politics of Protest* (Manchester: Manchester University Press, 2012).

32 Deborah Fink, "Not to Intrude": A Danish Perception on Gender and Class in Nineteenth-Century Dairying," *Agricultural History Society* 83, no. 4 (Fall 2009): 446–76.

33 Ibid., 447.

34 PP, *Royal Commission on the Employment of Children, Young Persons and Women in Agriculture,* (1867–9), 4068, xvii.

35 Government of France, "France 1896 Census," *International Population Census Publications: Series II, pre-1945* (1936).

36 Canning, *Languages of Labour and Gender*, 299.

37 Judith DeGroat, "The Public Nature of Women's Work: Definitions and Debates during the Revolution of 1848," *French Historical Studies* 20, no. 1 (Winter 1997): 35.

38 Canning, *Languages of Labour*, 268.

39 Ibid.

40 *Poor Man's Guardian*, March 16, 1833.

41 Barbara Taylor, *Eve and the New Jerusalem: Socialism and Feminism in the Nineteenth Century* (London: Virago, 1983).

42 Charles Sowerwine, "Workers and Women in France before 1914: The Debate over the Couriau Affair," *The Journal of Modern History* 55, no. 3 (September 1983), 414–15.

43 Ibid., 416.

44 Ibid., 441.

45 Quoted in ibid., 436.

46 Jane Jenson, "Paradigms and Political Discourse: Protective Legislation in France and the United States before 1914," *Canadian Journal of Political Science* 22, no. 2 (June 1989): 248.

47 Eric Hopkins, *Working-Class Self-Help in Nineteenth-Century England: Responses to Industrialization* (London: Routledge, 2016), 160–1.

48 Blanca Rodríguez-Ruiz and Ruth Rubio-Marín, "Introduction: Transition to Modernity, the Achievement of Female Suffrage, and Women's Citizenship," in *The Struggle for Female Suffrage in Europe: Voting to Become Citizens*, eds. Ruiz and Marín (Leiden: Brill, 2012), 19.

49 Ellen Carol Dubois, "Woman Suffrage Around the World: Three Phases of Suffragist Internationalism," in *Suffrage and Beyond: International Feminist Perspectives*, eds. Caroline Daley and Melanie Nolan (New York: New York University Press, 1994), 262.

50 Marguerite Bourat, "Women in Industry in France during the War," in *Proceedings of the Academy of Political Science in the City of New York: National Conference on War Economy* VIII, no. 1 (July 1918), 166.
51 Margaret R. Higonnet and Patrice L.-R. Higonnet, "The Double Helix," in *Behind the Lines: Gender and the Two World Wars*, eds. Margaret Randoph Higonnet, Jane Jenson, Sonya Michel, and Margaret Collins Weitz (New Haven, CT: Yale University Press, 1987), 31–47.
52 Treaty of Versailles, Part X111, Section II, Article 427-Seventh.
53 Marcelline J. Hutton, *Russian and West European Women, 1860–1939: Dreams, Struggles, and Nightmares* (Lanham, MD: Rowman & Littlefield, 2001), 199.

Chapter Nine

1 M. M. Bakhtin, *Rabelais and His World* (Bloomington: Indiana University Press, 1984).
2 Emile Durkheim, *The Elementary Forms of Religious Life* (New York, NY: Free Press, 1995).
3 Emma Griffin, "Sports and Celebrations in English Market Towns," *Historical Research* 75, no. 188 (May 2002), 195.
4 Robert Garner, *Animals, Politics, and Morality*, 2nd ed. (Manchester: Manchester University Press, 2004), 84–5.
5 Alain Faure, *Carême prenant: Du Carnival à Paris au XIXe siècle, 1800–1914* (Paris: Hachette, 1978).
6 Louis Chevalier, *Laboring Classes and Dangerous Classes in Paris During the First Half of the Nineteenth Century*, trans. Frank Jellinek (New York, NY: Howard Fertig, 1973).
7 W.Scott Haine, *The World of the Paris Café: Sociability Among the French Working Class, 1789–1914* (Baltimore, MD: Johns Hopkins University Press, 1996), 3–4.
8 Hugh Cunningham, *Leisure in the Industrial Revolution, c. 1750–c. 1850* (London: Croom Helm, 1980), 150.
9 Denis Poulot, *Le sublime ou le travailleur comme il est en 1870 et ce qu'il peut être: Question sociale* (Paris: Librairie internationale, 1870), 159.
10 Susan Barton, *Working-Class Organisations and Popular Tourism, 1840–1970* (Manchester: Manchester University Press, 2005), 51.
11 Derek B. Scott, *Sounds of the Metropolis: The 19th-Century Popular Music Revolution in London, New York, Paris and Vienna* (Oxford: Oxford University Press 2008), 51.
12 James Cannon, *The Paris Zone: A Cultural History* (London: Routledge, 2015), 88.
13 Granville Stanley Hall, *Youth: Its Education, Regimen, and Hygiene* (New York, NY: D. Appleton and Company, 1926), 143.
14 Paul R. Thompson, *The Edwardians: The Remaking of British Society* (London: Routledge, 1992), 195.
15 Louise McReynolds, *Russia at Play: Leisure Activities at the End of the Tsarist Era* (Ithaca, NY: Cornell University Press, 2003), 268.
16 Frank Trentmann, *Empire of Things: How We Became a World of Consumers, From the Fifteenth Century to the Twenty-first* (New York, NY: Harper, 2016), 214.
17 Martin Loiperdinger, "The Kaiser's Cinema: An Archeology of Attitudes and Audiences," in *A Second Life: German Cinema's First Decades*, eds. Thomas Elsaesser with Michael Wedel (Amsterdam: Amsterdam University Press, 1996), 43.
18 Michael Saler, *As If: Modern Enchantment and the Literary Prehistory of Virtual Reality* (Oxford: Oxford University Press, 2012), 27.
19 Cannon, *The Paris Zone*, 91.

20 Tony Collins, *Sport in Capitalist Society: A Short History* (New York, NY: Routledge, 2013), 6.
21 Ibid., 32.
22 Ibid., 48.
23 Ibid., 58–9.
24 Quoted in Christopher S. Thompson, *Tour de France: A Cultural History* (Berkeley: University of California Press, 2008), 147.
25 Ibid., 149–50.
26 David Martin and Roger Gynn, *The Olympic Marathon* (Champaign, IL: Human Kinetics, 2000), 63–81.
27 Catriona M. Parratt, *"More Than Mere Amusement": Working-Class Women's Leisure in England, 1750–1914* (Boston, MA: Northeastern University Press, 2001), 204.
28 Ibid., 207.
29 Lynn Abrams, *Workers' Culture in Imperial Germany: Leisure and Recreation in the Rhineland and Westphalia* (London: Routledge, 2002), 49.
30 Trentmann, *Empire of Things*, 148.
31 Alfred Marshall, *Principles of Economics*, 4th ed. (London: Macmillan and Co., 1898), 4:164.
32 Collins, *Sport in Capitalist Society*, 89.
33 W. Scott Haine, "Fighting on Two Fronts: The French Campaign to Eradicate Drunkenness in the Army and on the Home Front during World War I," paper presented at the Kettil Bruun Society, 22nd Annual Alcohol Epidemiology Symposium (Edinburgh, June 3–7, 1996).
34 Trentmann, *Empire of Things*, 274–6.
35 Richard Bessel, *Germany after the First World War* (Oxford: Clarendon Press, 1993), 144.
36 Ibid., 143.
37 Trentmann, *Empire of Things*, 149.
38 Alain Corbin, *L'avènement des loisirs, 1850–1960* (Paris: Aubier, 1995), 216.

FURTHER READINGS

Accampo, Elinor. *Industrialization, Family Life, and Class Relations: Saint Chamond, 1815–1914*. Berkeley: University of California Press, 1989.

Alexander, Lynn Mae. *Women, Work, and Representation: Needlewomen in Victorian Art and Literature*. Athens: Ohio University Press, 2003.

Allen, Robert C. *The British Industrial Revolution in Global Perspective*. Cambridge: Cambridge University Press, 2009.

Archer, John E. *Social Unrest and Popular Protest in England, 1780–1840*. Cambridge: Cambridge University Press, 2000.

Arnesen, Eric. *Waterfront Workers of New Orleans: Race, Class, and Politics, 1863–1923*. Urbana: University of Illinois Press, 1994.

August, Andrew. *The British Working Class, 1832–1940*. Harlow: Pearson Longman, 2007.

Bade, Klaus J. *Migration in European History*, translated by Allison Brown. Malden, MA: Blackwell, 2003.

Bade, Klaus J., Pieter C. Emmer, Leo Lucassen, and Jochen Oltmer, eds. *Encyclopedia of Migration and Minorities in Europe from the 17th Century to the Present*. Cambridge: Cambridge University Press, 2011.

Bale, John. *Sport, Space and the City*. London: Routledge, 1993.

Barringer, Tim. *Men at Work: Art and Labour in Victorian Britain*. New Haven, CT: Yale University Press, 2005.

Barton, Susan. *Working-Class Organisations and Popular Tourism 1840–1970*. Manchester: Manchester University Press, 2005.

Beaven, Brad. *Leisure, Citizenship and Working-Class Men in Britain 1850–1945*. Manchester: Manchester University Press, 2005.

Beik, Doris, and Paul Beik, eds. and trans. *Flora Tristan, Utopian Feminist: The Travel Diaries and Personal Crusade*. Bloomington: Indiana University Press, 1993.

Berg, Maxine. *The Machinery Question and the Making of Political Economy 1815–1848*. Cambridge: Cambridge University Press, 1982.

Berlanstein, Lenard R. *The Working People of Paris: 1871–1914*. Baltimore, MD: Johns Hopkins University Press, 1984.

Biernacki, Richard. *The Fabrication of Labour: Germany and Britain, 1640–1914*. Berkeley: University of California Press, 1995.

Binfield, Kevin, ed. *Writings of the Luddites*. Baltimore, MD: Johns Hopkins University Press, 2004.

Bourke, Joanna. *Working-Class Cultures in Britain, 1890–1960: Gender, Class, and Ethnicity*. London: Routledge, 1994.

Brinkmann, Tobias. "Why Paul Nathan Attacked Albert Ballin: The Transatlantic Mass Migration and the Privatization of Prussia's Eastern Border Inspection, 1886–1914." *Central European History* 43, no. 1 (2010): 47–83.

Canning, Kathleen. *Languages of Labour and Gender: Female Factory Work in Germany 1850–1914*. Ann Arbor: University of Michigan Press, 2002.

Carles, Emilie. *A Life of Her Own: The Transformation of a Countrywoman in Twentieth-Century France*, translated by Avriel H. Goldberger. New York, NY: Penguin, 1992.

Chaline, Jean-Pierre. "The Cotton Manufacturer in Normandy and England During the Nineteenth Century." *Textile History* 17, no. 1 (1986): 19–26.

Chenut, Helen Harden. *The Fabric of Gender: Working-Class Culture in Third Republic France*. University Park: Pennsylvania State University Press, 2005.

Clark, Anna. *The Struggle for the Breeches: Gender and the Making of the British Working Class*. Berkeley: University of California Press, 1995.

Coffin, Judith G. *The Politics of Women's Work: The Paris Garment Trades, 1750–1915*. Princeton, NJ: Princeton University Press, 1996.

Cohen, Margaret, and Christopher Prendergast. *Spectacles of Realism: Body, Gender, Genre*. Minneapolis: University of Minnesota Press, 1995.

Collins, Tony. *Sport in Capitalist Society: A Short History*. New York, NY: Routledge, 2013.

Corbin, Alain. *L'avènement des loisirs, 1850–1960*. Paris: Aubier, 1995.

Corbin, Alain. *Women for Hire: Prostitution and Sexuality in France after 1850*, translated by Alan Sheridan. Cambridge, MA: Harvard University Press, 1990.

Cottereau, Alain. "Droit et bon droit: Un droit des ouvriers instauré puis évincé par le droit du travail (France, XIXe siècle)." *Annales ESC* 57, no. 6 (November–December 2002): 1521–57.

Cross, Gary. *A Quest for Time: The Reduction of Work in Britain and France, 1840–1940*. Berkeley: University of California Press, 1989.

Cunningham, Hugh. *Time, Work and Leisure: Life Changes in England Since 1700*. Manchester: Manchester University Press, 2014.

Danahay, Martin A. *Gender at Work in Victorian Culture: Literature, Art and Masculinity*. Burlington, VT: Ashgate, 2005.

Daniel, Ute. *The War from Within: German Working-Class Women in the First World War*. Oxford: Berg, 1997.

Daunton, Martin J. *Housing the Workers, 1850–1914: A Comparative Perspective*. London: Bloomsbury, 2015.

Donnachie, Ian. *Robert Owen: Social Visionary*. Edinburgh: John Donald, 2000.

Downs, Laura Lee. *Manufacturing Inequality: Gender Division in the French and British Metalworking Industries, 1914–1939*. Ithaca, NY: Cornell University Press, 1995.

Ehrenreich, Barbara. *Dancing in the Street: A History of Collective Joy*. New York, NY: Metropolitan Books, 2007.

Engel, Barbara Alpern. *Between the Fields and the City: Women, Work, and Family in Russia, 1861–1914*. Cambridge: Cambridge University Press, 1994.

Facos, Michelle. *An Introduction to Nineteenth-Century Art*. New York, NY: Routledge, 2011.

Farr, James R. *Artisans in Europe, 1350–1914*. Cambridge: Cambridge University Press, 2000.

Farwell, Beatrice. *The Charged Image: French Lithographic Caricature, 1816–1848*. Santa Barbara, CA: Santa Barbara Museum of Art, 1989.

Frader, Laura L., and Sonya O. Rose, eds. *Gender and Class in Modern Europe*. Ithaca, NY: Cornell University Press, 1996.

Frobert, Ludovic. *Les Canuts ou la démocratie turbulente: Lyon, 1831–1834* Paris: Tallandier, 2009.

Fuchs, Rachel G. *Poor and Pregnant in Paris: Strategies for Survival in the Nineteenth Century*. New Brunswick, NJ: Routledge University Press, 1992.

Fuchs, Rachel G. *Gender and Poverty in Nineteenth-Century Europe*. Cambridge: Cambridge University Press, 2005.

Glickman, Rose L. *Russian Factory Women: Workplace and Society, 1880–1914.* Berkeley: University of California Press, 1984.
Green, Nancy. *Ready-to-Wear and Ready-to-Work: A Century of Immigrants in Paris and New York.* Durham, NC: Duke University Press, 1997.
Griffin, Carl J. *The Rural War: Captain Swing and the Politics of Protest.* Manchester: Manchester University Press, 2012.
Guillaumin, Émile. *The Life of a Simple Man*, translated by Margaret Crosland. Hanover: New Hampshire University Press, 1983.
Guillerme, André. *La naissance de l'industrie à Paris: Entre sueurs et vapeurs, 1780–1830.* Seyssel: Champ Vallon, 2007.
Gullickson, Gay L. *Spinners and Weavers of Auffay: Rural Industry and the Sexual Division of Labor in a French Village 1750–1850.* Cambridge: Cambridge University Press, 1986.
Gullickson, Gay. *Unruly Women of Paris: Images of the Commune.* Ithaca, NY: Cornell University Press, 1996.
Halleux, Robert. *Le savoir de la main: Savants et artisans dans l'Europe pré-industrielle.* Paris: Armand Colin, 2009.
Hamlin, Christopher. *Public Health and Social Justice in the Age of Chadwick: Britain 1800–1854.* Cambridge: Cambridge University Press, 1998.
Harzig, Christiane, and Dirk Hoerder. *What is Migration History?* Malden, MA: Polity Press, 2009.
Hilaire-Pérez, Liliane. *La pièce et le geste: Artisans, marchands et savoir technique à Londres au XVIIIe siècle.* Paris: Albin Michel, 2013.
Hobsbawm, Eric J. *The Age of Empire, 1875–1914.* New York, NY: Vintage, 1989.
Hobsbawm, Eric J. *The Age of Capital, 1848–1875.* New York, NY: Vintage, 1996.
Hobsbawm, Eric J. *The Age of Extremes, 1914–1991.* New York, NY: Vintage, 1996.
Hobsbawm, Eric J. *The Age of Revolution, 1789–1848.* New York, NY: Vintage, 1996.
Hobsbawm, Eric J., and George Rudé. *Captain Swing.* Harmondsworth: Penguin Books, 1973.
Hochstadt, Steve. *Mobility and Modernity: Migration in Germany, 1820–1989.* Ann Arbor: University of Michigan Press, 1999.
Hoffman, David L. *Peasant Metropolis: Social Identities in Moscow, 1919–1941.* Ithaca, NY: Cornell University Press, 1994.
Hopkins, Eric. *Working-Class Self-Help in Nineteenth-Century England: Responses to Industrialization.* London: Routledge, 2016.
Horn, Jeff, Leonard N. Rosenband, and Merritt Roe Smith, eds. *Reconceptualizing the Industrial Revolution.* Cambridge, MA: MIT Press, 2010.
Hornborg, Alf. *The Power of the Machine: Global Inequalities of Economy, Technology, and Environment.* Walnut Creek, CA: AltaMir, 2001.
Horne, Janet R. *A Social Laboratory for Modern France: The Musée Social and the Rise of the Welfare State.* Durham, NC: Duke University Press, 2002.
Huneault, Kristina. *Difficult Subjects: Working Women and Visual Culture, Britain 1880–1914.* Burlington, VT: Ashgate, 2002.
Hutton, Marcelline J. *Russian and West European Women, 1860–1939: Dreams, Struggles, and Nightmares.* Lanham, MD: Rowman & Littlefield, 2001.
Ittman, Karl. *Work, Gender and Family in Victorian England.* Houndmills: Macmillan, 1995.
Jarrige, François. *Au temps des "tueuses de bras": Les bris de machines à l'aube de l'ère industrielle.* Rennes, Presses universitaires de Rennes, 2009.
Joyce, Patrick, ed. *The Historical Meanings of Work.* Cambridge: Cambridge University Press, 1987.

Joyce, Patrick. *Work, Society and Politics: The Culture of the Factory in Later Victorian England*. New Brunswick, NJ: Rutgers University Press, 1980.

Katznelson, Ira, and Aristide Zolberg, eds. *Working-Class Formation: Nineteenth-Century Patterns in Western Europe and the United States*. Princeton, NJ: Princeton University Press, 1986.

Kelly, Alfred E., ed. and trans. *The German Worker: Working-Class Autobiographies from the Age of Industrialization*. Berkeley: University of California Press, 1987.

Kessler, Marni Reva. *Sheer Presence: The Veil in Manet's Paris*. Minneapolis: University of Minnesota Press, 2006.

Kushner, Nina. *Erotic Exchanges: The World of Elite Prostitution in Eighteenth-century Paris*. Ithaca, NY: Cornell University Press, 2013.

Laite, Julia. *Common Prostitutes and Ordinary Citizens: Commercial Sex in London, 1885–1960*. Basingstoke: Palgrave Macmillan, 2012.

Laroulandie, Fabrice. *Les ouvriers de Paris*. Paris: Éditions Christian, 1997.

Laurie, Bruce. *Working People of Philadelphia, 1800–1850*. Philadelphia, PA: Temple University Press, 1980.

Lefebvre, Philippe. *L'invention de la grande entreprise: Travail, hiérarchie, marché. France, fin XVIIIe–début XXe siècle*. Paris: Presses universitaires de France, 2003.

Lequin, Yves. *Les ouvriers de la région Lyonnaise (1848–1914)*. 2 volumes. Lyon: Presses universitaires de Lyon, 1977.

Levine-Clark, Marjorie. *Beyond the Reproductive Body: The Politics of Women's Health and Work in Early Victorian England*. Columbus: Ohio University Press, 2004.

Levine-Clark, Marjorie. *Unemployment, Welfare, and Masculine Citizenship: "So Much Honest Poverty" in Britain, 1870–1930*. Basingstoke: Palgrave Macmillan, 2015.

Lichtenstein, Nelson, et al. *Who Built America? Working People and the Nation's Economy, Politics, Culture, and Society*, vol. 2. New York, NY: Worth Publishers, 2000.

Lipton, Eunice. *Looking into Degas: Uneasy Images of Women and Modern Life*. Berkeley: University of California Press, 1986.

Liu, Tessie P. *The Weaver's Knot: The Contradictions of Class Struggle and Family Solidarity in Western France, 1750–1914*. Ithaca, NY: Cornell University Press, 1994.

Lucassen, Leo. *The Immigrant Threat: The Integration of Old and New Migrants in Western Europe Since 1850*. Urbana: University of Illinois Press, 2005.

MacLeod, Christine. *Heroes of Invention: Technology, Liberalism and British Identity (1750–1914)*. Cambridge: Cambridge University Press, 2007.

Magraw, Roger. *A History of the French Working Class*. 2 volumes. Oxford: Blackwell, 1992.

Malm, Andreas. *Fossil Capital: The Rise of Steam-Power and the Roots of Global Warming*. London: Verso, 2016.

Marks, Robert. *Origins of the Modern World: A Global and Environmental Narrative from the Fifteen to the Twenty-First Century*, 3rd ed. Lanham, MD: Rowman and Littlefield, 2015.

Massin, Robert. *Les Cris de la ville: Commerces ambulants et petits métiers de la rue*. Paris: Gallimard, 1978.

Maynes, Mary Jo. *Taking the Hard Road: Life Course in French and German Workers' Autobiographies in the Era of Industrialization*. Chapel Hill: University of North Carolina Press, 1995.

McReynolds, Louise. *Russia at Play: Leisure Activities at the End of the Tsarist Era*. Ithaca, NY: Cornell University Press, 2003.

Milliot, Vincent. *"Les Cris de Paris," ou le peuple travesti: les représentations des petits métiers parisiens (XVIe–XVIIIe siècles)*. Paris: Publications de la Sorbonne, 1995.

Moch, Leslie Page. *Moving Europeans: Migration in Western Europe Since 1650*. Bloomington: Indiana University Press, 2003.

Moch, Leslie Page. *The Pariahs of Yesterday: Breton Migrants in Paris*. Durham, NC: Duke University Press, 2012.

Mühlberg, Dietrich, ed. *Proletariat: Culture and Lifestyle in the 19th Century*, translated by Katherine Vanovitch. Leipzig: Édition Leipzig, 1988.

Nead, Lynda. *Victorian Babylon: People, Streets and Images in Nineteenth-century London*. New Haven, CT: Yale University Press, 2000.

Nicholas, Stephen, ed. *Convict Workers: Reinterpreting Australia's Past*. Cambridge: Cambridge University Press, 1988.

Nochlin, Linda. *Realism*. Harmondsworth: Penguin, 1971.

Nochlin, Linda. *Representing Women*. New York, NY: Thames and Hudson, 1999.

Nochlin, Linda. *Women Artists: The Linda Nochlin Reader*, edited by Maura Reilly. London: Thames & Hudson, 2015.

Noiriel, Gérard. *Workers in French Society in the 19th and 20th Centuries*. New York, NY: Berg, 1990.

Nye, David E. *American Technological Sublime*. Cambridge, MA: MIT Press, 1994.

Parratt, Catriona M. *"More Than Mere Amusement": Working-Class Women's Leisure in England, 1750–1914*. Boston, MA: Northeastern University Press, 2001.

Pomeranz, Kenneth. *The Great Divergence: China, Europe, and the Making of the Modern World Economy*. Princeton, NJ: Princeton University Press, 2000.

Rabinbach, Anson. *The Human Motor: Energy, Fatigue, and the Origins of Modernity*. New York, NY: Basic Books, 1990.

Rancière, Jacques. *The Nights of Labor: The Workers' Dream in Nineteenth-century France*, translated by John Drury. Philadelphia, PA: Temple University Press, 1989.

Randall, Adrian. *Before the Luddites: Custom, Community and Machinery in the English Woollen Industry, 1776–1809*. Cambridge: Cambridge University Press, 1991.

Ransel, David L., ed. and trans. *Olga Semyonova Tian-Shanskaia, Village Life in Late Tsarist Russia*. Bloomington: Indiana University Press, 1993.

Reberioux, Madeleine. *Images du travail: Peintures et dessins des collections françaises*. Paris: Éditions de la Réunion des musées nationaux, 1985.

Reid, Donald. *Paris Sewers and Sewermen: Realities and Representations*. Cambridge, MA: Harvard University Press, 1991.

Richardson, Sarah. *The Political Worlds of Women: Gender and Politics in Nineteenth-century Britain*. New York, NY: Routledge, 2013.

Sabel, Charles F., and Jonathan Zeitlin, eds. *World of Possibilities: Flexibility and Mass Production in Western Industrialization*. Cambridge: Cambridge University Press, 1997.

Saler, Michael. *As If: Modern Enchantment and the Literary Prehistory of Virtual Reality*. Oxford: Oxford University Press, 2012.

Sante, Luc. *The Other Paris*. New York, NY: Farrar, Straus and Giroux, 2015.

Scott, Derek B. *Sounds of the Metropolis: The 19th-Century Popular Music Revolution in London, New York, Paris and Vienna*. Oxford: Oxford University Press, 2008.

Scott, Joan Wallach. *Gender and the Politics of History*. New York, NY: Columbia University Press, 1988.

Scott, Joan Wallach. *The Glassworkers of Carmaux*. Cambridge, MA: Harvard University Press, 1980.

Sewell, William H., Jr. *Work and Revolution in France: The Language of Labor from the Old Regime to* 1848. Cambridge: Cambridge University Press, 1980.

Shorter, Edward, and Charles Tilly. *Strikes in France, 1830–1968*. Cambridge: Cambridge University Press, 1974.

Stanziani, Alessandro. *Bondage: Labor and Rights in Eurasia from the Sixteenth to the Early Twentieth Centuries*. New York, NY: Berghan, 2014.

Stearns, Peter N. *Paths to Authority: The Middle Class and the Industrial Labor Force in France, 1820–48*. Chicago: University of Illinois Press, 1978.

Steele, Valerie. *The Corset: A Cultural History*. New Haven, CT: Yale University Press, 2001.

Steidl, Annemarie, et al., eds. *European Mobility: Internal, International, and Transatlantic Moves in the 19th and the Early 20th Centuries*. Vienna: V & R Unipress, 2009.

Stewart, Mary Lynn. *Women, Work and the French State: Labour Protection and Social Patriarchy, 1879–1919*. Kingston: McGill-Queen's University Press, 1989.

Stone, Judith. *The Search for Social Peace: Reform Legislation in France, 1891–1914*. Albany: State University of New York Press, 1985.

Taylor, Barbara. *Eve and the New Jerusalem: Socialism and Feminism in the Nineteenth Century*. London: Virago, 1983.

Thompson, Dorothy, ed. *The Early Chartists*. London: Macmillan, 1971.

Thompson, Edward P. *Customs in Common: Studies in Traditional Popular Culture*. London: Merlin Press, 1991.

Thompson, Edward P. *The Making of the English Working Class*. Toronto: Penguin Books, (1963) 1991.

Thompson, Victoria E. *The Virtuous Marketplace: Women and Men, Money and Politics in Paris, 1830–1870*. Baltimore, MD: Johns Hopkins University Press, 2000.

Traugott, Mark, ed. and trans. *The French Worker: Autobiographies from the Early Industrial Era*. Berkeley: University of California Press, 1993.

Trentman, Frank. *Empire of Things: How We Became a World of Consumers, From the Fifteenth Century to the Twenty-first*. New York, NY: Harper, 2016.

Tresch, John. *The Romantic Machine: Utopian Science and Technology after Napoleon*. Chicago, IL: University of Chicago Press, 2012.

Valenze, Deborah M. *The First Industrial Woman*. Oxford: Oxford University Press, 1995.

Verdon, Nicola. *Rural Women Workers in Nineteenth-Century England: Gender, Work and Wages*. Rochester, NY: Boydell Press, 2002.

Verley, Patrick. *L'échelle du monde: Essai sur l'industrialisation de l'Occident*. Paris: Gallimard, 1997.

Von Tunzelmann, Nick. *Steam Power and British Industrialization to 1860*. Oxford: Clarendon Press, 1978.

Wilentz, Sean. *Chants Democratic: New York City and the Rise of the American Working Class*. Oxford: Oxford University Press, 1984.

Woollacott, Angela. *On Her Their Lives Depend: Munitions Workers in the Great War*. Berkeley: University of California Press, 1994.

Zelnick, Reginald E., ed. and trans. *A Radical Worker in Tsarist Russia: The Autobiography of Sëmen Ivanovich Kanatchikov*. Palo Alto, CA: Stanford University Press, 1986.

INDEX

agriculture 1–2, 7–9, 22, 33, 109, 111, 122, 133, 142–4
Americas 17, 22, 86, 93, 97, 104–6, 112, 160
Anti-Corn Law League 137
apprenticeship 7, 82, 88
    apprentices 52, 58, 65, 67–74, 99–100, 107, 136
artisans 8–11, 15, 17–24, 27, 52, 54–5, 58, 78, 91, 133, 136, 139. *See also* skill; workshops
    artisanal culture 67–8, 71, 73, 75, 76, 80, 87–9
    leisure 150, 158
association 16, 21, 69, 71, 75–9, 141, 145, 147, 152, 158

Babbage, Charles 19, 24
Birmingham 21, 55, 123
Blanqui, Adophe 19
Booth, Charles 128
Brazil 11, 53, 106

Cabet, Etienne 16, 20, 90, 91
capitalism 4, 22, 24, 27, 51–3, 58, 93–5, 115, 123, 129
catherinette 47–8
Chartism 9, 76, 124, 137–8, 151
children 45, 59, 80, 103. *See also* protective legislation
    care 61, 122–4, 126, 129, 162
    labor 6, 8, 52, 60, 63–5, 73, 77, 89, 134
    working hours 13, 134–5
cinema 14, 154–8, 163. *See also* urban
cities 7, 14, 21, 35, 39–40, 52, 55, 59, 75, 80
    conditions 115–21, 126–7
    leisure 149, 151, 154
    migration 62, 69, 108, 111
class consciousness 4, 14, 54
class struggle 4, 14, 27, 57
clothing trades 6–7, 12, 33, 38, 42, 47, 52, 57, 59, 73–4, 102, 141
coal industry 5, 8, 73, 86, 91, 108, 113. *See also* mining; protective legislation
    imagery 17, 34, 35

coerced labor 11, 112, 114. *See also* convict labor; serfdom; slavery
colonies 11, 17, 18, 22, 25–6, 53, 82, 93–5, 104, 113, 121. *See also* empires; imperialism
Combination Acts 7, 68
communism 83. *See also* Marx
compagnonnages 57, 65, 69, 71
concentration of labor 11, 91, 93, 95, 97
consumerism 21, 40, 161–2
    consumer economy 1, 5, 74, 150, 154
    consumers 10, 14, 65, 96
convict labor 112, 144
    prisoners of war 11, 113
corporations 71, 74–5, 78
cottage industry. *See* domestic industry
cotton 23, 29, 51, 55, 65
    manufacture 5–7, 20, 31, 32, 63, 78–9, 88, 124, 134–5
    thread 12, 17

Daumier, Honoré 37, 43–5, 48
Degas, Edgar 42, 45–8
degeneration 13, 121, 126–8, 131, 160
Dickens, Charles 19, 63, 115
division of labor 6–7, 19–20, 24, 73–4, 78, 86, 90–1, 136. *See also* Taylorism
    gendered 34, 57, 59, 82–3, 93, 133, 138–9
domestic industry 6, 10, 17, 19, 20, 23, 52, 62, 68, 75, 122, 141
domestic servants 9, 24, 51, 58–62, 100, 102–4
domestic violence 124
domesticity 34, 42, 73, 79–80, 119, 122–4, 131, 137, 140, 142, 144

economic crisis 9, 12, 68, 75, 136
education 14, 63–4, 106–7, 124–7, 147
    worker education 57, 76, 95, 103, 137, 161, 167
embroidery 48, 77, 78, 100
empires 2, 34, 51, 78, 100, 106–7, 112, 158, 161–2. *See also* colonies; imperialism
employers 6, 10–12, 30, 47, 52, 74, 96, 110

association 76–7
employer-employee relations 9, 14, 29, 38, 57, 62, 68, 79–83, 114, 135–6, 163
and women 102–3, 138–47
Engels, Friedrich 10–11, 24, 89, 115, 123, 125
ethnicity 3–5, 26, 57, 74, 76, 107–9, 161

factory 3, 11, 22, 31, 51–5, 58, 87, 90–1. *See also* Taylorism
   conditions 56, 59, 60, 63, 77, 82
   discipline 3, 22, 29, 79–80
   legislation 134–6, 141–2
   system 2, 12, 19–20, 22, 24, 86, 97, 122
   women 73, 74, 77–8, 103, 123–4
   work 2, 12, 20, 23, 28, 29, 67–74, 116
   workers 14, 23, 32, 58, 67
family 11, 14, 17, 23–5, 53, 63, 67, 73, 76, 115. *See also* domesticity; male breadwinner model
   and men 105–7
   migration 105–7, 114
   and women 12, 31, 33, 43, 59, 62, 100, 102–3
famine 9, 16, 28, 101
fashion 6, 31, 33, 35, 37–42, 46, 48
feminism 142, 145–7
feminization 7, 35, 42
Fourier, Charles 16, 23, 27, 76, 86, 90
France 56, 64, 77, 86–7, 120, 141–2, 155, 159–60. *See also* revolutions
   artisans 21, 55, 57, 65, 69
   corporate system 7, 68, 71, 74, 78
   gender 12, 35–41, 48, 55, 57, 60–2, 139, 147–8
   industrialization 19, 20, 23, 31
   labor 24, 74–5, 81–3, 88, 89, 96
   mobility 100–2, 104, 113
   socialism 16–17, 26–7
   welfare 120, 130, 136
French Section of the Socialist International 82, 141
friendly societies 9, 75, 76, 152. *See also* mutual aid

garment trades. *See* clothing trades
gender 3, 34–5, 47, 49, 131, 146–7. *See also* male breadwinner model; sexuality
   division of labor 34, 57, 59, 74, 82–3, 93, 133, 138–9
   family and 12, 31, 33, 43, 59, 62, 71, 74, 100, 102–3

femininity 34, 35, 40, 42, 45, 48, 137
imagery 32, 33, 37–50
masculinity 7, 34, 35, 82, 123–4, 135, 137, 139
roles 4, 119, 122–6, 129
skill and status 6–7, 41, 58–9, 138–9, 142–3, 145
space 34, 40, 55, 57, 151
women 33, 41, 124, 139, 140
Germany 56, 77–8, 160–2. *See also* Prussia
   industry 7, 14, 17, 79, 93, 133
   mobility 99, 104, 106–14
   social politics 56, 82, 96, 130–1, 141, 146
   women 133, 140–4, 147–8
   workers 21, 57, 58–9, 65, 69
Grand National Consolidated Trade Union (GNCTU) 9, 138–9, 145
Great Britain 3, 26, 56, 101, 113, 119, 120, 130
   industry 2, 5–9, 12–14, 17, 133, 149
   leisure 151–3, 155, 158–9, 161–2
   organized labor 69, 71, 74, 80, 82, 87, 96, 124, 134, 138, 144
   women 42–3, 48, 144, 148
great depression (1870s–1890s) 93, 127, 130
guilds 7, 9, 38, 65, 68, 78

hours of work 9, 10, 52, 59, 62, 73, 83, 112, 121, 162
   regulation 13, 56, 123, 134–5, 141–2, 147

imperialism 2, 3, 28, 95–6, 116. *See also* colonies; empires
India 2, 17, 22, 25, 95
industrial revolution 1, 8, 12–14, 18, 55, 149
industrialization 1–22, 31, 93, 102, 131, 133–4, 159
   deindustrialization 9, 101
   social effects 63, 68, 77, 95, 115–6, 122–3
injury, at workplace 13, 19, 45, 55–6, 157
Ireland 2, 9, 28, 101, 112

journeymen 8, 52, 68, 71, 73–5, 78, 91, 100, 136

labor 4, 10, 14, 15–17, 58, 135–6. *See also* children; division of labor; ethnicity; gender; migration; pay; skill; work
   agricultural 7, 28–9, 55, 56, 101–2, 134
   alienation 2, 16, 19, 24, 26, 58, 89–91, 115
   coerced 11, 24–6, 52–3, 112

day/casual 28, 53, 54, 64
demand 19, 33–4, 52–3, 101, 102, 105, 107, 109, 111–12, 114, 120, 142–4
discipline 3, 6, 19, 20, 22, 29, 41, 68, 74, 79–80, 92
female 6, 12, 59–61, 122–4, 134
labor-intensive 6, 52, 74, 143
labor movement 11, 14, 27, 57, 82, 85, 124, 141
manual 11, 12, 15, 20, 22, 33–4, 43, 48, 86, 96–7, 160
organization of 11, 21, 23, 77, 86, 97
supply 22, 52, 87, 93, 106, 112, 140, 142–4, 154
sweated 52, 61, 75
value 2, 10, 24, 27, 133, 139, 148
Labour Party 56, 82, 146
laissez-faire 13, 56, 68, 78–80, 135, 141
Lanté, Louis-Marie 38–40, 46
laundresses 37, 38, 43–7, 151
Le Chapelier Law 68
leisure 149–63. *See also* cinema; music halls; print culture
cafés 42, 78, 149, 151–5, 162–3
carnival 149–51, 153, 159, 161, 163
football 150, 151, 158, 160, 162
music 14, 80, 149, 151, 153–8
radio 149–50, 162–3
reading 154, 157, 163
sites 150, 154, 155
sports 155, 158, 160
liberalism 15, 20, 25–6, 96, 136–7, 146
linen 17, 31, 101
London 10, 21, 35, 55, 76, 90, 138
conditions 10, 55, 57, 62, 117–28, 151
Cries of London 35–7
leisure 151–5, 160
Luddites 8, 10, 23, 88, 134, 144
Lyon 15, 145, 146, 155
manufacture 6, 21, 27, 31, 55, 69, 73, 136

machines 12, 20. *See also* sewing machine
imagery 42–4, 58
impact on workers 8, 14, 15, 16, 24, 74, 79–80, 83, 87–9, 96–7
machine-breaking 8, 10, 22–3, 81, 133–4, 142–3, 148
mechanization 2, 5–6, 11, 13, 19, 22–3, 52, 85–7, 92–3, 95, 144–5
male breadwinner model 12, 34, 76, 122–4, 126, 129
Malthus, Thomas 13, 16

Manchester 52, 55, 96, 108, 117
conditions 117, 119, 123, 124
leisure sites 151, 154
textiles 20, 31, 32, 79, 101
Marx, Karl 4–5, 10, 14, 24, 27, 28, 58, 85, 89, 115
masculinity. *See* gender
masters 6, 8, 11, 52, 56, 65, 67–75, 145
Mayhew, Henry 117
Mechanics Institutes 76, 152
mechanization. *See* machines
men 76, 109, 125, 129, 136–9, 145, 148. *See also* gender; male breadwinner model; skill
bodies 34, 55–6, 86, 120, 128
journeymen 8, 52, 65, 68–71, 73–5, 78, 91, 100
and machines 19, 24, 85, 89–90, 92
middle-class 42, 45
and work 10, 22, 32, 38, 57, 64, 93, 110, 143
metalworking 23, 82, 112
Michelet, Jules 19, 28, 89–90, 115, 119
migration 19, 59, 62, 99–112, 114, 117, 120
mining 5, 73, 75, 102, 108–9, 111–14, 139–40, 147. *See also* coal
conditions 77, 78, 119, 123, 140–1
mobility 28, 53, 69, 99–114, 158
morality 16, 19, 20, 23, 27–9, 45, 77–80, 86, 92, 119–23, 127–30, 139, 154–5, 158–61
Moscow 57, 62, 64, 73, 111
motherhood 12, 34, 148
music hall 14, 151, 153, 154, 155, 158, 162
mutual aid 9, 75–6, 80, 145
mutualism 21, 27

New Lanark 23, 63–4
New York 9, 56, 76, 117, 120, 124, 151, 153

Owen, Robert 16, 23, 57, 63–4, 76, 90, 138

Paris 21, 45, 52, 55–8, 75–6, 78, 95–6, 117, 120, 136, 152–9, 162
cris de Paris 35–8
protest 88, 144, 151
trades 6, 7, 10, 31, 33, 47–8, 79
workers 20, 38, 40, 42, 60, 62, 69, 71, 103
Paris Commune 62, 127, 141, 159
paternalism 12, 26, 30, 79–80

pay 8, 9, 24, 52, 59, 62, 93, 96, 113, 160, 162, 163
   children's 63, 65
   equal 10, 139, 148
   low-paid 7, 9, 24, 57, 69, 73–6, 89, 137, 142
   piece rates 6, 52, 72, 75, 82, 138
   women's 32, 59, 112, 139, 145–7
peasantry 1, 2, 11, 17, 28–59, 73, 89, 91, 136
   mobility 100, 101, 103, 105, 109, 111–12. *See also* agriculture
peddlers 9, 35–8
phalanstery 16, 23, 27, 103
Philipon, Charles 40-3, 45
plantations 6, 22, 25, 53, 95, 106
political economy 3, 11, 13, 23, 80–2, 124, 133–42, 147–8, 152
political parties 13, 14, 27, 56, 82, 96, 137, 141, 146–7, 162
politics 4, 13, 16, 23, 80–82, 124, 133–42, 147–8, 152
poor laws 111, 129, 137, 143
population growth 28, 37, 86, 100, 102, 112, 114
   urban 52, 117, 136, 151
poverty 3, 10, 16, 23, 54, 77, 109, 111, 116–21, 126–31, 161
power looms 7, 19, 79, 81–2, 92–3, 134, 139, 145
print culture 11, 31, 33–42, 48
printing 11, 79, 88–9, 145–6, 153
progress 5, 11, 13, 15, 24, 28–9, 48, 78–9, 85–7, 93, 96
proletarianization 6, 7, 8, 89, 90
prostitution 7, 42, 45–6, 53, 59, 62, 127, 154, 162
protective legislation 13, 95, 123, 135, 139–44, 147
protest 8–9, 12, 23, 31, 75, 87, 89, 93, 96, 130, 133, 136–7, 143–5. *See also* machines, machine-breaking; strikes
Prussia 9, 59, 99, 105–9, 141
public health 85, 116–22, 129–31, 151, 161
putting-out system. *See* domestic industry

railroads 5–6, 7, 16, 23, 87, 149, 153
   rail industry 12, 55, 99, 110, 111, 112
rationalization of work 19, 22, 42, 82, 83, 85, 87
ready-to-wear 6–7, 73, 74. *See also* clothing trades
religion 4–5, 14, 57, 81, 150
   Catholicism 69, 77, 108, 142, 144, 150
   Judaism 57, 58, 69, 106–7
revolutions
   1848 27, 43, 88, 91, 112, 134, 136–7, 160–1
   American 53
   French 7, 24, 27, 29, 37, 53, 68, 160
   revolutionary ideas 62, 65, 78, 97, 162
   Russian 83, 114, 162
Ricardo, David 13, 16, 23
right to work 27, 136, 138
Russia 11, 24, 51, 56, 57, 62, 64, 65, 73, 76, 83, 148
   leisure 155, 157, 161–2
   migration 103, 106–7, 109, 111–12, 113, 114

Saint-Simon, Henri de 10, 76, 90
Say, Jean-Baptiste 16, 24–5
separate spheres. *See* domesticity
serfdom 11, 24, 52, 62, 73, 111–12
sewing 6, 41, 43, 48, 60, 62, 144
sewing machine 6, 7, 31, 52, 59, 61–2, 93
sexual harassment 59, 74, 77, 78, 102
   assault 7
sexuality 12, 42, 45, 47, 77–8, 119
SFIO. *See* French Section of the Socialist International
silk industry 21, 27, 31, 60, 69, 76, 101, 136, 141, 144
skill 5–7, 27, 30, 51, 52–4, 58, 64–5, 69, 73–6, 82–3, 85–9, 110, 123, 142, 145. *See also* deskilling; Taylorism
   gender 41, 48, 55, 59, 80, 82, 133, 138–9, 142, 145
   skilled workers 10, 20, 21, 24, 59–60, 67, 96–7, 106, 109, 111–12, 152
   unskilled workers 7, 20, 22, 59, 79, 80, 106, 134
slavery, as institution 11, 22, 24–5, 52–3, 106
   as metaphor 24, 28, 58, 89–90, 134, 146
social Darwinism 126
Social Democratic Party, Germany (SPD) 56, 82, 141, 157, 161
socialism 10–11, 15, 16–7, 22, 23, 26, 27, 62, 76, 90, 96–7, 130, 136, 141, 146–8
social reform 23, 56, 90, 120–1, 134, 139–44, 154
SPD. *See* Social Democratic Party; Germany
spinning 31–2, 73–4, 139
   machinery 5, 6, 13, 29, 89, 90, 134
   spinning jenny 17, 31, 81

sports. *See* leisure
steam power 5–6, 22–4, 31, 79, 86, 105, 139
　engine 58, 86, 105, 111, 115
　looms 7, 19, 79, 82, 92–3, 134, 139, 145
　ships 2, 5, 7, 106, 114
strikes 9, 10, 14, 52, 55–6, 80–3, 97, 133, 135–8, 146. *See also* protest
　women and 138–9, 144–5
suffrage 95, 137, 143, 146, 147. *See also* vote
sweated industry 52, 61, 75, 93, 141

tailoring 6–7, 10, 38, 61, 71, 73, 74, 138, 146
Taylorism 7, 29, 30, 95, 97
technology 2, 5, 6, 8, 12, 16–17, 52, 85–97, 133. *See also* machines; skill
　and gender 139, 142–3
　and leisure 155, 162
　and progress 13–15
Ten Hours Act 134–5
textile mills 5–6, 20, 31, 51–2, 73–4, 77–8, 81
textiles 2, 6, 12, 17, 23, 33, 87, 102, 134, 140. *See also specific textiles*; spinning; weaving
Tour de France
　and cycling 159–60
　and labor 57, 65, 69
trades 4, 6–12, 14, 20, 21, 29, 35–7, 51–2, 55–7, 62, 68–9, 72–6, 103, 122, 138, 144. *See also specific trades*
Tristan, Flora 56–7, 62

unemployment 2, 74–5, 96–7, 103, 112, 116, 129–30, 136
unfree labor. *See* coerced labor; serfdom; slavery
unions 9, 82, 96–7, 124, 137–8, 146–8, 157, 161
　gender 124, 137, 139, 142, 145–6
　legalization 13, 56, 82, 96
　membership 73, 81
United States 12, 14, 23, 63, 76, 154–5
　immigration 101, 104, 105–7, 109–10
　industrialization 2, 6, 7, 13, 15, 17–8, 20, 21, 93
　labor movement 9, 57, 96, 97

suffrage 130, 147, 148
work 28–9, 86–7, 115
urban 55, 86, 150–4, 157. *See also* cities
　industries and workers 21, 28, 33, 35–7, 47–8, 54, 88
　living conditions 3, 117, 119–22, 126
　urbanization 8, 52, 100–3, 108, 110, 114–15, 122, 123, 131, 149
Ure, Andrew 19, 90
utopian socialism 10, 16, 63, 76

Villermé, Louis René 23, 77, 120
vote 9, 27, 56, 59, 82, 146, 148. *See also* suffrage

wars 23, 62, 100, 104, 107, 111, 160–1
　First World War 2, 7, 12–13, 29, 35, 48, 80–3, 93, 97–9, 112–4, 147–8, 161–3
　Franco–Prussian 109, 142, 159
　Second World War 93, 148
weaving 5, 10, 21, 31, 73, 74, 93, 101, 139. *See also* steam
women 6, 12, 33–43, 47–8, 55, 57, 59–62, 102, 103, 122–4, 134, 138–48. *See also* family; feminism; gender; labor, prostitution; sexual harassment; skill
wool 13, 29, 31, 64, 81, 88, 144
work 60. *See also* artisans; division of labor; factory; gender; labor; trades
　culture 3, 28, 41, 47, 54, 65, 67–83
　imagery 32–50
　workers' rights 9, 20, 24, 62, 146
　workforce 6–12, 22–3, 29, 33, 47, 52–3, 59, 71, 73, 82, 92–3, 99, 113–14, 124, 129, 148, 161–2
　working hours (*see* hours of work)
workshops 7, 10, 21, 24, 27, 29, 35, 40–1, 48, 55, 58, 69, 80, 86, 136, 150

Yorkshire 17, 73, 88, 134
youth 100, 112, 113, 123, 154

Zola, Emile 45, 55, 60–1